James Hamblin Smith

Elementary Trigonometry

James Hamblin Smith
Elementary Trigonometry
ISBN/EAN: 9783743344198
Manufactured in Europe, USA, Canada, Australia, Japa
Cover: Foto ©Paul-Georg Meister /pixelio.de

Manufactured and distributed by brebook publishing software (www.brebook.com)

James Hamblin Smith

Elementary Trigonometry

ELEMENTARY TRIGONOMETRY

BY

J. HAMBLIN SMITH, M.A.

GONVILLE AND CAIUS COLLEGE,
AND LATE LECTURER AT ST. PETER'S COLLEGE, CAMBRIDGE

NEW EDITION, REVISED

RIVINGTONS
London, Oxford, and Cambridge
1874

PREFACE

I HAVE attempted in this work to explain and illustrate the principles of that portion of Plane Trigonometry which precedes De Moivre's Theorem. The method of explanation is similar to that adopted in my ELEMENTARY ALGEBRA. The examples, progressive and easy, have been selected chiefly from College and University Examination Papers, but I am indebted for many to the works of several German writers, especially those of Dienger, Meyer, Weiss, and Wiegand. I have carried on the subject somewhat beyond the limits set by the Regulations for the Examination of Candidates for Honours in the Previous Examination for two reasons: first, because I hope to see those limits extended, secondly, that my work may be more useful to those who are reading the subject in Schools and to Candidates in the Local Examinations.

J. HAMBLIN SMITH.

CAMBRIDGE, 1870.

CONTENTS

CHAPTER I.
On the Measurement of Lines 1

CHAPTER II.
On the Ratio of the Circumference of a Circle to the Diameter 5

CHAPTER III.
On the Measurement of Angles 10

CHAPTER IV.
On the Method of Converting the Measures of Angles from one to another System of Measurement . 18

CHAPTER V.
On the Use of the Signs + and − to denote Contrariety of Direction 26

CHAPTER VI.
On the Trigonometrical Ratios 32

CHAPTER VII.
On the Changes in Sign and Magnitude of the Trigonometrical Ratios of an Angle as it increases from 0° to 360° 39

CHAPTER VIII.
On Ratios of Angles in the First Quadrant . . 46

CHAPTER IX.
On the Relations between the Trigonometrical Ratios for the same Angle 54

CONTENTS.

CHAPTER X.
Comparison of Trigonometrical Ratios for different Angles 65

CHAPTER XI.
On the Solution of Trigonometrical Equations . . 73

CHAPTER XII.
On the Trigonometrical Ratios of two Angles . . 83

CHAPTER XIII.
On the Trigonometrical Ratios for multiple and sub-multiple Angles 99

CHAPTER XIV.
On Logarithms 112

CHAPTER XV.
On Trigonometrical and Logarithmic Tables . . 125

CHAPTER XVI.
On the Relations between the Sides of a Triangle and the Trigonometrical Ratios of the Angles of the Triangle 142

CHAPTER XVII.
On the Solution of right-angled Triangles . . 154

CHAPTER XVIII.
On the Solution of Triangles other than right-angled 164

CHAPTER XIX.
Measurement of Heights and Distances . . . 178

CHAPTER XX.
Propositions relating to the Areas of Triangles, Polygons, and Circles 187

Answers 206
Appendix 222

ELEMENTARY TRIGONOMETRY.

CHAPTER I.

On the Measurement of Lines.

1. To measure a line AB we fix upon some line as a standard of linear measurement: then if AB contains the standard line p times, p is called the *measure* of AB, and the magnitude of AB is represented algebraically by the symbol p. (See *Algebra*, Art. 33.)

Since the standard contains itself once, its measure is *unity*, and it will be represented by 1.

2. Two lines are *commensurable* when a line can be taken as the standard of measurement (or, as it is commonly called, the unit of length) such that it is contained in each an exact number of times.

3. If the measures of two lines AB, CD be p and q respectively, the ratio $AB : CD$ is represented by the fraction $\dfrac{p}{q}$. (See *Algebra*, Arts. 341, 342.)

Examples.—I.

(1) If the unit of length be an inch, by what number will 4 feet 6 inches be represented?

(2) If 7 inches be taken as the unit of length, by what number will 15 feet 2 inches be represented?

(3) If 192 square inches be represented by the number 12, what is the unit of linear measurement?

(4) If 1000 square inches be represented by the number 40, what is the unit of linear measurement?

(5) If 216 cubic inches be represented by the number 8, what is the unit of linear measurement?

(6) If 2000 cubic inches be represented by the number 16, what is the unit of linear measurement?

(7) If a yards be the unit of length, what is the measure of b feet?

(8) A line referred to different units of length has measures 5 and 4; the first unit is 6 inches, what is the other?

(9) A line referred to three different units of length has measures 1, 36, 12 respectively. The unit in the first case is a yard: what is it in the others?

(10) Express the ratio between $3\frac{1}{4}$ inches and $3\frac{1}{2}$ yards.

(11) If the measure of m yards be c, what is the measure of n feet?

4. Now suppose the measures of the sides of a right-angled triangle to be p, q, r respectively, the right angle being subtended by that side whose measure is r.

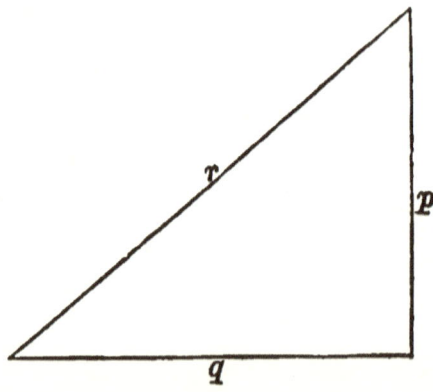

Then since the geometrical property of such a triangle, established by Euclid I. 47, may be extended to the case in which the sides are represented by *numbers* or symbols standing for numbers,

$$p^2 + q^2 = r^2.$$

If any two of the numerical quantities involved in this equation are given, we can determine the third.

For example, if $r=5$ and $q=3$,
$$p^2 + 9 = 25,$$
$$\therefore p^2 = 16,$$
$$\therefore p = 4.$$

EXAMPLES.—II.

(1) The hypotenuse being 51 yards, and one of the sides containing the right angle 24 yards, find the other side.

(2) The sides containing the right angle being 8 feet and 6 feet, find the hypotenuse.

(3) A rectangular field measures 225 yards in length, and 120 yards in breadth; what will be the length of a diagonal path across it?

(4) A rectangular field is 300 yards long and 200 yards broad; find the distance from corner to corner.

(5) A rectangular plantation, whose width is 88 yards, contains $2\frac{1}{2}$ acres; find the distance from corner to corner across the plantation.

(6) The sides of a right-angled triangle are in Arithmetical Progression and the hypotenuse is 20 feet; find the other sides.

(7) The sides of a right-angled triangle are in Arithmetical Progression; shew that they are proportional to 3, 4, 5.

(8) A ladder, whose foot rests in a given position, just reaches a window on one side of a street, and when turned about its foot, just reaches a window on the other side. If the two positions of the ladder be at right angles to each other, and the heights of the windows be 36 and 27 feet respectively, find the width of the street and the length of the ladder.

(9) In a right-angled isosceles triangle the hypotenuse is 12 feet, find the length of each of the other sides.

(10) What is the length of the diagonal of a square, whose side is 5 inches?

(11) The area of a square is 390625 square feet; what is the diagonal?

(12) Each side of an equilateral triangle is 13; find the length of the perpendicular dropped from one of the angles on the opposite side.

(13) If ABC be an equilateral triangle and the length of AD, a perpendicular on BC, be 15; find the length of AB.

(14) The radius of a circle is 37 inches; a chord is drawn in the circle: if the length of this chord be 70 inches, find its distance from the centre.

(15) The distance of a chord in a circle from the centre is 180 inches; the diameter of the circle is 362 inches: find the length of the chord.

(16) The length of a chord in a circle is 150 feet, and its distance from the centre is 308 feet; find the diameter of the circle.

(17) If ABC be an isosceles right-angled triangle, C being the right angle, show that
$$AC : AB = 1 : \sqrt{2}.$$

(18) If DEF be an equilateral triangle and a perpendicular DG be dropped on EF, show that
$$EG : ED : DG = 1 : 2 : \sqrt{3}.$$

CHAPTER II.

On the Ratio of the Circumference of a Circle to the Diameter.

5. It is evident that a straight line can be compared as to its length with a circular arc, and that consequently the ratio between such lines can be represented in the form of a fraction.

6. We must assume as an axiom that an arc is greater than the chord subtending it: that is, if ABD be part of the circumference of a circle cut off by the straight line AD, the length of ABD is greater than the length of AD.

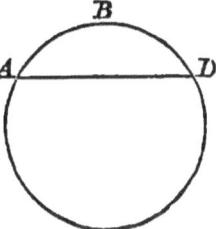

7. A figure enclosed by any number of straight lines is called a *polygon*.

8. A *regular* polygon is one in which all the sides and angles are equal.

9. The *perimeter* of a polygon is the sum of the sides. Hence if AB be one of the sides of a regular polygon of n sides the perimeter of the polygon will be $n \cdot AB$.

10. The circumference of a circle is greater than the perimeter of any polygon which can be inscribed in the circle, but as the number of sides of such a polygon is increased the perimeter of the polygon approaches nearer to the circumference of the circle, as will appear from the following illustration.

Let AB be the side of a regular hexagon $ABDEFG$ inscribed in a circle.

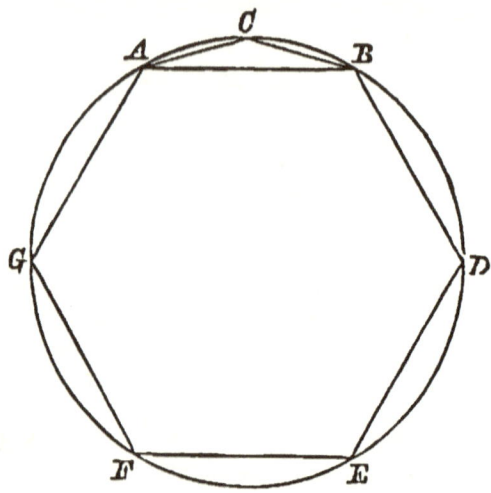

Then AB is equal to the radius of the circle. EUCL. IV. 15.

Now the arc ACB is greater than AB, and the circumference of the circle is therefore larger than the perimeter of the hexagon.

Hence

the circumference is greater than six times the radius, and greater than *three times the diameter*.

Now suppose C to be the middle point of the arc AB.

Join AC, CB.

These will be sides of a regular dodecagon or figure of 12 sides inscribed in the circle.

Now AC, CB are together *greater than AB*: but AC, CB are together *less than the arc ACB*.

Hence the perimeter of the dodecagon will be less than the circumference of the circle, but will approximate more nearly than the perimeter of the hexagon to the circumference of the circle.

So the larger the number of sides of a polygon inscribed in a circle, the more nearly does the perimeter of the polygon approach to the circumference of the circle; and when the number of sides is infinitely large, the perimeter of the polygon will become ultimately equal to the circumference of the circle.

11. *To shew that the circumference of a circle varies as the radius.*

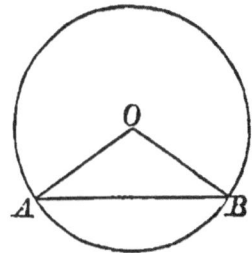 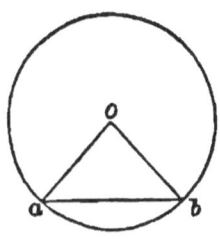

Let O and o be the centres of two circles.

Let AB, ab be sides of regular polygons of n sides inscribed in the circles, P, p the perimeters of the polygons, and C, c the circumferences of the circles.

Then OAB, oab are similar triangles.

$$\therefore OA : oa :: AB : ab$$
$$:: n \cdot AB : n \cdot ab$$
$$:: P : p.$$

Now when n is very large the perimeters of the polygons may be regarded as equal to the circumferences of the circles;

$$\therefore OA : oa :: C : c.$$

Hence it follows that the circumference of a circle varies as the radius of the circle.

12. Since the circumference varies as the radius, the ratio $\dfrac{\text{circumference}}{\text{radius}}$ is the same for all circles, and therefore the ratio $\dfrac{\text{circumference}}{\text{diameter}}$ is the same for all circles.

13. Def. The ratio $\dfrac{\text{circumference}}{\text{diameter}}$ is denoted by the symbol π.

14. The value of this numerical quantity π cannot be determined exactly, but it has been *approximately* determined by various methods.

If we take a piece of string which will exactly go round a penny, and another piece which will exactly stretch across the diameter of the penny: if we then set off along a straight line seven lengths of the first string, and on another straight line by the side of the first we set off twenty-two lengths of the second string, we shall find that the two lines are very nearly equal. Hence 22 diameters are nearly equal to 7 circumferences, that is the ratio $\dfrac{\text{circumference}}{\text{diameter}} = \dfrac{22}{7}$ nearly, or in other words the fraction $\dfrac{22}{7}$ is a rough approximation to the value of π.

The fraction $\dfrac{355}{113}$ gives a closer approximation.

The accurate value of the ratio to 5 places of decimals is 3·14159.

15. Suppose we call the radius of a circle r: then the diameter $= 2r$.

Now $\dfrac{\text{circumference}}{\text{diameter}} = \pi$;

$\therefore \dfrac{\text{circumference}}{2r} = \pi$;

$\therefore$ circumference $= 2\pi r$.

Hence arc of semicircle $= \pi r$,

and arc of quadrant $= \dfrac{\pi r}{2}$.

Examples.—III.

In the following examples the value of π may be taken as $\frac{22}{7}$.

(1) The diameter of a circle is 5 feet, what is its circumference?

(2) The circumference of a circle is 542 ft. 6 in., what is its radius?

(3) The driving-wheel of a locomotive-engine of diameter 6 feet makes 2 revolutions in a second: find approximately the number of miles per hour at which the train is going.

(4) Supposing the earth to be a perfect sphere whose circumference is 25000 miles, what is its diameter?

(5) The diameter of the Sun is 883220 miles, what is its circumference?

(6) The circumference of the moon is 6850 miles, what is its radius?

(7) Find the length of an arc which is $\frac{1}{12}$ of the whole circumference, if the radius is 12 ft. 6 in.

(8) Find the length of an arc which is $\frac{5}{7}$ of the whole circumference, if the diameter is 21 feet.

(9) The circumference of a circle is 150 feet, what is the side of a square inscribed in it?

(10) The circumference of a circle is 200 feet, what is the side of a square inscribed in it?

(11) A water-wheel, whose diameter is 12 feet, makes 30 revolutions per minute. Find approximately the number of miles per hour traversed by a point on the circumference of the wheel.

(12) A mill-sail, whose length is 21 feet, makes 15 revolutions per minute. How many miles per hour does the end of the sail traverse?

CHAPTER III.

On the Measurement of Angles.

16. TRIGONOMETRY was originally, as the name imports, the science which furnished methods for determining the magnitude of the sides and angles of triangles, but it has been extended to the treatment of all theorems involving the consideration of angular magnitudes.

17. Euclid defines a plane rectilineal angle as the inclination of two straight lines to each other, which meet, but are not in the same straight line. Hence the angles of which Euclid treats are less than two right angles.

In Trigonometry the term *angle* is used in a more extended sense, the magnitude of angles in this science being unlimited.

18. An angle in Trigonometry is defined in the following manner.

Let WQE be a fixed straight line, and QP a line which revolves about the fixed point Q, and which at first coincides with QE.

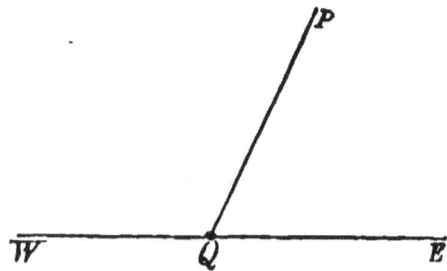

Then when QP is in the position represented in the figure, we say *that it has described the angle PQE.*

The advantage of this definition is that it enables us to consider angles not only greater than two right angles, but greater than four right angles, viz. such as are described by the revolving line when it makes more than one complete revolution.

19. In speaking of a trigonometrical angle we must take into account the position from which the line that has described the angle started.

Suppose for instance that QP, starting from the position QE and revolving in a direction contrary to that in which the hands of a watch revolve, has come into the position indicated in the figure. It has then described an angle EQP greater than two right angles.

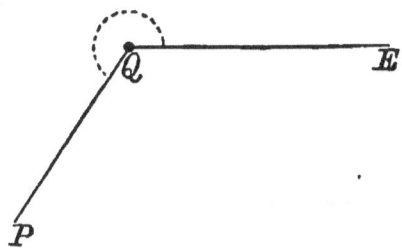

20. The magnitudes of angles are represented by numbers expressing how many times the given angles contain a certain angle fixed upon as the unit of angular measure.

When we speak of an angle θ we mean an angle which contains the unit of angular measurement θ times.

21. There are three modes of measuring angles, called

   I.   The Sexagesimal or English method,
  II.   The Centesimal or French method,
 III.   The Circular Measure,

which we now proceed to describe in order.

I. *The Sexagesimal Method.*

22. In this method we suppose a right angle to be divided into 90 equal parts, each of which parts is called a *degree*, each degree to be divided into 60 equal parts, each of which is called a *minute*, and each minute to be divided into 60 equal parts, each of which is called a *second*. Then the magnitude

of an angle is expressed by the number of degrees, minutes and seconds, which it contains. Degrees, minutes and seconds are marked respectively by the symbols °, ′, ″ : thus, to represent 14 degrees, 9 minutes, 37·45 seconds, we write

$$14^\circ . 9' . 37'' \cdot 45.$$

23. We can express the measure of an angle (expressed in degrees, minutes and seconds) in degrees and decimal parts of a degree by the following process.

Let the given angle be $39^\circ . 5' . 33''$,

$$\begin{array}{r|l} 60 & 33\cdot \\ \hline 60 & 5\cdot 55 \\ \hline & \cdot 0925 \end{array}$$

∴ $39^\circ . 5' . 33'' = 39\cdot 0925$ degrees.

EXAMPLES.—IV.

Express as the decimal of a degree the following angles.

(1) $24^\circ . 16' . 5''$,   (4) $5' . 28''$,

(2) $37^\circ . 2' . 43''$,   (5) $375^\circ . 4'$,

(3) $175^\circ . 0' . 14''$,   (6) $78^\circ . 12' . 4''$.

II. *The Centesimal Method.*

24. In this method we suppose a right angle to be divided into 100 equal parts, each of which parts is called a *grade*, each grade to be divided into 100 equal parts, each of which is called a *minute*, and each minute to be divided into 100 equal parts, each of which is called a *second*. Then the magnitude of an angle is expressed by the number of grades, minutes and seconds, which it contains. Grades, minutes and seconds are marked respectively by the symbols ᵍ, ′, ″: thus, to represent 35 grades, 56 minutes, 84·53 seconds, we write $35^g . 56' . 84'' \cdot 53$.

The advantage of this method is that we can write down the minutes and seconds as the decimal of a grade by inspection.

Thus, if the given angle be $14^g . 19' . 57"$,

$$\text{since } 19' = \frac{19}{100} \text{ of a grade} = \cdot 19 \text{ grades,}$$

$$\text{and } 57" = \frac{57}{10000} \text{ of a grade} = \cdot 0057 \text{ grades,}$$

$$14^g . 19' . 57" = 14 \cdot 1957 \text{ grades.}$$

25. If the number expressing the minutes or seconds has only one significant digit, we must prefix a cipher to occupy the place of tens before we write down the minutes and seconds as the decimal of a grade.

Thus $\quad\quad\quad 25^g . 9' . 54" = 25^g . 09 . 54'$
$$= 25 \cdot 0954 \text{ grades,}$$

and $\quad\quad\quad 36^g . 8' . 4" = 36^g . 08' . 04"$
$$= 36 \cdot 0804 \text{ grades.}$$

EXAMPLES.—V.

Express as decimals of a grade the following angles:

(1) $25^g . 14' . 25"$, (4) $15' . 7" \cdot 45$,

(2) $38^g . 4' . 15"$, (5) $425^g . 13' . 5" \cdot 54$,

(3) $214^g . 3' . 7"$, (6) $2^g . 2' . 2" \cdot 22$.

26. The Centesimal Method was introduced by the French Mathematicians in the 18th century. The advantages that would have been obtained by its use were not considered sufficient to counterbalance the enormous labour which must have been spent on the re-arrangement of the Mathematical Tables then in use.

III. *The Circular Measure.*

27. In selecting a unit of angular measurement we may take any angle whose magnitude is invariable. Such an angle is that which is subtended at the centre of a circle by an arc equal to the radius of the circle, as we shall now prove.

28. *To shew that the angle subtended at the centre of a circle by an arc equal to the radius of the circle is the same for all circles.*

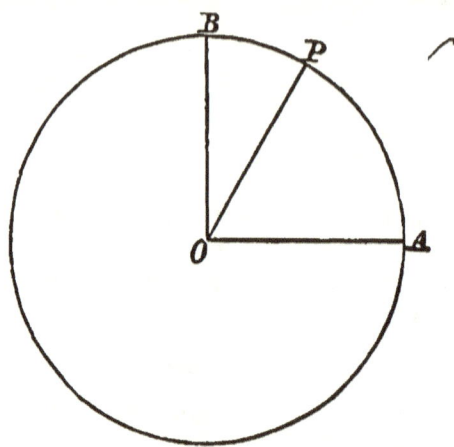

Let O be the centre of a circle, whose radius is r;

AB the arc of a quadrant, and therefore AOB a right angle;

AP an arc equal to the radius AO.

Then, $AP = r$ and $AB = \dfrac{\pi r}{2}$. (Art. 15.)

Now, by Euc. VI. 33,

$$\frac{\text{angle } AOP}{\text{angle } AOB} = \frac{\text{arc } AP}{\text{arc } AB},$$

or,
$$\frac{\text{angle } AOP}{\text{a right angle}} = \frac{r}{\dfrac{\pi r}{2}}$$

$$= \frac{2r}{\pi r}$$

$$= \frac{2}{\pi}.$$

Hence angle $AOP = \dfrac{2 \text{ right angles}}{\pi}$

Thus the magnitude of the angle AOP is independent of r and is therefore the same for all circles.

ON THE MEASUREMENT OF ANGLES.

29. In the Circular System of measurement the unit of angular measurement may be described as

(1) The angle subtended at the centre of a circle by an arc equal to the radius of the circle,

or, which is the same thing, as we proved in Art. 28, as

(2) The angle whose magnitude is the πth part of two right angles.

30. It is important that the beginner should have a clear conception of the size of this angle, and this he will best obtain by considering it relatively to the magnitude of that angular unit which we call a degree.

Now the unit of circular measure

$$= \frac{\text{two right angles}}{\pi} = \frac{180^\circ}{3 \cdot 14159} = 57^\circ \cdot 2958 \text{ nearly.}$$

Now if BC be the quadrant of a circle, and if we suppose the arc BC to be divided into 90 equal parts, the right angle BAC will be divided by the radii which pass through these points into 90 equal angles, each of which is called a degree.

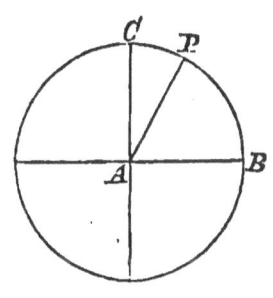

A radius AP meeting the arc at a certain point between the 57th and 58th divisions, reckoned from B, will make with AB an angle equal in magnitude to the unit of circular measure.

Hence an angle whose circular measure is 2 contains rather more than 114 degrees, and one whose circular measure is 3 contains nearly 172 degrees, or rather less than two right angles.

31. Since the unit of circular measure $= \dfrac{2 \text{ right angles}}{\pi}$,

π times the unit of circular measure $= 2$ right angles.

Hence

an angle whose circular measure is π is equal to 2 right angles,

.... $\dfrac{\pi}{2}$ .... a right angle,

.... 2π .... 4 right angles.

32. *To shew that the circular measure of an angle is equal to a fraction which has for its numerator the arc subtended by that angle at the centre of any circle, and for its denominator the radius of that circle.*

Let EOD be any angle.

About O as centre and with any radius, describe a circle cutting OE in A, and OD in R.

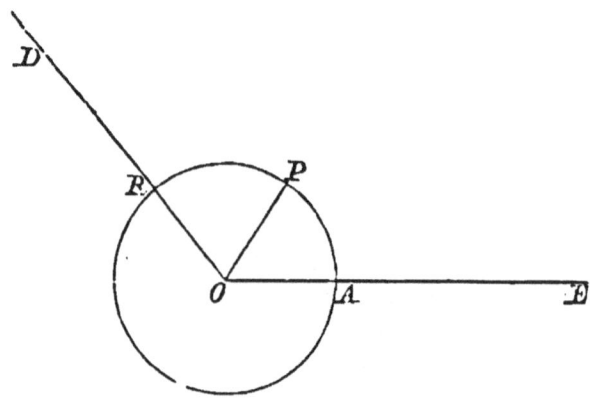

Make angle AOP equal to the unit of circular measure.

Then arc AP = radius AO (Art. 29).

Now, by Euc. VI. 33,

$$\frac{\text{angle } AOR}{\text{angle } AOP} = \frac{AR}{AP};$$

$$\therefore \text{ angle } AOR = \frac{AR}{AP} \cdot \text{angle } AOP$$

$$= \frac{AR}{AO} \cdot \text{angle } AOP$$

$$= \frac{\text{arc}}{\text{radius}} \cdot \text{unit of circular measure};$$

$\therefore$ the circular measure of angle AOR

$$= \frac{\text{arc}}{\text{radius}}.$$

33. The units in the three systems when expressed in terms of one common standard, two right angles, stand thus:

the unit in the Sexagesimal Method $=\dfrac{1}{180}$ of two right angles,

the unit in the Centesimal Method $=\dfrac{1}{200}$ of two right angles,

the unit in the Circular Method $=\dfrac{1}{\pi}$ of two right angles.

34. It is not usual to assign any distinguishing mark to angles estimated by the Third Method, but for the purpose of stating the relation between the three units in a clear and concise form, we shall use the symbol 1^c to express the unit of circular measure.

Then we express the relation between the units thus:

$$1^u : 1^g : 1^c = \dfrac{1}{180} : \dfrac{1}{200} : \dfrac{1}{\pi}.$$

CHAPTER IV.

On the Method of Converting the Measures of Angles from one to another System of Measurement.

35. WE proceed to explain the process for converting the measures of angles from each of the three systems of measurement described in Chap. III. to the other two.

36. *To convert the measure of an angle expressed in degrees to the corresponding measure in grades.*

Let the given angle contain D degrees.

$$1 \text{ degree} = \frac{1}{90} \text{ of a right angle};$$

$$\therefore D \text{ degrees} = \frac{D}{90} \text{ of a right angle}$$

$$= \frac{D}{90} \text{ of 100 grades}$$

$$= \frac{100D}{90} \text{ grades}$$

$$= \frac{10D}{9} \text{ grades.}$$

Hence we obtain the following rule: *If an angle be expressed in degrees, multiply the measure in degrees by 10, divide the result by 9, and you obtain the measure of the angle in grades.*

Ex. How many grades are contained in the angle $24°.51'.45''$?

$$24°.51'.45'' = 24\cdot8625 \text{ degrees}$$

$$\begin{array}{r|l} & 10 \\ \hline 9 & 248\cdot625 \\ \hline \text{grades} & 27\cdot625 \end{array}$$

∴ the angle contains $27^g.62'.50''$.

EXAMPLES.—VI.

Find the number of grades, minutes and seconds in the following angles:

(1) $27°.15'.46''$.   (2) $157°.4'.9''$.
(3) $24'.18''$.   (4) $19°.0'.18''$.
(5) $143°.9'$.   (6) $28°$.
(7) $10°.25'.48''$.   (8) $27°.38'.12''$.
(9) $300°.15'.58''$.   (10) $422°.7'.22''$.

37. *To convert the measure of an angle expressed in grades to the corresponding measure in degrees.*

Let the given angle contain G grades.

$$1 \text{ grade} = \frac{1}{100} \text{ of a right angle};$$

$$\therefore G \text{ grades} = \frac{G}{100} \text{ of a right angle}$$

$$= \frac{G}{100} \text{ of 90 degrees}$$

$$= \frac{90G}{100} \text{ degrees}$$

$$= \frac{9G}{10} \text{ degrees.}$$

Hence we obtain the following rule: *If an angle be expressed in grades, multiply the measure in grades by 9, divide the result by 10, and you obtain the measure of the angle in degrees.*

Ex. How many degrees are contained in the angle $42^g.34'.56''$?

$$42^g.34'.56' = 42\cdot3456 \text{ grades}$$

$$\begin{array}{r} 9 \\ \hline 10 \mid 381\cdot1104 \end{array}$$

degrees $38\cdot11104$
$$\overline{60}$$
minutes $6\cdot66240$
$$\overline{60}$$
seconds $39\cdot74400$

∴ the angle contains $38°.6'.39''\cdot744$.

Examples.—VII.

Find the number of degrees, minutes, and seconds in the following angles:

(1) $19^g.45'.95''$.   (2) $124^g.5'.8''$.
(3) $29^g.75'$.   (4) $15^g.0'.15''$.
(5) $154^g.7'.24''$.   (6) 43^g.
(7) $38^g.71'.20''\cdot3$.   (8) $50^g.76'.94''\cdot3$.
(9) $170^g.63'.27''$.   (10) $324^g.13'.88''\cdot7$.

38. *If the number of degrees in an angle be given, to find its circular measure.*

Let the given angle contain D degrees.

$$1° = \frac{1}{180} \text{ of two right angles}$$

$$= \frac{1}{180} \text{ of } \pi \text{ units of circular measure}$$

$$= \frac{\pi}{180} \text{ units of circular measure;}$$

$$\therefore D° = \frac{D\pi}{180} \text{ units of circular measure.}$$

CONVERTING MEASURES OF ANGLES.

Hence we obtain the following rule:

If an angle be expressed in degrees, multiply the measure in degrees by π, divide the result by 180, and you obtain the circular measure of the angle.

Ex. Find the circular measure of $45°.15'$;

$$45°.15' = 45\cdot 25 \text{ degrees};$$

∴ circular measure required is

$$\frac{45\cdot 25 \times \pi}{180} = \frac{4525\pi}{18000} = \frac{905\pi}{3600} = \frac{181\pi}{720}.$$

EXAMPLES.—VIII.

Express in circular measure the following angles:

(1) $60°$.   (2) $22°.30'$.   (3) $11°.15'$.   (4) $270°$.

(5) $315°$.   (6) $24°.13'$.   (7) $95°.20'$.   (8) $12°.5'.4''$.

(9) The angles of an equilateral triangle.

(10) The angles of an isosceles right-angled triangle.

39. *If the circular measure of an angle be given to find the number of degrees which it contains.*

Let θ be the given circular measure.

$$1^c = \frac{1}{\pi} \text{ of two right angles}$$

$$= \frac{1}{\pi} \text{ of 180 degrees}$$

$$= \frac{180}{\pi} \text{ degrees};$$

$$\therefore \theta^c = \frac{\theta \cdot 180}{\pi} \text{ degrees}.$$

Hence we obtain the following rule:

If an angle be expressed in circular measure, multiply the measure by 180, divide the result by π, and you obtain the measure of the angle in degrees.

Ex. Express in degrees the angle whose circular measure is $\frac{5\pi}{8}$.

The measure in degrees $= \frac{5\pi \times 180}{8 \times \pi} = \frac{900}{8} = 112 \cdot 5$ degrees.

Examples.—IX.

Express in degrees, &c. the angles whose circular measures are

(1) $\frac{\pi}{2}$. (2) $\frac{\pi}{3}$. (3) $\frac{\pi}{4}$. (4) $\frac{\pi}{6}$. (5) $\frac{2\pi}{3}$.

(6) $\frac{1}{2}$. (7) $\frac{1}{3}$. (8) $\frac{1}{4}$. (9) $\frac{1}{6}$. (10) $\frac{2}{3}$.

40. Similar rules will hold with respect to the equations for connecting the centesimal and the circular systems, 200 being put in the place of 180: thus

circular measure of an angle containing G grades $= G \cdot \frac{\pi}{200}$,

number of grades in the angle whose

circular measure is $\theta = \theta \cdot \frac{200}{\pi}$.

Examples.—X.

Express in circular measure the following angles:

(1) 50^g. (2) 25^g. (3) $6^g . 25'$. (4) 250^g.

(5) 500^g. (6) $13^g . 5' . 5''$. (7) $24^g . 15' . 2'' \cdot 15$.

(8) $125^g . 0' . 13''$. (9) $3'$. (10) $5''$.

Examples.—XI.

Express in grades, &c. the angles whose circular measures are

41. We shall now give a set of Miscellaneous Examples to illustrate the principles explained in this and the two preceding Chapters.

EXAMPLES.—XII.

(*Note.* Circular measure is not introduced till Ex. 17.)

1. If the unit of angular measurement be $5°$, what is the measure of $22\frac{1}{2}°$?

2. If an angle of $42\frac{1}{2}°$ be represented by 10, what is the unit of measurement?

3. An angle referred to different units has measures in the ratio 8 to 5; the smaller unit is $2°$, what is the other? Express the unit in terms of the other.

4. An angle referred to different units has measures in the ratio 7 to 6; the smaller unit is $3°$, what is the other? Express each unit in terms of the other.

5. If half a right angle be taken as the unit of angular measurement, what is the measure of an angle of $42°$?

6. Compare the angles $13°.13'.48''$ and $14^g.7^v$.

7. If D be the number of degrees in any angle and G the number of grades, show that $G = D + \frac{1}{9}D$.

8. An equilateral triangle is divided into two triangles by a line bisecting one side; express the angles of these two triangles in degrees and grades respectively.

9. If the angles of a triangle are in Arithmetical Progression, show that one of them is $60°$.

10. Reduce $39^g\cdot012$ to degrees, minutes and seconds.

11. If there be m English minutes in an angle, find the number of French seconds in the same angle.

12. What fraction of a right angle must be the unit in order that an angle of $5°.33'.20''$ may be represented by 5?

13. What must be the unit angle if the sum of the measures of a degree and a grade is 1?

14. If there be three angles in arithmetical progression, and the number of grades in the greatest be equal to the number of degrees in the sum of the other two, the angles are as 11 : 19 : 27.

15. Prove that $\dfrac{180^0}{\sqrt{3}} = 115^{\text{g}}.47'$ nearly.

16. The three angles of a triangle are in arithmetical progression, and the number of grades in the least : the number of degrees in the greatest :: 2 : 9. Find the angles.

17. It being given that the angle subtended by an arc equal to the radius is $57^{\circ}29577$, find the ratio of the circumference of a circle to its diameter.

18. Two angles of a triangle are in magnitude as 2 : 3. If the third angle be a right angle, express the angles of this triangle in each of the three systems of measurement.

19. Two straight lines drawn from the centre of a circle contain an angle subtended by an arc which is to the whole circumference as 13 : 27; express this angle in degrees.

20. An arc of a circle is to the whole circumference as 17 : 54; express in grades the angle which the arc subtends at the centre of the circle.

21. Determine in grades the magnitude of the angle subtended by an arc two feet long at the centre of a circle whose radius is 18 inches.

22. One angle of a triangle is 2 in circular measure, and another is 20^0: find the number of grades in the third.

23. An arc of a circle, whose radius is 7 inches, subtends an angle of $15^0.39'.7''$; what angle will an arc of the same length subtend in a circle whose radius is 2 inches?

24. What is the circular measure of $11^{\text{g}}.30'$ if $\pi = \dfrac{355}{113}$?

25. If the numerical value of an angle measured by the circular system be $\left(\dfrac{\pi}{3}\right)^2$, how many degrees does it contain?

26. The whole circumference of one circle is just long enough to subtend an angle of one grade at the centre of another circle: what part of the latter circumference will subtend an angle of $1°$ at the centre of the former circle?

27. Taking 4 right angles as the unit, what number will represent $1°$, 1^g, 1^c respectively?

28. The earth being supposed a sphere of which the diameter is 7980 miles, find the length of $1°$ of the meridian.

29. If half a right angle be the unit of angular measurement, express the angles whose measures are

$$\frac{3}{2},\ 4,\ \pi,\ 4n+\frac{1}{3},$$

(1) in degrees, (2) in units of circular measure.

30. If the unit be an angle subtended at the centre of a circle by an arc three times as large as the radius, what number will represent an angle of $45°$?

31. Express in degrees:
   (1) The angle of a regular hexagon.
   (2) The angle of a regular pentagon.

32. Express in grades:
   (1) The angle of a regular pentagon.
   (2) The angle of a regular octagon.

33. Express in circular measure:
   (1) The angle of an equilateral triangle.
   (2) The angle of a regular hexagon.

34. Find the circular measure of the angle of a regular polygon of n sides.

35. The radius of a circle is 18 feet, find the length of an arc which subtends an angle of $10°$ at the centre.

36. The angles in one regular polygon are twice as many as those in another polygon, and an angle of the former : an angle of the latter :: 3 : 2. Find the number of the sides in each.

CHAPTER V.

On the Use of the Signs + and − to denote Contrariety of Direction.

42. In a science which deals with the distances measured from a fixed point it is convenient to have some means of distinguishing a distance, measured in one direction from the point, from a distance, measured in a direction exactly opposite to the former. This contrariety of direction we can denote by prefixing the Algebraic signs + and − to the symbols denoting the lengths of the measured lines.

43. It must also be observed that magnitudes of things cannot properly be made subject to the rules and operations of Algebra, as these rules and operations have only been proved for algebraical symbols. We must therefore find some algebraical representative for any magnitude before we subject it to algebraical operations: such a representative is the measure of that magnitude with the proper sign prefixed.

44. We explained in Chapters I. and III. the principles of algebraical representation as applied to the *measures* of lines and angles, and we have now to explain the rules by which we are enabled to express *contrariety of direction* in the case of lines and angles by employing the signs + and −.

45. Suppose that two straight roads *NS*, *WE* intersect one another at right angles at the point *O*.

A traveller comes along *SO* with the intention of going to *E*.

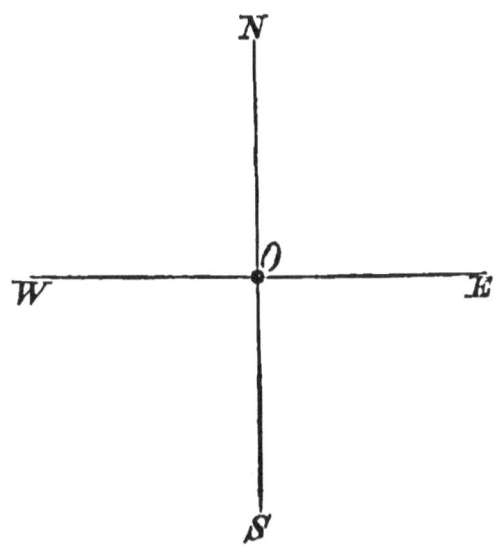

Suppose *OE* to represent a distance of 4 miles

and *OW* to represent a distance of 4 miles,

and suppose the traveller to walk at the rate of 4 miles an hour.

If on coming to *O* he makes a mistake and turns to the left instead of the right he will find himself at the end of an hour at *W*, 4 miles *further* from *E* than he was when he reached *O*.

So far from making progress *towards* his object, he has walked *away from it:* so far from *gaining* he has *lost* ground.

In Algebraic language we express the distinction between the distance he ought to have traversed and the distance he did traverse by saying that *OE* represents a *positive* quantity and *OW* a *negative* quantity.

46. Availing ourselves of the advantages afforded by the use of the signs + and − to indicate the directions of lines, we make the following conventions:

(1) Let O be a fixed point in any straight line BOA.

$$B \quad\quad\quad O \quad\quad\quad A$$

Then, if distances measured from O in the direction OA be considered *positive*, distances measured from O in the direction OB will properly be considered *negative*.

Hence if OA and OB be equal and the measure of each be m, the complete algebraical representative of OA is m, whereas that of OB is $-m$.

The direction in which the positive distances are measured is quite indifferent, but when once it has been fixed, the negative distances must lie in the contrary direction.

(2) Let O be a fixed point in which two lines AB, CD cut one another at right angles.

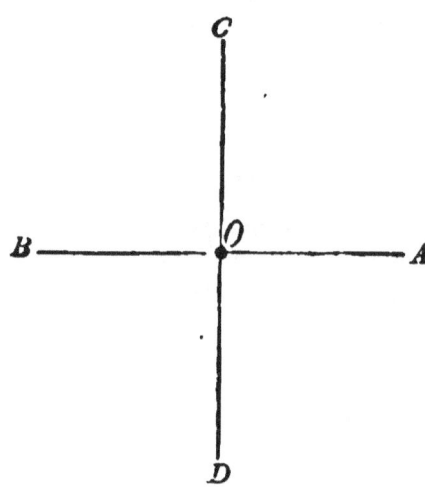

Then, if we regard lines measured along OA and OC as *positive*, we shall properly regard lines measured along OB and OD as *negative*.

This convention is extended to lines *parallel* to AB or CD in the following manner:

CONTRARIETY OF DIRECTION. 29

Lines parallel to *CD* are positive when they lie above *AB*, negative .... below *AB*.

Lines parallel to *AB* are positive when they lie on the right of *CD*, negative when they lie on the left of *CD*.

47. We may now proceed to explain how the position of a point may be determined.

NS and *WE* are two lines cutting each other at right angles in the point *O*.

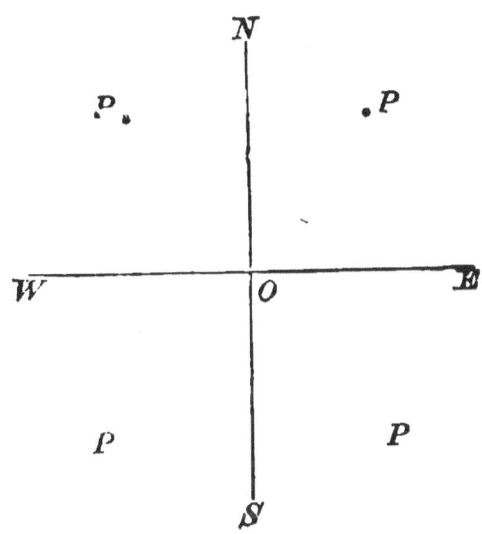

The position of a point *P* is said to be known, when the lengths of the perpendiculars dropped from it on the lines *NS* and *WE* are known, provided that we also know on which side of each of the lines *NS* and *WE* the point *P* lies.

If the perpendicular dropped from *P* to *WE* be *above* *WE* it is reckoned *positive*.

If the perpendicular dropped from *P* to *WE* be *below* *WE* it is reckoned *negative*.

If the perpendicular dropped from *P* to *NS* be on the *right* of *NS* it is reckoned *positive*.

If the perpendicular dropped from *P* to *NS* be on the *left* of *NS* it is reckoned *negative*.

CONTRARIETY OF DIRECTION.

48. Angles in Trigonometry must be considered not with respect to their magnitude only, but also with reference to their mode of generation; that is to say, we shall have to consider whether they are traced out by the revolution of the generating line *from right to left or from left to right*.

49. Let a line OP starting from the position OE revolve about O in the direction $ENWSE$; that is, in a direction contrary to that in which the hands of a watch revolve.

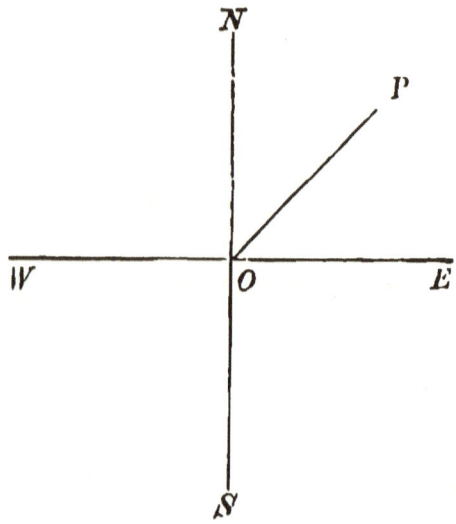

Then all angles so traced out are considered *positive*.

When OP reaches the line

ON it will have traced out a right angle,
OW .... two right angles,
OS .... three right angles,
OE .... four right angles.

If we suppose the line to revolve in the direction $ESWNE$, we may properly account the angles traced out by it to be *negative* angles.

For the sake of clearness we shall call OP the *revolving* line, and OE the *primitive* line.

50. Now suppose P to be a point in the revolving line OP.

Let a perpendicular let fall from P meet the line EW in the point M, and let this be done in each of the four quarters made by the intersection of NS and WE, as in the diagrams in the next article.

Then in the first quarter PM is positive and OM is positive,

.... second........ PM is positive and OM is negative,

.... third .... PM is negative and OM is negative,

.... fourth......... PM is negative and OM is positive.

Note.—When we say that a line PM *is* positive or negative we mean that its measure has the + or − sign prefixed to indicate the direction in which it is drawn.

Thus if the measure of PM be p, the complete algebraical representative of PM will be p or $-p$ according as PM is above or below WE.

So also if the measure of OM be q, the complete algebraical representative of OM will be q or $-q$, according as OM is on the right or left of NS.

CHAPTER VI.

On the Trigonometrical Ratios.

51. LET the line OP revolving from the position OE about O from right to left describe the angle EOP, which we shall call the Angle of Reference.

From P let fall the perpendicular PM on the line EOW.

We then obtain a right-angled triangle POM, which we shall call The Triangle of Reference.

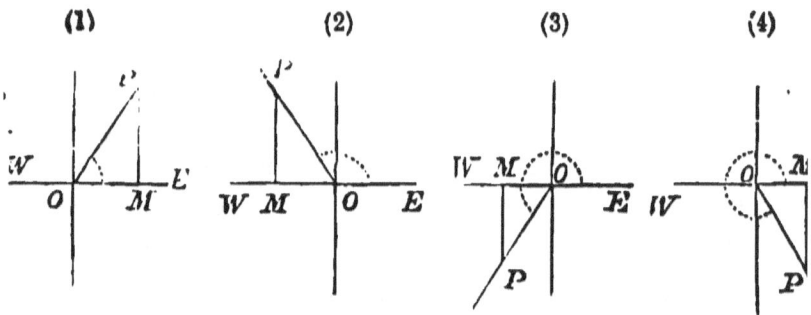

In fig. (1) the angle of reference is an acute angle.

In fig. (2) it is an obtuse angle.

In fig. (3) it is greater than two right angles but less than three right angles.

In fig. (4) it is greater than three right angles but less than four right angles.

Then the ratio

(1) $\dfrac{PM}{OP}$ is defined to be the *sine* of the angle EOP,

(2) $\dfrac{OM}{OP}$ .... *cosine* ....

(3) $\dfrac{PM}{OM}$ .... *tangent* ....

(4) $\dfrac{OP}{PM}$ .... *cosecant* ....

(5) $\dfrac{OP}{OM}$ .... *secant* ....

(6) $\dfrac{OM}{PM}$ .... *cotangent* ....

52. It will be observed that

$$\text{cosecant } EOP = \frac{1}{\text{sine } EOP},$$

$$\text{secant } EOP = \frac{1}{\text{cosine } EOP},$$

$$\text{cotangent } EOP = \frac{1}{\text{tangent } EOP}.$$

53. The words sine, cosine, &c. are abbreviated, and the Trigonometrical Ratios of an angle A are thus written:

sin A, cos A, tan A, cosec A, sec A, cot A.

54. The defect of the cosine of an angle from unity is called the *versed sine*, thus,

versed sine $EOP = 1 - \cos EOP$.

The words versed sine are abbreviated to *versin*.

55. The powers of the Trigonometrical Ratios are expressed in the following way:

(sin $A)^2$ is written thus, $\sin^2 A$,

(cos $A)^3$ is written thus, $\cos^3 A$,

and so for the other ratios.

56. We have given the Ratio-definitions in the most *general* form, but we shall for the present confine the attention of the student to the *particular* cases of the Ratios of Acute and Obtuse Angles, with which we are chiefly concerned in this treatise.

Ratios for Acute Angles.

57. The six Trigonometrical Ratios are *arithmetical* quantities, denoting the relations existing between the sides of a right-angled triangle, which we call the Triangle of Reference, taken two by two.

58. Let us now look at the *order* in which the sides are taken to form the ratios which we call the *sine* and the *cosine* of an acute angle.

Referring to fig. (1) of Art. 51,

$$\text{sine } EOP = \frac{PM}{OP},$$

$$\text{cosine } EOP = \frac{OM}{OP}.$$

In each case the *denominator* of the fraction is formed by that side of the triangle of reference which is *opposite to the right angle*.

Of the two other sides we may call PM the side *opposite* to the angle of reference, so as to distinguish it from OM the side *adjacent* to the angle of reference.

Hence in determining the ratio which we call the *sine* of a given acute angle we must take as the *numerator* of the fraction that side of our triangle of reference which is *opposite* to the given angle; and in determining the ratio which we call the *cosine* of a given acute angle we must take as the *numerator* of the fraction that side of our triangle of reference which is *adjacent* to the given angle: the denominator being in both cases that side of the triangle which *subtends the right angle* of the triangle.

Note.—Omitting the word *acute* in this Article the remarks will be applicable to all the diagrams of Art. 51.

59. If the remarks given in the preceding Article be clearly understood, the student will find no difficulty in writing down the ratios for the sine and the cosine of a given acute angle, whatever may be the position in which the triangle of reference for that angle may stand.

Suppose PM to be perpendicular to OM,

DN to be perpendicular to PM.

Then POM, PDN, DMN are three right-angled triangles.

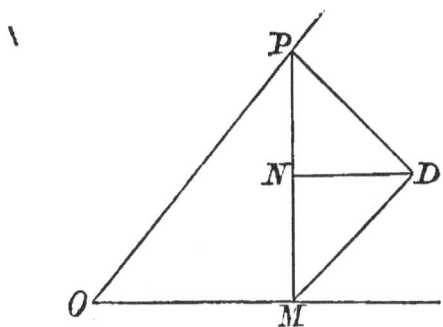

Now $\quad \sin POM = \dfrac{PM}{OP}: \cos POM = \dfrac{OM}{OP}.$

$\quad\quad \sin OPM = \dfrac{OM}{OP}: \cos OPM = \dfrac{PM}{OP}.$

Also $\quad \sin DPN = \dfrac{DN}{PD}: \cos DPN = \dfrac{PN}{PD}.$

$\quad\quad \sin PDN = \dfrac{PN}{PD}: \cos PDN = \dfrac{DN}{PD}.$

And $\quad \sin DMN = \dfrac{DN}{DM}: \cos DMN = \dfrac{MN}{DM}.$

$\quad\quad \sin NDM = \dfrac{NM}{DM}: \cos NDM = \dfrac{DN}{DM}.$

60. When once the student has acquired facility in fixing on the lines which form the ratios called the *sine* and the *cosine*, he will be able to determine the other four ratios without any trouble.

EXAMPLES.—XIII.

(1) Let ABC be a triangle. Draw from B a perpendicular BD on AC, and let it be *within* the triangle. Then write the following ratios:

$$\sin BAD, \cos BAD, \tan BAD;$$
$$\sin ABD, \cot ABD, \operatorname{cosec} ABD;$$
$$\sin BCD, \sin CBD, \tan BCD.$$

(2) Let ABC be a right-angled triangle, having B as the right angle, and let the angles be denoted by the letters $A, B, C,$ and the sides respectively opposite to them by the letters a, b, c.

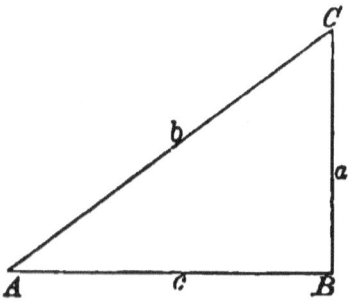

Shew that

$a = b \cdot \sin A = b \cdot \cos C = c \cdot \tan A = c \cdot \cot C,$

$b = a \cdot \operatorname{cosec} A = a \cdot \sec C = c \cdot \sec A = c \cdot \operatorname{cosec} C,$

$c = a \cdot \cot A = a \cdot \tan C = b \cdot \cos A = b \cdot \sin C.$

Note.—These results are worthy of notice, as being of frequent use in a later part of the subject.

61. *The trigonometrical ratios remain unchanged so long as the angle is the same.*

ON THE TRIGONOMETRICAL RATIOS. 37

Let EOB be any angle.

In OB take any points P, P' and draw $PM, P'M'$ at right angles to OE.

Then, since $PM, P'M'$ are parallel,
the triangles $OPM, OP'M'$ are similar.

Hence
$$\frac{PM}{OP} = \frac{P'M'}{OP'};$$

i.e. the value of the sine of EOB is the same so long as the angle is the same, and this result holds good for the other ratios.

The figure represents the simplest case, where the given angle is less than a right angle, but the conclusion is true for all angles.

Ratios for Obtuse Angles.

62. Suppose ACB to be an obtuse angle. Draw AD at right angles to BC produced.

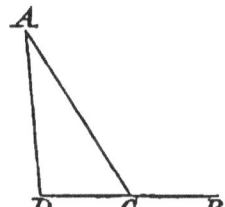

Then, regarding ACB as an angle described by CA revolving round C from the position CB,

$$\sin ACB = \frac{AD}{AC},$$

$$\cos ACB = \frac{CD}{AC}.$$

Now suppose the measures of AD, AC, DC to be p, q, r respectively.

Then the complete algebraical representative of AD is $+p$,
.... of AC is $+q$,
.... of CD is $-r$.

for CD is measured from C in a direction *exactly opposite* to that of *the primitive line* CB.

$$\therefore \sin ACB = \frac{p}{q}, \quad \cos ACB = -\frac{r}{q}.$$

63. In the application of Algebra to Geometry it is the practice of most writers to use the geometrical representative of a magnitude where the algebraical representative ought to be employed. Thus suppose p and q to be the measures of two lines AB, CD, we often find the fraction $\dfrac{AB}{CD}$ where we ought in strictness to find the fraction $\dfrac{p}{q}$. This loose method of notation is, however, sometimes less cumbersome, and we shall therefore retain it at the risk of a slight want of clearness.

64. Whenever we represent the ratios of lines *algebraically* we must be careful to put the *complete* algebraical representative for each line. This cannot be too strongly impressed on a beginner, and we therefore give another illustration of it

Let EOW be the primitive line and a diameter of a circle,

NOS a diameter at right angles to EOW,

and POP' any other diameter.

Draw PM and $P'M'$ at right angles to EOW.

Let p be the measure of PM and $P'M'$,

r the measure of the radius.

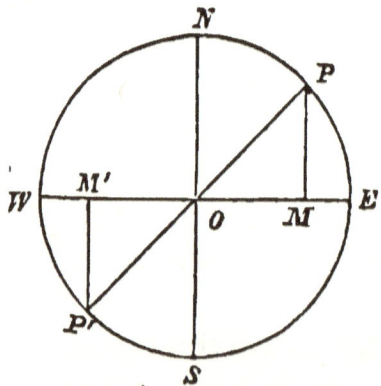

Then the ratio $PM : PO$ is represented algebraically by $\dfrac{p}{r}$,

but .... $P'M' : P'O$ .... by $\dfrac{-p}{r}$.

CHAPTER VII.

On the changes in Sign and Magnitude of the Trigonometrical Ratios of an Angle as it increases from 0° to 360°.

65. LET *NS*, *WE* bisect each other at right angles in the point *O*, and let a line equal in length to *OE* be supposed to revolve in the positive direction from *OE* round the fixed point *O*.

Let *r* be the measure of *OE*.

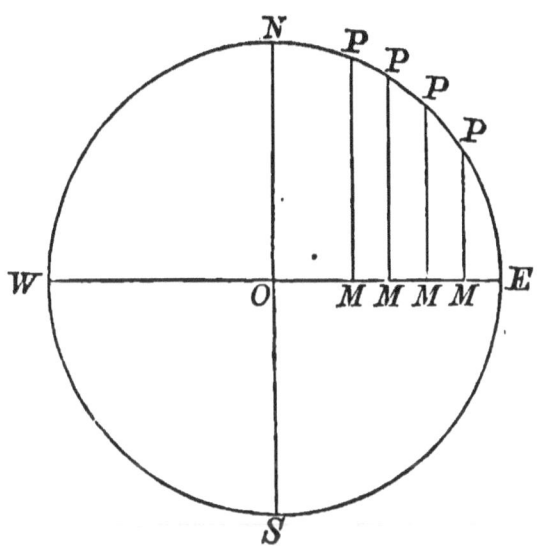

As the revolving line passes from the position *OE* to the positions *ON*, *OW*, *OS*, *OE*, the extremity traces out a circle *ENWS*.

40 CHANGES IN SIGN AND MAGNITUDE.

If we take a succession of points in EN, as P, P, P, P, and from them let fall perpendiculars PM, PM, PM, PM on the line OE, and do the same in the other quadrants, it is clear that

In passing from E to N,

$\qquad PM$ continually increases from zero to r,

$\qquad OM$ continually decreases from r to zero.

In passing from N to W,

$\qquad PM$ continually decreases from r to zero,

$\qquad OM$ continually increases from zero to r.

In passing from W to S,

$\qquad PM$ continually increases from zero to r,

$\qquad OM$ continually decreases from r to zero.

In passing from S to E,

$\qquad PM$ continually decreases from r to zero,

$\qquad OM$ continually increases from zero to r.

Again,

PM is positive in the first and second quadrants,

$\qquad$ negative in the third and fourth.

OM is positive in the first and fourth quadrants,

$\qquad$ negative in the second and third.

OP is always positive, and always $= r$.

66. *To trace the changes in sign and magnitude of the sine of an angle as the angle increases from $0°$ to $360°$.*

Let NOS, EOW be two diameters of a circle at right angles.

Let a radius OP, whose measure is r, by revolving from OE trace out any angle EOP, and denote this angle by A.

From P draw PM at right angles to EOW.

$\qquad$ Then $\qquad\qquad \sin A = \dfrac{PM}{OP}.$

CHANGES IN SIGN AND MAGNITUDE.

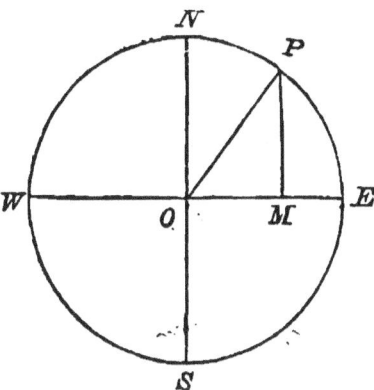

As A increases from $0°$ to $90°$, OP revolves from OE to ON,

$\therefore PM$ increases from 0 to r and is positive,

OP is always $= r$ ...... positive;

$\therefore \sin A$ increases from 0 to 1 ...... positive.

As A increases from $90°$ to $180°$, OP revolves from ON to OW,

$\therefore PM$ decreases from r to 0 and is positive,

OP is always $= r$ ...... positive;

$\therefore \sin A$ decreases from 1 to 0 ...... positive.

As A increases from $180°$ to $270°$, OP revolves from OW to OS,

$\therefore PM$ increases from 0 to r and is negative,

OP is always $= r$ ...... positive;

$\therefore \sin A$ increases from 0 to 1 ...... negative.

As A increases from $270°$ to $360°$, OP revolves from OS to OE,

$\therefore PM$ decreases from r to 0 and is negative,

OP is always $= r$ ...... positive;

$\therefore \sin A$ decreases from 1 to 0 ...... negative.

67. *To trace the changes in the sign and magnitude of the cosine of an angle as the angle increases from 0° to 360°.*

Making the same construction as in Art. 66,

$$\cos A = \frac{OM}{OP}.$$

As A increases from 0° to 90°, OP revolves from OE to ON,

∴ OM decreases from r to 0 and is positive,

OP is always $= r$ ...... positive;

∴ $\cos A$ decreases from 1 to 0 ...... positive.

As A increases from 90° to 180°, OP revolves from ON to OW,

∴ OM increases from 0 to r and is negative,

OP is always $= r$ ...... positive;

∴ $\cos A$ increases from 0 to 1 ...... negative.

As A increases from 180° to 270°, OP revolves from OW to OS,

∴ OM decreases from r to 0 and is negative,

OP is always $= r$ ...... positive;

∴ $\cos A$ decreases from 1 to 0 ...... negative.

As A increases from 270° to 360°, OP revolves from OS to OE,

∴ OM increases from 0 to r and is positive,

OP is always $= r$ ...... positive;

∴ $\cos A$ increases from 0 to 1 ...... positive.

68. *To trace the changes in the sign and magnitude of the tangent of an angle as the angle increases from 0° to 360°.*

Making the same construction as in Art. 66,

$$\tan A = \frac{PM}{OM}.$$

As A increases from $0°$ to $90°$, OP revolves from OE to ON,

∴ PM increases from 0 to r and is positive,

OM decreases from r to 0 ...... positive;

∴ $\tan A$ increases from 0 to ∞ ...... positive.

As A increases from $90°$ to $180°$, OP revolves from ON to OW,

∴ PM decreases from r to 0 and is positive,

OM increases from 0 to r ...... negative;

∴ $\tan A$ decreases from ∞ to 0 ...... negative.

As A increases from $180°$ to $270°$, OP revolves from OW to OS,

∴ PM increases from 0 to r and is negative,

OM decreases from r to 0 ...... negative;

∴ $\tan A$ increases from 0 to ∞ ...... positive.

As A increases from $270°$ to $360°$, OP revolves from OS to OE,

∴ PM decreases from r to 0 and is negative,

OM increases from 0 to r ...... positive;

∴ $\tan A$ decreases from ∞ to 0 ...... negative.

Note.—The symbol ∞ is used to denote numbers which are infinitely great, and the symbol 0 is used to denote numbers which are infinitely small. When we say that $\dfrac{r}{0} = \infty$ we mean that if any finite number r be divided by a number infinitely small the quotient is a number infinitely great.

69. When A is less than, but very nearly equal to $90°$, $\tan A$ is very large and positive, and when A is very little greater than $90°$, $\tan A$ is very large and negative. This is expressed by saying that the tangent of an angle changes sign in passing through the value ∞.

To explain this more clearly we give another method of tracing the changes in the sign and magnitude of $\tan A$, as A increases from $0°$ to $180°$.

Let NOS, EOW be two diameters of a circle at right angles.

Suppose a line OP revolving from the position OE to trace out any angle EOP, and denote this angle by A.

Draw EC, WD at right angles to EOW, and let them meet the revolving line in any points P, P.

Let the measure of OE be r.

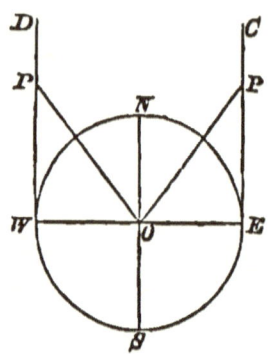

Then as A increases from $0°$ to $90°$,

$$\tan A = \frac{EP}{OE},$$

EP increases from 0 to ∞ and is positive,

OE is always $= r$ ...... positive;

$\therefore \tan A$ increases from 0 to ∞ ...... positive.

As A increases from $90°$ to $180°$,

$$\tan A = \frac{WP}{OW},$$

WP decreases from ∞ to 0 and is positive,

OW is always $= r$ ...... negative;

$\therefore \tan A$ decreases from ∞ to 0 ...... negative.

Thus as the revolving line passes from one side of ON to the other, $\tan A$ changes from $+\infty$ to $-\infty$.

70. The changes of the cosecant, secant and cotangent should be traced for himself by the student for practice.

CHANGES IN SIGN AND MAGNITUDE. 45

71. We now present the changes of the Trigonometrical Ratios in a convenient tabular form.

Columns 1, 3, 5, 7, 9 give the values of the ratios for the particular values of the angle placed above the columns.

Columns 2, 4, 6, 8 give the signs of the ratios as the angle passes from 0° to 90°, from 90° to 180°, from 180° to 270°, and from 270° to 360

A	0°		90°		180°		270°		360°
sin A	0	+	1	+	0	−	−1	−	0
cos A	1	+	0	−	−1	−	0	+	1
tan A	0	+	∞	−	0	+	∞	−	0
cosec A	∞	+	1	+	∞	−	−1	−	∞
sec A	1	+	∞	−	−1	−	∞	+	1
cot A	∞	+	0	−	∞	+	0	−	∞

72. The sine and cosine are never greater than unity.

The cosecant and secant are never less than unity.

The tangent and cotangent have all values from zero to infinity.

73. The Trigonometrical Ratios change sign in passing through the values 0 and ∞ and for no other values.

74. From the results given in the table (Art. 71) we are led to the following conclusion, which will be more fully explained hereafter.

If the value of a Trigonometrical Ratio be given, we cannot fix on one angle to which it exclusively belongs.

Thus if the given value of sin A be $\frac{1}{2}$, we know, since sin A passes through all values from 0 to 1 as A increases from 0° to 90°, that *one* value of A lies between 0° and 90°. But since we also know that the value of sin A passes through all values between 1 and 0 as A increases from 90° to 180°, it is evident that there is *another* value of A between 90 and 180° for which

$$\sin A = \frac{1}{2}.$$

CHAPTER VIII.

On Ratios of Angles in the First Quadrant.

75. WE have now to treat of the values of the Trigonometrical Ratios for some particular angles in the first quadrant. These angles, which we shall take in their proper order, as they are traced out by the revolving line, are 0°, 30°, 45°, 60°, 90°.

76. The signs of all the ratios for an angle in the first quadrant are positive.

77. *To find the Trigonometrical Ratios for an angle of 0°.* We have already proved in the preceding Chapter that

$\sin 0° = 0,$ $\cos 0° = 1,$ $\tan 0° = 0.$
$\operatorname{cosec} 0° = \infty,$ $\sec 0° = 1,$ $\cot 0° = \infty.$

78. *To find the Trigonometrical Ratios for an angle of 30°.*

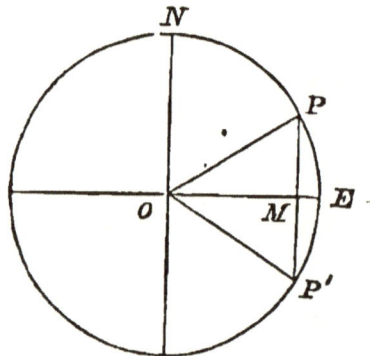

Let OP revolving from the position OE describe an angle EOP equal to one-third of a right angle, that is an angle of 30°.

ANGLES IN THE FIRST QUADRANT.

Draw the chord PMP' at right angles to OE, and join OP'.

Then angle $OP'P = OPP' = 90° - POM = 60°$.

Thus POP' is an equilateral triangle, and OM bisects PP';

$$\therefore OP = 2PM.$$

Let the measure of PM be m.

Then the measure of OP is $2m$.

And the measure of OM is $\sqrt{(4m^2 - m^2)} = \sqrt{(3m^2)} = m \cdot \sqrt{3}$.

Then $\qquad \sin 30° = \dfrac{PM}{OP} = \dfrac{m}{2m} = \dfrac{1}{2}$,

$$\cos 30° = \dfrac{OM}{OP} = \dfrac{m\sqrt{3}}{2m} = \dfrac{\sqrt{3}}{2},$$

$$\tan 30° = \dfrac{PM}{OM} = \dfrac{m}{m\sqrt{3}} = \dfrac{1}{\sqrt{3}}.$$

So also $\qquad \text{cosec } 30° = 2, \text{ sec } 30° = \dfrac{2}{\sqrt{3}}, \text{ cot } 30° = \sqrt{3}$.

79. *To find the Trigonometrical Ratios for an angle of $45°$.*

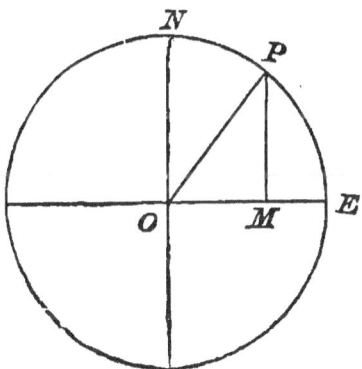

Let OP revolving from the position OE describe an angle EOP equal to half a right angle, that is an angle of $45°$.

Draw PM at right angles to OE.

Then since POM and OPM are together equal to a right angle, and POM is half a right angle, OPM is also half a right angle.

Thus POM is an isosceles triangle, and $OM = PM$.

Let the measure of OM be m.

Then the measure of PM is m.

And the measure of OP is $\sqrt{(m^2 + m^2)} = \sqrt{(2m^2)} = m\sqrt{2}$.

Then
$$\sin 45° = \frac{PM}{OP} = \frac{m}{m\sqrt{2}} = \frac{1}{\sqrt{2}},$$

$$\cos 45° = \frac{OM}{OP} = \frac{m}{m\sqrt{2}} = \frac{1}{\sqrt{2}},$$

$$\tan 45° = \frac{PM}{OM} = \frac{m}{m} = 1.$$

So also $\operatorname{cosec} 45° = \sqrt{2}$, $\sec 45° = \sqrt{2}$, $\cot 45° = 1$.

80. *To find the Trigonometrical Ratios for an angle of 60°.*

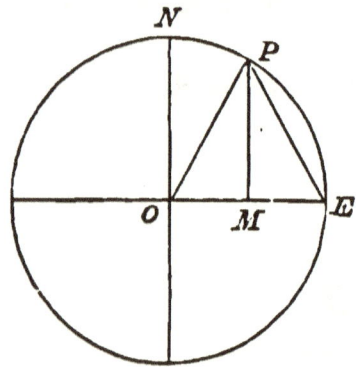

Let OP revolving from the position OE describe an angle EOP equal to two-thirds of a right angle, that is an angle of 60°.

Draw PM at right angles to OE and join PE.

Then POE is an equilateral triangle and PM bisects OE,
$$\therefore OP = 2OM.$$

Let the measure of OM be m.

Then the measure of OP is $2m$.

And the measure of PM is $\sqrt{(4m^2 - m^2)} = \sqrt{(3m^2)} = m\sqrt{3}$.

Then $\quad \sin 60° = \dfrac{PM}{OP} = \dfrac{m\sqrt{3}}{2m} = \dfrac{\sqrt{3}}{2},$

$$\cos 60° = \dfrac{OM}{OP} = \dfrac{m}{2m} = \dfrac{1}{2},$$

$$\tan 60° = \dfrac{PM}{OM} = \dfrac{m\sqrt{3}}{m} = \sqrt{3}.$$

So also $\quad \operatorname{cosec} 60° = \dfrac{2}{\sqrt{3}}, \quad \sec 60° = 2, \quad \cot 60° = \dfrac{1}{\sqrt{3}}.$

81. *To find the Trigonometrical Ratios for an angle of* 90°.

We have already proved in the preceding Chapter that

$$\sin 90° = 1, \quad \cos 90° = 0, \quad \tan 90° = \infty,$$
$$\operatorname{cosec} 90° = 1, \quad \sec 90° = \infty, \quad \cot 90° = 0.$$

EXAMPLES.—XIV.

If $\alpha = 0°$, $\beta = 30°$, $\gamma = 45°$, $\delta = 60°$, $\theta = 90°$, find the numerical values of the following expressions:

(1) $\cos \alpha . \sin \gamma . \cos \delta.$

(2) $\sin \theta . \cos \dfrac{\pi}{4} . \operatorname{cosec} \delta.$

(3) $\sin \dfrac{\pi}{2} + \cos \dfrac{\pi}{6} - \sec \alpha.$

(4) $\sin \dfrac{\pi}{3} . \operatorname{cosec} \dfrac{\pi}{2} . \sec \delta$

(5) $(\sin \theta - \cos \theta + \operatorname{cosec} \beta)\left(\cos \theta + \sec \dfrac{\pi}{4} + \cot \delta\right).$

Also prove the following:

(6) $(\sin \delta - \sin \gamma)(\cos \beta + \cos \gamma) = \sin^2 \beta.$

(7) $\cot^2 \dfrac{\pi}{4} - \cot^2 \dfrac{\pi}{6} = \dfrac{\sin^2 \dfrac{\pi}{6} - \sin^2 \dfrac{\pi}{4}}{\sin^2 \dfrac{\pi}{4} . \sin^2 \dfrac{\pi}{6}}.$

(8) $\left(\sin \dfrac{\pi}{6} + \cos \dfrac{\pi}{6}\right)\left(\sin \dfrac{\pi}{3} - \cos \dfrac{\pi}{3}\right) = \cos \dfrac{\pi}{3}.$

(10) $\tan^2 \dfrac{\pi}{3} - \tan^2 \dfrac{\pi}{6} = \dfrac{\sin^2 \dfrac{\pi}{3} - \sin^2 \dfrac{\pi}{6}}{\cos^2 \dfrac{\pi}{3} \cdot \cos^2 \dfrac{\pi}{6}}$.

82. We are now able to give some simple examples of the practical use of Trigonometry in the measurement of heights and distances.

83. The values of the sines, cosines, tangents and the other ratios have been calculated for all angles succeeding each other at intervals of 1', and the results registered in Tables.

Instruments have been invented for determining:

1. The angle which the line joining two distant objects subtends at the eye of the observer.

2. The angle which a line joining the eye of the observer and a distant object makes with the horizontal plane.

If the object be *above* the observer the angle is called the Angle of *Elevation*.

If the object be *below* the observer the angle is called the Angle of *Depression*.

84. *To find the height of an object standing on a horizontal plane, the base of the object being accessible.*

Let PQ be a vertical column.

From the base P measure a horizontal line AP.

Then observe the angle of elevation QAP.

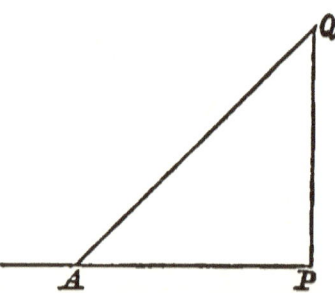

We can then determine the height of the column, for

$$QP = AP \cdot \tan QAP.$$

85. To find the breadth of a river.

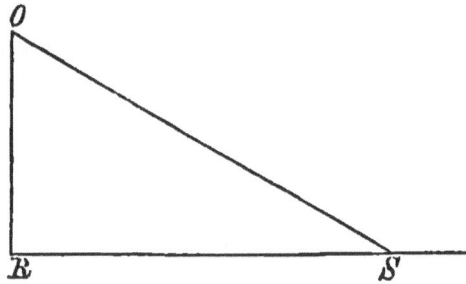

Let RS be the horizontal line joining two objects on the opposite banks.

From O, a point in a vertical line with R, observe the angle of depression OSR.

Then if OR be measured we can determine the length of RS, for

$$RS = \frac{OR}{\tan OSR}.$$

86. To find the height of a flag-staff on the top of a tower.

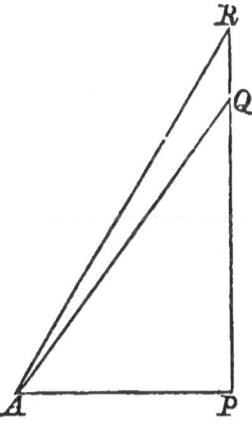

Let RQ be the flag-staff.

From P the base of the tower measure a horizontal line AP.

Observe the angles RAP and QAP.

Then we can find the length of RQ, for
$$RQ = RP - QP$$
$$= AP \cdot \tan RAP - AP \cdot \tan QAP.$$

87. *To find the altitude of the Sun.*

The altitude of the Sun is measured by the angle between a horizontal line and a line passing through the centre of the Sun.

If AB be a stick standing at right angles to the horizontal plane QR, and QB the shadow of the stick on the horizontal plane, a line joining QA will pass through the centre of the Sun.

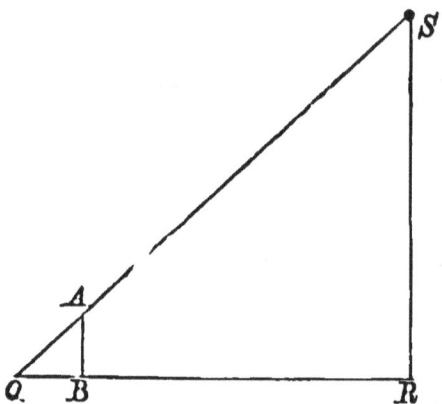

Then if we measure AB and QB we shall know the altitude of the Sun, for

$$\tan SQR = \frac{AB}{QB}.$$

Examples.—XV.

(1) At a point 200 feet from a tower and on a level with its base the angle of elevation of its summit is found to be $60°$: what is the height of the tower?

(2) What is the height of a tower whose top appears at an elevation of $30°$ to an observer 140 feet from its foot on a horizontal plane, his eye being 5 feet from the ground?

(3) Determine the altitude of the Sun when the length of a vertical stick is to the length of its shadow as $\sqrt{3} : 1$.

(4) At 300 feet measured horizontally from the foot of a steeple the angle of elevation of the top is found to be $30°$. What is the height of the steeple?

ANGLES IN THE FIRST QUADRANT. 53

(5) From the top of a rock 245 feet above the sea the angle of depression of a ship's hull is found to be 30°. How far is the ship distant?

(6) From the top of a hill there are observed two consecutive milestones, on a horizontal road, running from the base. The angles of depression are found to be 45° and 30°. Find the height of the hill.

(7) A flag-staff stands on a tower. I measure from the bottom of the tower a distance of 100 feet. I then find that the top of the flag-staff subtends an angle of 45° and the top of the tower an angle of 30° at my place of observation. What is the height of the flag-staff?

(8) From the summit of a tower whose height is 108 feet, the angles of depression of the top and bottom of a vertical column, standing on a level with the base of the tower, are found to be 30° and 60°. Find the height of the column.

(9) A person observes the elevation of a tower to be 60°, and on receding from it 100 yards further he finds the elevation to be 30°. Required the height of the tower.

(10) A stick 10 feet in length is placed vertically in the ground, and the length of its shadow is 25 feet. Find the altitude of the Sun, having given $\tan 25° = \cdot 4$.

(11) A spire stands on a tower in the form of a cube whose edge is 35 feet. From a point 23 feet above the level of the base of the tower, and 20 yards distant from the tower, the elevation of the top of the spire is found to be 56°. 34'. Find the height of the spire, having given $\tan 56°. 34' = 1\cdot 5$.

(12) The length of a kite string is 250 yards and the angle of elevation of the kite is 30°. Find the height of the kite.

(13) The height of a house-top is 60 feet. A rope is stretched from it and is inclined at an angle of 40°. 30' to the ground. Find the length of the rope, if $\sin 40°. 30' = \cdot 65$.

(14) A tower on the bank of a river is 120 feet high, and the angle of elevation of the top of the tower from the opposite bank is 20°; find the river's breadth if $\tan 20° = \cdot 35$.

(15) The altitude of the Sun is 36°. 30': what is the length of the shadow of a man 6 ft. high, if $\tan 36°. 30' = \cdot 745$?

CHAPTER IX.

On the Relations between the Trigonometrical Ratios for the same Angle.

88. LET EOP be any angle traced by OP revolving from the position OE, and let a perpendicular PM be dropped on OE or EO produced, thus

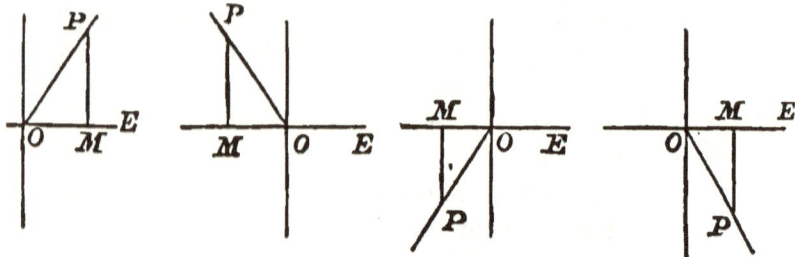

Let the angle EOP be denoted by A.

Then we can prove the following relations:

I. $\tan A = \dfrac{\sin A}{\cos A}$.

For $\tan A = \dfrac{PM}{OM} = \dfrac{\frac{PM}{OP}}{\frac{OM}{OP}} = \dfrac{\sin A}{\cos A}$.

II. $\sin^2 A + \cos^2 A = 1$.

For $\sin^2 A + \cos^2 A = \dfrac{PM^2}{OP^2} + \dfrac{OM^2}{OP^2}$

$= \dfrac{PM^2 + OM^2}{OP^2} = \dfrac{OP^2}{OP^2} = 1.$

RATIOS FOR THE SAME ANGLE.

III. $\sec^2 A = 1 + \tan^2 A$.

For $\sec^2 A = \dfrac{OP^2}{OM^2} = \dfrac{OM^2 + PM^2}{OM^2} = 1 + \dfrac{PM^2}{OM^2} = 1 + \tan^2 A$.

IV. $\operatorname{cosec}^2 A = 1 + \cot^2 A$.

For $\operatorname{cosec}^2 A = \dfrac{OP^2}{PM^2} = \dfrac{PM^2 + OM^2}{PM^2} = 1 + \dfrac{OM^2}{PM^2} = 1 + \cot^2 A$.

89. We shall now give a number of easy examples by which the student may become familiar with the formulæ which we have just obtained.

He must observe that these formulæ hold good for all magnitudes of the angle which we have represented by the letter A, that is, not only

$$\sin^2 A + \cos^2 A = 1,$$

but also $\sin^2 \theta + \cos^2 \theta = 1,$

and $\sin^2 x + \cos^2 x = 1,$

and $\sin^2 45^\circ + \cos^2 45^\circ = 1,$

and $\sin^2 60^\circ + \cos^2 60^\circ = 1,$

and $\sin^2 \dfrac{\pi}{2} + \cos^2 \dfrac{\pi}{2} = 1.$

And similarly for the other formulæ.

90. If then any angle be represented by θ, we know from Art. 88,

(1) $\tan \theta = \dfrac{\sin \theta}{\cos \theta}$.

(2) $\sin^2 \theta + \cos^2 \theta = 1$.

(3) $\sec^2 \theta = 1 + \tan^2 \theta$.

(4) $\operatorname{cosec}^2 \theta = 1 + \cot^2 \theta$.

And we also know from Art. 52,

(5) $\operatorname{cosec} \theta = \dfrac{1}{\sin \theta}$.

(6) $\sec \theta = \dfrac{1}{\cos \theta}$.

(7) $\cot \theta = \dfrac{1}{\tan \theta}$.

91. Ex. 1. Show that $\sec\theta - \tan\theta \cdot \sin\theta = \cos\theta$.

$$\sec\theta - \tan\theta \cdot \sin\theta = \frac{1}{\cos\theta} - \frac{\sin\theta}{\cos\theta} \cdot \sin\theta, \text{ by form (6) and (1)},$$

$$= \frac{1}{\cos\theta} - \frac{\sin^2\theta}{\cos\theta}$$

$$= \frac{1 - \sin^2\theta}{\cos\theta}$$

$$= \frac{\cos^2\theta}{\cos\theta}, \text{ by (2)},$$

$$= \cos\theta.$$

Ex. 2. Show that $\cot\alpha - \sec\alpha\,\operatorname{cosec}\alpha\,(1 - 2\sin^2\alpha) = \tan\alpha$.

$$\cot\alpha - \sec\alpha \cdot \operatorname{cosec}\alpha\,(1 - 2\sin^2\alpha)$$

$$= \frac{\cos\alpha}{\sin\alpha} - \frac{1}{\cos\alpha} \cdot \frac{1}{\sin\alpha}(1 - 2\sin^2\alpha), \text{ by (7, 6, 5)},$$

$$= \frac{\cos\alpha}{\sin\alpha} - \frac{1}{\cos\alpha \cdot \sin\alpha} + \frac{2\sin^2\alpha}{\cos\alpha \cdot \sin\alpha}$$

$$= \frac{\cos^2\alpha - 1 + 2\sin^2\alpha}{\cos\alpha \cdot \sin\alpha}$$

$$= \frac{\cos^2\alpha - (\sin^2\alpha + \cos^2\alpha) + 2\sin^2\alpha}{\cos\alpha \cdot \sin\alpha}, \text{ by (1)},$$

$$= \frac{\cos^2\alpha - \sin^2\alpha - \cos^2\alpha + 2\sin^2\alpha}{\cos\alpha \cdot \sin\alpha}$$

$$= \frac{\sin^2\alpha}{\cos\alpha \cdot \sin\alpha}$$

$$= \frac{\sin\alpha}{\cos\alpha}$$

$$= \tan\alpha.$$

It will be observed that in working these examples we commenced by expressing the other ratios in terms of the sine and cosine, and the beginner will find this the simplest course in most cases.

Examples.—XVI.

Prove the following relations:

(1) $\cos\theta . \tan\theta = \sin\theta$. (2) $\sin\theta . \cot\theta = \cos\theta$.

(3) $\sin a . \sec a = \tan a$. (4) $\cos a . \operatorname{cosec} a = \cot a$.

(5) $(1+\tan^2\theta). \cos^2\theta = 1$. (6) $(1+\cot^2\theta). \sin^2\theta = 1$.

(7) $\dfrac{\tan^2 a}{1+\tan^2 a} = \sin^2 a$. (8) $\dfrac{\operatorname{cosec}^2 a - 1}{\operatorname{cosec}^2 a} = \cos^2 a$.

(9) $\tan x + \cot x = \sec x . \operatorname{cosec} x$.

(10) $\dfrac{\cos x . \operatorname{cosec} x . \tan x}{\sin x . \sec x . \cot x} = 1$.

(11) $\cos x + \sin x . \tan x = \sec x$.

(12) $\dfrac{\cos\theta}{\tan\theta . \cot^2\theta} = \sin\theta$. (13) $(\cos^2\theta - 1)(\cot^2\theta + 1) = -1$.

(14) $\cot^2 a - \cos^2 a = \cot^2 a . \cos^2 a$.

(15) $\sec^2 a . \operatorname{cosec}^2 a = \sec^2 a + \operatorname{cosec}^2 a$.

(16) $\sin^2\phi + \sin^2\phi . \tan^2\phi = \tan^2\phi$.

(17) $\cot^2\phi . \sin^2\phi + \sin^2\phi = 1$.

(18) $\sec^2\phi - 1 = \sin^2\phi . \sec^2\phi$.

(19) $\sin^2\phi = 2\operatorname{versin}\phi - \operatorname{versin}^2\phi$.

(20) $\dfrac{\sec\theta - 1}{\sec\theta} = \operatorname{versin}\theta$.

92. We shall next show how to express the cosine, tangent and other ratios in terms of the sine.

Since $\quad \sin^2\theta + \cos^2\theta = 1,$

$$\cos^2\theta = 1 - \sin^2\theta\,;$$

$$\therefore\ \cos\theta = \pm\sqrt{(1-\sin^2\theta)}.$$

Again $\quad \tan\theta = \dfrac{\sin\theta}{\cos\theta}$

$$= \dfrac{\sin\theta}{\pm\sqrt{(1-\sin^2\theta)}}\cdot$$

Also
$$\operatorname{cosec}\theta = \frac{1}{\sin\theta},$$

$$\sec\theta = \frac{1}{\cos\theta} = \frac{1}{\pm\sqrt{(1-\sin^2\theta)}},$$

$$\cot\theta = \frac{1}{\tan\theta} = \frac{\pm\sqrt{(1-\sin^2\theta)}}{\sin\theta}.$$

The double sign before the root-symbols is to be explained thus. For an assigned value of $\sin\theta$ we shall have more than one value of θ (Art. 74). Hence we have an ambiguity when we endeavour to find $\cos\theta$ from the known value of $\sin\theta$. The double sign may *generally* be omitted in the examples which we shall hereafter give.

93. We shall now give two examples of another method of arriving at expressions for the other ratios in terms of a particular ratio. These examples should be carefully studied.

(1) *To express the other trigonometrical ratios in terms of the sine.*

Let PAM be an angle whose sine is s, a numerical quantity.

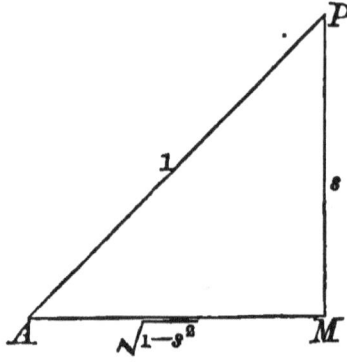

Let PM be drawn perpendicular to AM.

Then if AP be represented by 1,

PM will be represented by s,

and AM will therefore be represented by $\sqrt{1-s^2}$.

Then denoting PAM by A,

$$\cos A = \frac{AM}{AP} = \frac{\sqrt{1-s^2}}{1} = \sqrt{1-s^2} = \sqrt{1-\sin^2 A},$$

$$\tan A = \frac{PM}{AM} = \frac{s}{\sqrt{1-s^2}} = \frac{\sin A}{\sqrt{1-\sin^2 A}},$$

and similarly the other ratios may be expressed in terms of $\sin A$.

(2) *To express the other trigonometrical ratios in terms of the tangent.*

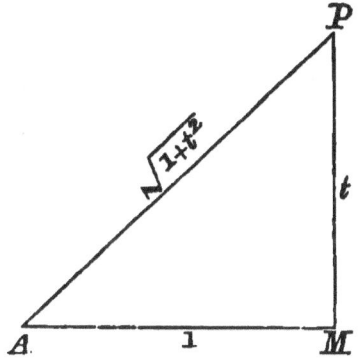

Making the same construction as in the preceding Article,

Let $\tan A = t$.

Then if AM be represented by 1, PM will be represented by t, and AP will be represented by $\sqrt{1+t^2}$.

Therefore $\sin A = \dfrac{PM}{AP} = \dfrac{t}{\sqrt{1+t^2}} = \dfrac{\tan A}{\sqrt{1+\tan^2 A}}$,

$\cos A = \dfrac{AM}{AP} = \dfrac{1}{\sqrt{1+t^2}} = \dfrac{1}{\sqrt{1+\tan^2 A}}$,

and similarly the other ratios may be found.

Examples.—XVII.

(1) Express the other trigonometrical ratios in terms of the cosine.

(2) Express the other trigonometrical ratios in terms of the cosecant.

(3) Express the other trigonometrical ratios in terms of the secant.

(4) Express the other trigonometrical ratios in terms of the cotangent.

94. *If any one of the Trigonometrical ratios be given the others may be found.*

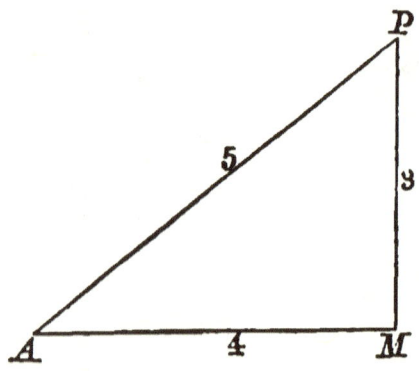

Thus suppose $\sin A = \frac{3}{5}$.

If PAM represent the angle, and PM be perpendicular to AM, we may represent PM by 3, AP by 5, and consequently AM by $\sqrt{25-9}$ or 4.

Then
$$\cos A = \frac{4}{5},$$
$$\tan A = \frac{3}{4},$$
$$\operatorname{cosec} A = \frac{5}{3},$$
$$\sec A = \frac{5}{4}.$$

RATIOS FOR THE SAME ANGLE.

95. If $\tan A = \dfrac{a}{b}$, to find $\sin A$ and $\cos A$.

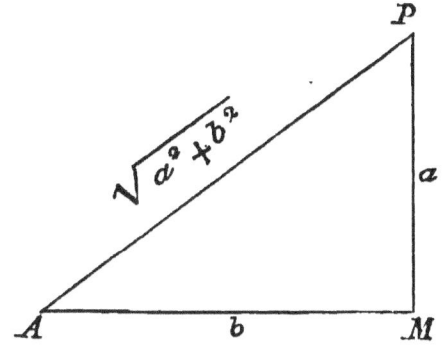

If PAM represent the angle, and PM be perpendicular to AM, we may represent PM by a, AM by b, and consequently AP by $\sqrt{a^2+b^2}$.

Then
$$\sin A = \frac{a}{\sqrt{a^2+b^2}},$$

$$\cos A = \frac{b}{\sqrt{a^2+b^2}}.$$

EXAMPLES.—XVIII.

(1) Given $\sin a = \dfrac{2}{3}$: find $\cos a$ and $\tan a$.

(2) Given $\cos a = \dfrac{4}{5}$: find $\sin a$ and $\tan a$.

(3) Given $\operatorname{cosec} \theta = \dfrac{4}{3}$: find $\cos \theta$ and $\tan \theta$.

(4) Given $\sin \theta = \dfrac{1}{\sqrt{3}}$: find $\cos \theta$ and $\tan \theta$.

(5) Given $\tan a = \dfrac{a^2}{b^2}$: find $\operatorname{cosec} a$ and $\sec a$.

(6) Given $\cos a = \dfrac{a}{b}$: find $\tan a$ and $\operatorname{cosec} a$.

(7) Given $\sin \theta = a$: find $\tan \theta$ and $\sec \theta$.

(8) Given $\cos\theta = b$: find $\tan\theta$ and $\csc\theta$.

(9) Given $\sin\theta = \cdot 6$: find $\cos\theta$ and $\cot\theta$.

(10) Given $\cos\theta = \cdot 5$: find $\cot\theta$ and $\csc\theta$.

(11) Given $\csc\theta = 2\cdot 4$: find $\cos\theta$ and $\cot\theta$.

(12) Given $\sec\theta = 1\cdot 03$: find $\sin\theta$ and $\tan\theta$

(13) Given $\sin\phi = \dfrac{99}{101}$: find $\cos\phi$ and $\cot\phi$.

(14) Given $\cos\phi = \dfrac{20}{101}$: find $\sin\phi$ and $\tan\phi$.

(15) Given $\operatorname{versin}\theta = \dfrac{1}{13}$: find $\sin\theta$ and $\sec\theta$.

96. We may here give the geometrical solutions of the problem of constructing an angle when its sine, cosine or tangent is given.

(1) *Given that the sine of an angle is $\dfrac{a}{b}$, to construct the angle.*

The sine of an angle cannot be greater than *unity*,

∴ a is not greater than b.

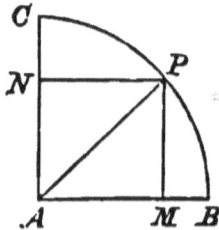

Draw a line $AB = b$, and describe a circle with centre A and radius AB.

Let BAC be a quadrant of this circle.

Mark off on AC the line $AN = a$.

RATIOS FOR THE SAME ANGLE. 63

Draw NP, PM at right angles to AC, AB.

Then PAM is the angle required: for

$$\sin PAM = \frac{PM}{AP} = \frac{AN}{AP} = \frac{a}{b}.$$

(2) *Given that the cosine of an angle is $\frac{a}{b}$, to construct the angle.*

Making the same construction as before,

PAN is the angle required: for

$$\cos PAN = \frac{AN}{AP} = \frac{a}{b}.$$

(3) *Given that the tangent of an angle is $\frac{a}{b}$, to construct the angle.*

Take a line $AM = b$, and draw $PM = a$ at right angles to AM (fig. in Art. 95).

Join AP. Then PAM is the angle required: for

$$\tan PAM = \frac{PM}{AM} = \frac{a}{b}.$$

97. We shall now give a set of examples similar to those in Ex. XVI. but presenting in some cases more difficulty.

EXAMPLES.—XIX.

Prove the following relations:

(1) $\sin A = \dfrac{1}{\sqrt{(1 + \cot^2 A)}}.$

(2) $\cos A = \dfrac{1}{\sqrt{(1 + \tan^2 A)}}.$

(3) $\cos x = \dfrac{\cot x}{\sqrt{(1 + \cot^2 x)}}.$

(4) $\tan x \cdot \cos x = \sqrt{(1 - \cos^2 x)}.$

(5) $\cos\phi = \dfrac{\sqrt{(\operatorname{cosec}^2\phi - 1)}}{\operatorname{cosec}\phi}$.

(6) $\tan\phi = \sqrt{\left(\dfrac{1 - \cos^2\phi}{\cos^2\phi}\right)}$.

(7) $\sin^2 a = (1 + \cos a) \cdot \operatorname{versin} a$.

(8) $\tan^2 a - \tan^2 \beta = \dfrac{\cos^2 \beta - \cos^2 a}{\cos^2 \beta \cdot \cos^2 a}$.

(9) $\cot^2 a - \cot^2 \beta = \dfrac{\sin^2 \beta - \sin^2 a}{\sin^2 a \cdot \sin^2 \beta}$.

(10) $\sin^2\theta \cdot \tan^2\theta + \cos^2\theta \cdot \cot^2\theta = \tan^2\theta + \cot^2\theta - 1$.

(11) $\sec^4\theta + \tan^4\theta = 1 + 2\sec^2\theta \cdot \tan^2\theta$.

(12) $\operatorname{cosec}\theta(\sec\theta - 1) - \cot\theta(1 - \cos\theta) = \tan\theta - \sin\theta$.

(13) $\cot^2 b + \tan^2 b = \sec^2 b \operatorname{cosec}^2 b - 2$.

(14) $\cot^2 A - \cos^2 A = \cos^4 A \operatorname{cosec}^2 A$.

(15) $\tan^2\theta - \sin^2\theta = \sin^4\theta \sec^2\theta$.

(16) $(\sec\theta - \operatorname{cosec}\theta)(1 + \cot\theta + \tan\theta) = \dfrac{\sec^2\theta}{\operatorname{cosec}\theta} - \dfrac{\operatorname{cosec}^2\theta}{\sec\theta}$.

(17) $\dfrac{\operatorname{cosec}\theta}{\sec\theta} + \dfrac{\sec\theta}{\operatorname{cosec}\theta} = \sec\theta \cdot \operatorname{cosec}\theta$.

(18) $\cos\theta(\tan\theta + 2)(2\tan\theta + 1) = 2\sec\theta + 5\sin\theta$.

(19) $\cos x(2\sec x + \tan x)(\sec x - 2\tan x) = 2\cos x - 3\tan x$

(20) $(\operatorname{cosec}\theta - \cot\theta)^2 = \dfrac{1 - \cos\theta}{1 + \cos\theta}$.

(21) $\dfrac{\sec\theta \cdot \cot\theta - \operatorname{cosec}\theta \cdot \tan\theta}{\cos\theta - \sin\theta} = \operatorname{cosec}\theta \cdot \sec\theta$.

(22) $\sec\theta + \operatorname{cosec}\theta \cdot \tan^3\theta(1 + \operatorname{cosec}^2\theta) = 2\sec^3\theta$.

(23) $(\sin\theta + \sec\theta)^2 + (\cos\theta + \operatorname{cosec}\theta)^2 = (1 + \sec\theta \cdot \operatorname{cosec}\theta)^2$.

(24) $\dfrac{1 + (\operatorname{cosec}\theta \cdot \tan\phi)^2}{1 + (\operatorname{cosec}a \cdot \tan\phi)^2} = \dfrac{1 + (\cot\theta \cdot \sin\phi)^2}{1 + (\cot a \cdot \sin\phi)^2}$.

(25) $(3 - 4\sin^2 A)(1 - 3\tan^2 A) = (3 - \tan^2 A)(4\cos^2 A - 3)$.

CHAPTER X.

Comparison of Trigonometrical Ratios for different Angles.

98. THE COMPLEMENT of an angle is that angle which must be added to it to make a right angle.

Thus the complement of 60^0 is 30^0, because $60^0 + 30^0 = 90^0$, and the complement of $14^0.36'.15''$ is $75^0.23'.45''$.

Also the complement of 80^g is 20^g, because $80^g + 20^g = 100^g$, and the complement of $42^g.5'.28''$ is $57^g.94'.72''$.

And the complement of $\dfrac{\pi}{6}$ is $\dfrac{\pi}{3}$, because $\dfrac{\pi}{6} + \dfrac{\pi}{3} = \dfrac{\pi}{2}$.

So generally, if α, β, γ be the measures of an angle in the three systems,

$$\text{complement of the angle} = 90^0 - \alpha = 100^g - \beta = \dfrac{\pi}{2} - \gamma.$$

Hence if the angle be negative (see Art. 48), and its measures be $-\alpha, -\beta, -\gamma$ in the three systems,

$$\text{complement of the angle} = 90^0 - (-\alpha) = 100^g - (-\beta) = \dfrac{\pi}{2} - (-\gamma)$$

$$= 90^0 + \alpha = 100^g + \beta = \dfrac{\pi}{2} + \gamma.$$

EXAMPLES.—XX.

1. Find the complements of the following angles:

(1) $24^0.14'.42''$. (2) $43^0.2'.57''$.

(3) $64^0.0'.14''$. (4) $82^0.4'.15''$.

(5) 125°. 15'. 42". (6) 178°. 27'. 34".
(7) 195°. (8) 254°.
(9) −25°. (10) −245°.

2. Find the complements of the following angles:

(1) 32ᵍ. 23'. 24". (2) 95ᵍ. 3'. 75".
(3) 46ᵍ. 0'. 84". (4) 2ᵍ. 5'. 4".
(5) 135ᵍ. 2 . 5". (6) 169ᵍ. 0'. 3".
(7) 243ᵍ. (8) 357ᵍ.
(9) −35ᵍ. (10) −245ᵍ.

3. What are the complements of the following angles?

(1) $\frac{\pi}{4}$. (2) $\frac{\pi}{3}$. (3) $\frac{3\pi}{5}$. (4) $-\frac{\pi}{4}$. (5) $-\frac{3\pi}{4}$.

99. *To compare the Trigonometrical Ratios of an angle and its complement.*

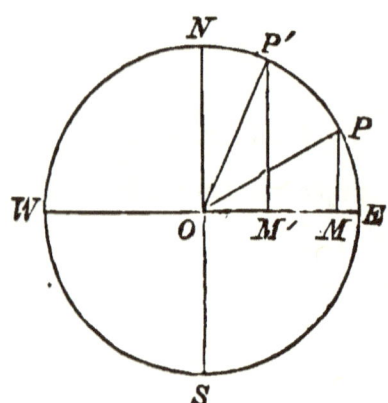

Let NOS, EOW be two diameters of a circle at right angles.

Let a radius OP revolving from OE trace out the angle $POE = A$.

Next, let the radius revolve from OE to ON and back again through an angle $NOP' = A$.

Then angle $EOP' = 90° - A$.

Draw PM and $P'M'$ at right angles to EO.

Now angle $OP'M' = NOP' = A = POE$.

Hence the triangles $P'OM'$ and OPM are equal in all respects (Eucl. I. 26).

Therefore

$$\sin(90° - A) = \sin EOP' = \frac{P'M'}{OP'} = \frac{OM}{OP} = \cos EOP = \cos A,$$

$$\cos(90° - A) = \cos EOP' = \frac{OM'}{OP'} = \frac{PM}{OP} = \sin EOP = \sin A,$$

$$\tan(90° - A) = \tan EOP' = \frac{P'M'}{OM'} = \frac{OM}{PM} = \cot EOP = \cot A.$$

And similarly it may be shown that

$$\operatorname{cosec}(90° - A) = \sec A, \quad \sec(90° - A) = \operatorname{cosec} A,$$

$$\cot(90° - A) = \tan A.$$

This is a proposition of great practical importance. We have only proved it for the case in which A is less than 90°, but the conclusions hold good for all values of A.

100. The SUPPLEMENT of an angle is that angle which must be added to it to make two right angles.

Thus the supplement of 60° is 120°, because $60° + 120° = 180°$, and the supplement of 24°. 43'. 17'' is 155°. 16'. 43''.

Also the supplement of 80^g is 120^g, because $80^g + 120^g = 200^g$, and the supplement of 114^g. 3'. 15` is $85^g$. 96`. 85``.

And the supplement of $\frac{\pi}{8}$ is $\frac{7\pi}{8}$, because $\frac{\pi}{8} + \frac{7\pi}{8} = \pi$.

So, generally, if a, β, γ be the measures of an angle in the three systems,

supplement of the angle $= 180° - a = 200^g - \beta = \pi - \gamma$.

Hence if the angle be negative and its measures be $-a$, $-\beta$, $-\gamma$ in the three systems,

supplement of the angle $= 180° - (-a) = 200^g - (-\beta) = \pi - (-\gamma)$

$$= 180° + a = 200^g + \beta = \pi + \gamma.$$

Examples.—XXI.

1. Find the supplements of the following angles:

   (1) $34°. 12'. 49''$. (2) $132°. 24'. 47''$.

   (3) $146°. 0'. 41''$. (4) $28°. 15'. 4''$.

   (5) $179°. 59'. 59''$. (6) $100°. 49'. 53''$.

   (7) $245°$. (8) $437°. 3'. 4''$.

   (9) $-49°$. (10) $-355°$.

2. Find the supplements of the following angles:

   (1) $132^g. 32'. 42''$. (2) $195^g. 2'. 57''$.

   (3) $3^g. 97'. 98''$. (4) $65^g. 12'. 8''$.

   (5) $154^g. 3'. 6''$. (6) $174^g. 0'. 4''$.

   (7) 275^g. (8) $527^g. 2'. 14''$.

   (9) -35^g. (10) -325^g.

3. What are the supplements of the following angles?

   (1) $\dfrac{\pi}{2}$. (2) $\dfrac{\pi}{3}$. (3) $\dfrac{4\pi}{5}$. (4) $-\dfrac{\pi}{4}$. (5) $-\dfrac{3\pi}{4}$.

4. Find the difference between the supplement of the complement of an angle and the complement of its supplement.

101. *To compare the Trigonometrical Ratios of an angle and its supplement.*

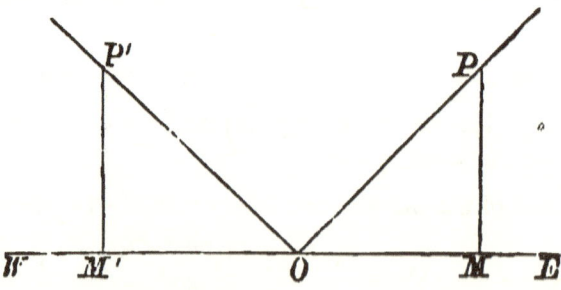

Let the angle $EOP = A$.

RATIOS FOR DIFFERENT ANGLES. 69

Produce EO to W, and make the angle $P'OW = A$.

Take $OP' = OP$, and draw PM, $P'M'$ at right angles to EW.

Then the triangles PMO, $P'M'O$ are geometrically equal. (Eucl. I. 26.)

Therefore

$$\sin(180° - A) = \sin EOP' = \frac{P'M'}{OP'} = \frac{PM}{OP} = \sin A,$$

$$\cos(180° - A) = \cos EOP' = \frac{OM'}{OP'} = \frac{-OM}{OP} = -\cos A,$$

$$\tan(180° - A) = \tan EOP' = \frac{P'M'}{OM'} = \frac{PM}{-OM} = -\tan A.$$

And similarly the other ratios may be compared.

102. *To shew that* $\sin(90° + A) = \cos A$, *and*

$$\cos(90° + A) = -\sin A.$$

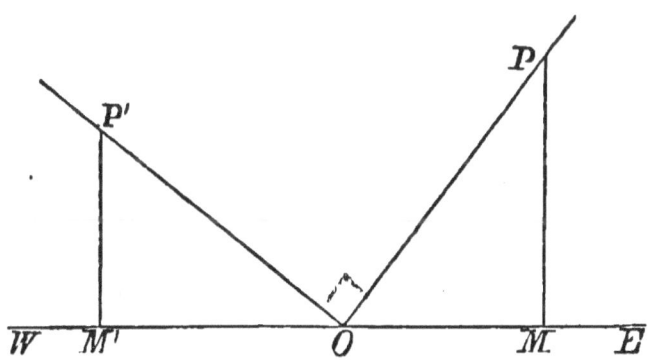

Let the angle $EOP = A$.

Draw OP' at right angles to OP, and make $OP' = OP$.

Draw PM and $P'M'$ at right angles to EOW.

Then since the angles $P'OM'$ and POM make up a right angle, and the angles OPM and POM make up a right angle,

Angle $P'OM' = $ angle OPM.

Also right angle $P'M'O$ = right angle PMO, and side $P'O$ = side PO, opposite equal angles in each;

∴ the triangles $P'OM'$, OPM are equal in all respects, and
$$P'M' = OM, \text{ and } OM' = PM.$$

Then $\sin(90° + A) = \sin EOP' = \dfrac{P'M'}{OP'} = \dfrac{OM}{OP} = \cos A,$

and $\cos(90° + A) = \cos EOP' = \dfrac{OM'}{OP'} = \dfrac{-PM}{OP} = -\sin A.$

103. *To shew that* $\sin(180° + A) = -\sin A$, *and*
$$\cos(180° + A) = -\cos A.$$

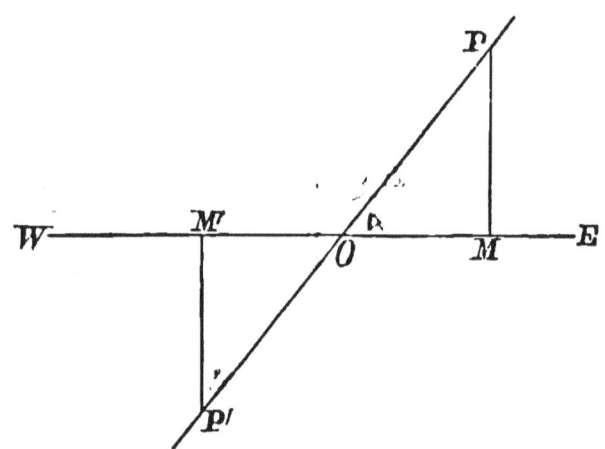

Let the angle $EOP = A$.

Produce EO to W and PO to P', making $OP' = OP$.

Draw PM, $P'M'$ at right angles to EW.

Then the angle EOP' measured in the positive direction $= 180° + A$.

The triangles POM, $P'OM'$ are geometrically equal.

Now $\sin(180° + A) = \sin EOP' = \dfrac{P'M'}{OP'} = \dfrac{-PM}{OP} = -\sin A,$

and $\cos(180° + A) = \cos EOP' = \dfrac{OM'}{OP'} = \dfrac{-OM}{OP} = -\cos A.$

104. To shew that $\sin(-A) = -\sin A$, and
$$\cos(-A) = \cos A.$$

Let the angle $EOP = A$.

Draw PM at right angles to EW, and produce PM to P' making $MP' = MP$.

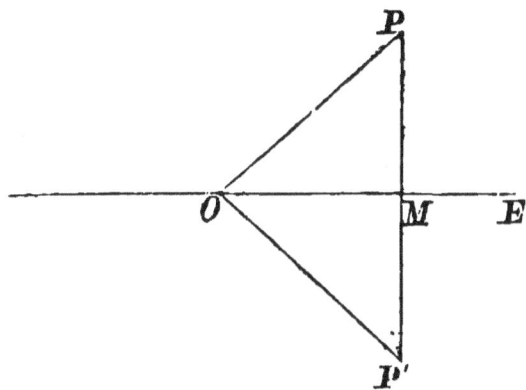

Join OP'.

Then the triangles POM, $P'OM$ are geometrically equal, and the angle EOP', which is numerically equal to EOP, will, if regarded as measured in a negative direction, be represented by $-A$.

Now $\quad \sin(-A) = \sin EOP' = \dfrac{P'M}{OP'} = \dfrac{-PM}{OP} = -\sin A,$

and $\quad \cos(-A) = \cos EOP' = \dfrac{OM}{OP'} = \dfrac{OM}{OP} = \cos A.$

105. To shew that $\sin(360° - A) = -\sin A$, and
$$\cos(360° - A) = \cos A.$$

Making the same construction as in the preceding Article, angle EOP' measured in the positive direction $= 360° - A$.

Then $\quad \sin(360° - A) = \sin EOP' = \dfrac{P'M}{OP'} = \dfrac{-PM}{OP} = -\sin A,$

and $\quad \cos(360° - A) = \cos EOP' = \dfrac{OM}{OP'} = \dfrac{OM}{OP} = \cos A.$

Examples.—XXII.

1. Prove the following relations:

(1) $\sec(180° - A) = -\sec A$,   (2) $\csc\left(\dfrac{\pi}{2} + \theta\right) = \sec\theta$,

(3) $\tan(180° + A) = \tan A$,   (4) $\sec(\pi + \theta) = -\sec\theta$,

(5) $\tan(-\theta) = -\tan\theta$,   (6) $\cot(2\pi - \theta) = -\cot\theta$.

2. State and prove the relations subsisting between the cosecants of $B°$ and $(90 + B)°$, also of ϕ and $\pi + \phi$.

3. State and prove the relations subsisting between the secants of $A°$ and $(90 + A)°$, also of θ and $\dfrac{\pi}{2} - \theta$.

106. With reference to the Trigonometrical Ratios of different angles discussed in this chapter it is to be observed that for an angle in the

First Quadrant all the Ratios are Positive,

Second .... all are Negative except the Sine and Cosecant,

Third .... Tangent and Cotangent,

Fourth .... Cosine and Secant.

Also the following relations must be specially noticed:

$\sin A = \sin(180° - A) = -\sin(180° + A) = -\sin(360° - A) = -\sin(-A)$,
$\cos A = -\cos(180° - A) = -\cos(180° + A) = \cos(360° - A) = \cos(-A)$,
$\tan A = -\tan(180° - A) = \tan(180° + A) = -\tan(360° - A) = -\tan(-A)$

Examples.—XXIII.

Find the values of the following Ratios:

(1) $\sin 120°$,   (2) $\cos 120°$,   (3) $\sin 135°$,   (4) $\cos 135°$,

(5) $\sin 150°$,   (6) $\cos 150°$,   (7) $\sin 225°$,   (8) $\sin 240°$,

(9) $\tan 300°$,   (10) $\csc 300°$,   (11) $\sec 315°$,   (12) $\cot 330°$.

CHAPTER XI.

On the Solution of Trigonometrical Equations.

107. THE Solution of a Trigonometrical Equation is the process of finding what angle an unknown letter representing an angular magnitude must stand for in order that the equation may be true.

(1) Suppose we have to find the value of θ which will satisfy the equation

$$\cos \theta + \sec \theta = \frac{5}{2}.$$

Our first step is to put $\dfrac{1}{\cos \theta}$ in the place of $\sec \theta$, so that we may have only one function of the unknown angle in the equation: thus

$$\cos \theta + \frac{1}{\cos \theta} = \frac{5}{2}.$$

We then proceed to solve the equation just as we should solve an algebraical equation in which x occupied the place of $\cos \theta$: thus

$$2 \cos^2 \theta + 2 = 5 \cos \theta,$$

$$2 \cos^2 \theta - 5 \cos \theta = -2,$$

$$\cos^2 \theta - \frac{5}{2} \cos \theta = -1,$$

$$\cos^2 \theta - \frac{5}{2} \cos \theta + \frac{25}{16} = \frac{9}{16},$$

$$\cos \theta - \frac{5}{4} = \pm \frac{3}{4},$$

$$\cos \theta = 2 \text{ or } \frac{1}{2}.$$

Now the value 2 is inadmissible, for the cosine of every angle is not greater than 1.

The other value $\frac{1}{2}$ is the value of the cosine of 60°. (Art. 80.)

Hence $\qquad \cos \theta = \cos 60°$.

That is, *one* value of θ which satisfies the equation is 60°.

We shall explain hereafter our reason for writing the word *one* in italics.

(2) *To solve the equation* $3 \sin \theta = 2 \cos^2 \theta$.

$$3 \sin \theta = 2(1 - \sin^2 \theta);$$

$$\therefore 3 \sin \theta = 2 - 2 \sin^2 \theta,$$

or $\quad 2 \sin^2 \theta + 3 \sin \theta = 2,$

$$\sin^2 \theta + \frac{3}{2} \sin \theta = 1,$$

$$\sin^2 \theta + \frac{3}{2} \sin \theta + \frac{9}{16} = \frac{25}{16},$$

$$\sin \theta + \frac{3}{4} = \pm \frac{5}{4},$$

$$\sin \theta = \frac{1}{2} \text{ or } -2.$$

The value -2 is inadmissible, for the sine of an angle cannot be numerically greater than 1.

The other value $\frac{1}{2}$ is the value of the sine of 30°. (Art. 78.)

Hence $\qquad \sin \theta = \sin 30°$.

That is, *one* value of θ which satisfies the equation is 30°.

EXAMPLES.—XXIV.

Find a value of θ which will satisfy the following equations:

(1) $\sin\theta + \cos\theta = 0$. (2) $\sin\theta - \cos\theta = 0$.

(3) $\sin\theta = \tan\theta$. (4) $\cos\theta = \cot\theta$.

(5) $2\sin\theta = \tan\theta$. (6) $3\sin\theta = 2\cos^2\theta$.

(7) $\sin\theta + \cos^2\theta \cdot \text{cosec}\,\theta = 2$. (8) $\tan\theta = 4 - 3\cot\theta$.

(9) $4\sec^2\theta - 7\tan^2\theta = 3$.

(10) $\cos\theta \cdot \text{cosec}\,\theta + \sin\theta \cdot \sec\theta = \dfrac{4}{\sqrt{3}}$.

(11) $3\sin^2\theta - \cos^2\theta + (\sqrt{3} + 1)(1 - 2\sin\theta) = 0$.

(12) $3\cos^2\theta - \sin^2\theta + (\sqrt{3} + 1)(1 - 2\cos\theta) = 0$.

(13) $\sec\theta \cdot \text{cosec}\,\theta + 2\cot\theta = 4$. (14) $\sin\theta + \cos\theta = \sqrt{2}$.

(15) $\cot^2\theta + 4\cos^2\theta = 6$.

(16) $\tan\theta + \cot\theta = 2$. (17) $\sin\theta - \cos\theta = \sqrt{2}$.

(18) $\sin\theta + \cos\theta = 2\sqrt{2}\sin\theta\cos\theta$.

(19) $\sqrt{3} \cdot \sin\theta = \sqrt{3} - \cos\theta$. (20) $\tan^2\theta + 4\sin^2\theta = 3$.

108. We have already stated (Art. 74) that if the value of a Trigonometrical Ratio be given we cannot fix on *one* particular angle to which it exclusively belongs. This statement was confirmed by many of the conclusions at which we arrived in Chap. x. For instance, since

$$\sin(180° - A) = \sin A,$$

it follows that the sines of the angles A and $180° - A$ have the same value, that is, if we know that $\sin A = \dfrac{1}{2}$, A may have either of *two* values, one of which is $30°$ and the other $150°$.

Now we know that

$$\sin(180° - A) = \sin A \text{ and } \operatorname{cosec}(180° - A) = \operatorname{cosec} A,$$

$$\cos(360° - A) = \cos A \text{ and } \sec(360° - A) = \sec A,$$

$$\tan(180° + A) = \tan A \text{ and } \cot(180° + A) = \cot A.$$

Thus for each given value of any one of the Trigonometrical Ratios there are *two* angles and two only between 0° and 360° for which that Ratio is the same in magnitude and sign.

109. Suppose OE to be the primitive line, and OP the revolving line, and let the angle EOP, less than 360°, be denoted by A.

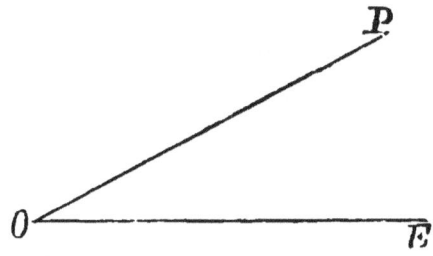

Now suppose OP to make a *complete* revolution, that is, to start from the position indicated in the diagram and to revolve till it comes back to that position.

Then the revolving line will have described an angle $360° + A$.

Our triangle of reference will then be the same for an angle $360° + A$ as for an angle A.

Hence, $\qquad \sin(360° + A) = \sin A,$

and $\qquad \cos(360° + A) = \cos A.$

And the same holds good for the other Ratios.

OF TRIGONOMETRICAL EQUATIONS. 77

Hence, expressing ourselves for brevity in the symbols of the circular system, if a be the circular measure of an angle for which any one of the trigonometrical ratios has an assigned value,

$2\pi + a$ will represent an angle for which the value of that particular ratio is the same.

Now let the revolving line make a second complete revolution, then it will have described an angle

$$2\pi + 2\pi + a, \text{ or, } 4\pi + a.$$

And so $4\pi + a$ will represent an angle for which the value of the above-mentioned ratio will be the same.

And, generally, if the revolving line, after having traced out the angle a makes n revolutions,

$2n\pi + a$ will represent an angle for which the value of any particular ratio is the same as it is for a.

Now since n may have any integral value from 1 to ∞, there will be an infinite number of angles for which the value of any one of the Trigonometrical ratios is the same as it is for the angle a.

Again, if a be the circular measure of an angle traced out by a line revolving in the positive direction, $-(2\pi - a)$ will be the measure of an angle traced out by the line revolving in the *negative* direction, for which the triangle of reference will be the same as for the positive angle a.

If the line then make n complete revolutions in the negative direction, $-2n\pi - (2\pi - a)$ will represent an angle for which the value of any particular ratio is the same as it is for a.

We can now explain the way in which general expressions are found for all angles which have a given trigonometrical ratio.

110. *To find a general expression for all angles which have a given sine.*

Let a be an angle whose sine is given.

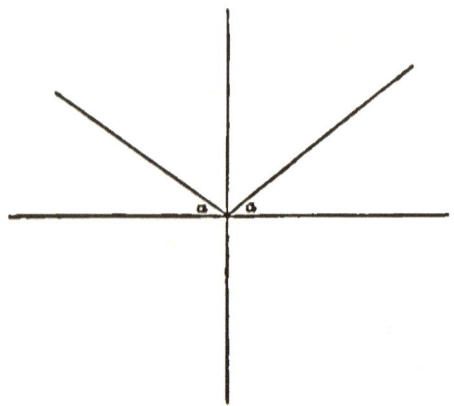

First, reckoning in the positive direction,
$$a \text{ and } \pi - a$$
are angles with the same sine. (Art. 101.)

Also $\left.\begin{array}{l}2n\pi + a \\ \text{and} \quad 2n\pi + (\pi - a)\end{array}\right\}$ .... (1)

are angles with the same sine. (Art. 109.)

Secondly, reckoning in the negative direction,
$$-(2\pi - a) \text{ and } -\{2\pi - (\pi - a)\},$$
that is, $\quad -(2\pi - a) \text{ and } -(\pi + a),$
are angles with the same sine.

Also $\left.\begin{array}{l}-2n\pi - (2\pi - a) \\ \text{and} \quad -2n\pi - (\pi + a)\end{array}\right\}$ .... (2)

are angles with the same sine, n being any positive integer.

Now the angles in (1) and (2) may be arranged thus:
$$2n\pi + a, \ (2n+1)\pi - a, \ -(2n+2)\pi + a, \ -(2n+1)\pi - a,$$
all of which, and no others, are included in the formula
$$n\pi + (-1)^n \cdot a,$$
where n is zero or any positive or negative integer, which is therefore the general expression for all angles which have a given sine.

OF TRIGONOMETRICAL EQUATIONS. 79

111. *To find a general expression for all angles which have a given cosine.*

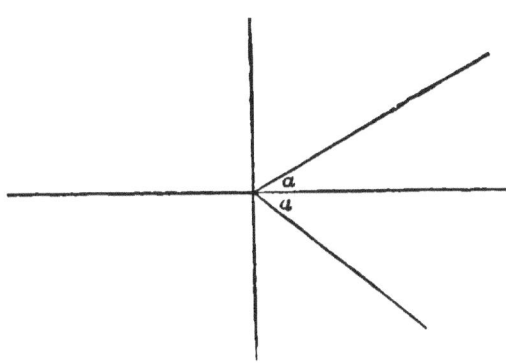

Let a be an angle whose cosine is given.

First, reckoning in the positive direction,

$$a \text{ and } 2\pi - a$$

are angles with the same cosine. (Art. 105.)

$$\left.\begin{array}{ll} \text{Also} & 2n\pi + a \\ \text{and} & 2n\pi + (2\pi - a) \end{array}\right\} \dots\dots\dots\dots\dots\dots\dots\dots\dots\dots\dots(1)$$

are angles with the same cosine. (Art. 109.)

Secondly, reckoning in a negative direction,

$$-(2\pi - a) \text{ and } -a$$

are angles with the same cosine.

$$\left.\begin{array}{ll} \text{Also} & -2n\pi - (2\pi - a) \\ \text{and} & -2n\pi - a \end{array}\right\} \dots\dots\dots\dots\dots\dots\dots\dots\dots(2)$$

are angles with the same cosine, n being any positive integer.

Now the angles in (1) and (2) may be arranged thus:

$$2n\pi + a, \ (2n+2)\pi - a, \ -(2n+2)\pi + a, \ -2n\pi - a,$$

all of which, and no others, are included in the formula

$$2n\pi \pm a,$$

which is therefore the general expression for all angles which have a given cosine.

112. *To find a general expression for all angles which have a given tangent.*

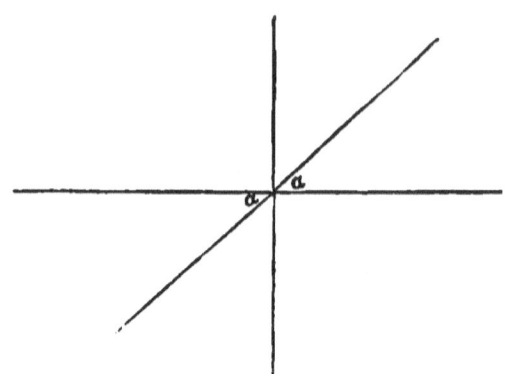

Let a be an angle whose tangent is given.

First, reckoning in the positive direction,

$$a \text{ and } \pi + a$$

are angles with the same tangent. (Art. 108.)

$$\left. \begin{array}{l} \text{Also } 2n\pi + a \\ \text{and } \quad 2n\pi + (\pi + a) \end{array} \right\} \quad \dots\dots\dots\dots\dots\dots\dots\dots\dots \text{(1)}$$

are angles with the same tangent. (Art. 109.)

Secondly, reckoning in the negative direction,

$$-(2\pi - a) \text{ and } -(\pi - a)$$

are angles with the same tangent.

$$\left. \begin{array}{l} \text{Also } -2n\pi - (2\pi - a) \\ \text{and } \quad -2n\pi - (\pi - a) \end{array} \right\} \quad \dots\dots\dots\dots\dots\dots\dots \text{(2)}$$

are angles with the same tangent, n being any positive integer.

Now the angles in (1) and (2) may be arranged thus:

$$2n\pi + a, \ (2n+1)\pi + a, \ -(2n+2)\pi + a, \ -(2n+1)\pi + a,$$

all of which, and no others, are included in the formula

$$n\pi + a,$$

which is therefore the general expression for all angles which have a given tangent.

OF TRIGONOMETRICAL EQUATIONS.

113. We shall now explain how to express the Trigonometrical Ratios of any angle in terms of the ratios of a positive angle less than a right angle.

First, when the given angle is *positive*.

If the angle is greater than $360°$, subtract from it $360°$ or any multiple of $360°$, and the ratios for the resulting angle are the same as for the original angle.

Thus we obtain an angle less than $360°$, and if this angle be greater than $180°$, we may subtract $180°$ from it, and the ratios for the resulting angle will be the same in magnitude, but the signs of all but the tangent and cotangent will be changed. (Art. 106.)

Thus we obtain an angle less than $180°$, and if this angle be greater than $90°$, we may replace it by its supplement, and the ratios for the resulting angle will be the same in magnitude, but the signs of all but the sine and cosecant will be changed. (Art. 106.)

Thus

$$\sin 675° = \sin(360° + 315°) = \sin 315° = -\sin 135° = -\sin 45°,$$

$$\tan 960° = \tan(720° + 240°) = \tan 240° = \tan 60°.$$

Secondly, when the angle is *negative*.

Add $360°$ or any multiple of $360°$ so as to obtain a positive angle, for which the ratios will be the same as for the original angle, and then proceed as before.

If the given angle be less than $180°$, apply the formulæ obtained from Art. 104.

Ex. $\sin(-825°) = \sin(1080° - 825°) = \sin 255° = -\sin 75°$.

$\tan(-135°) = -\tan 135° = -\tan 45°$.

EXAMPLES.—XXV

Find the values of the following ratios:

(1) $\sin 480°$.　　(2) $\cos 480°$.　　(3) $\sin 495°$.

(4) $\cos 495°$.　　(5) $\sin 870°$.　　(6) $\cos 870°$.

S. T.

(7) $\sin 945°$. (8) $\sin 960°$. (9) $\tan 1020°$.

(10) $\operatorname{cosec} 1380°$. (11) $\sec 1395°$. (12) $\cot 1410°$.

(13) $\cos 420°$. (14) $\sec 750°$. (15) $\tan 945°$.

(16) $\sin 1200°$. (17) $\sin 1485°$. (18) $\cos 1470°$.

(19) $\sin 7\pi$. (20) $\sec 8\pi$. (21) $\operatorname{cosec} 930°$.

(22) $\cot 1140°$. (23) $\tan 1305°$. (24) $\operatorname{cosec} 1740°$.

(25) $\sin(-240°)$. (26) $\cot(-675°)$. (27) $\sec(-135°)$.

(28) $\tan(-225°)$. (29) $\operatorname{cosec}(-690°)$. (30) $\cos(-120°)$.

Examples.—XXVI.

Write down the general value of θ which satisfies the following equations:

(1) $\sin \theta = 1$.

(2) $\cos \theta = 1$.

(3) $\sin \theta = \dfrac{1}{\sqrt{2}}$.

(4) $\tan \theta = \sqrt{3}$.

(5) $3 \sin \theta = 2 \cos^2 \theta$.

(6) $2 \sin \theta = \tan \theta$.

(7) $\tan^2 \theta + 4 \sin^2 \theta = 3$.

(8) $\cos^2 \theta = \sin^2 \theta$.

(9) $\tan \theta = 4 - 3 \cot \theta$.

(10) $\sec^2 \theta - \dfrac{5}{2} \sec \theta + 1 = 0$.

114. The symbol $\sin^{-1} x$ denotes an angle whose sine is x,

$\cos^{-1} x$ .... cosine is x,

and a similar notation is used for the other ratios.

Hence if we know that, for instance, $\tan \theta = \dfrac{2}{3}$, we may write the general value of θ thus:

$$\theta = n\pi + \tan^{-1} \dfrac{2}{3}.$$

CHAPTER XII.

On the Trigonometrical Ratios of two Angles.

115. WE now proceed to explain the Trigonometrical Functions of the Sum and Difference of two angles. These functions are the most important in the subject, and the student will find that his subsequent progress will depend much on the way in which he has read this Chapter.

116. We shall first establish the following formulæ:

$\sin (A + B) = \sin A \cdot \cos B + \cos A \cdot \sin B$,

$\cos (A + B) = \cos A \cdot \cos B - \sin A \cdot \sin B$,

$\sin (A - B) = \sin A \cdot \cos B - \cos A \cdot \sin B$,

$\cos (A - B) = \cos A \cdot \cos B + \sin A \cdot \sin B$;

by means of which we can express the sine and cosine of the sum or difference of two angles in terms of the sines and cosines of the angles themselves.

The *diagrams* which we shall employ are only applicable to the cases in which A and B are both positive and less than $90°$, also, when we are considering the sum of the angles, $A + B$ is less than $90°$, and when we are considering the difference of the angles, A is greater than B. The *formulæ* are however true for all values of A and B. Particular cases may be proved by special constructions of the diagrams, but it is beyond the scope of this treatise to enter into detail on this and similar points.

117. *To shew that*

$$\sin(A+B) = \sin A \cdot \cos B + \cos A \cdot \sin B,$$

and

$$\cos(A+B) = \cos A \cdot \cos B - \sin A \cdot \sin B.$$

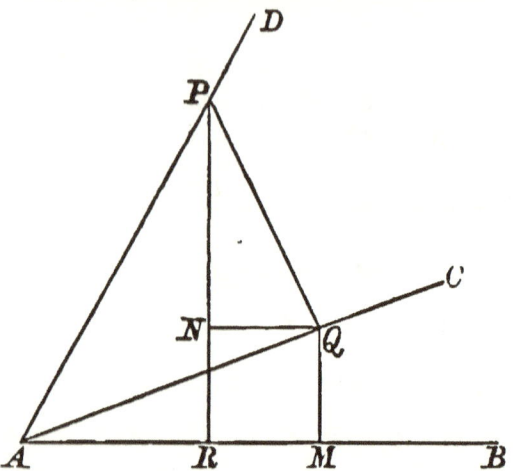

Let the angle BAC be represented by A and CAD by B. Then the angle BAD will be represented by $A+B$.

From P^*, any point in AD, draw PR at right angles to AB and PQ at right angles to AC.

From Q draw QM at right angles to AB, and QN at right angles to PR.

Then angle $QPN = 90° - PQN = NQA = QAM = A$.

Now
$$\sin(A+B) = \sin PAR = \frac{RP}{AP}$$

$$= \frac{RN+NP}{AP} = \frac{QM+NP}{AP} = \frac{QM}{AP} + \frac{NP}{AP}$$

$$= \frac{QM}{AQ} \cdot \frac{AQ}{AP} + \frac{NP}{PQ} \cdot \frac{PQ}{AP}$$

$$= \sin A \cdot \cos B + \cos A \cdot \sin B.$$

$$\cos(A+B) = \cos PAR = \frac{AR}{AP}$$

$$= \frac{AM-MR}{AP} = \frac{AM-NQ}{AP} = \frac{AM}{AP} - \frac{NQ}{AP}$$

$$= \frac{AM}{AQ} \cdot \frac{AQ}{AP} - \frac{NQ}{PQ} \cdot \frac{PQ}{AP}$$

$$= \cos A \cdot \cos B - \sin A \cdot \sin B.$$

* P is taken in the line bounding the angle under consideration, that is, BAD.

RATIOS OF TWO ANGLES.

118. *To shew that*
$$\sin(A-B) = \sin A . \cos B - \cos A . \sin B,$$
and
$$\cos(A-B) = \cos A . \cos B + \sin A . \sin B.$$

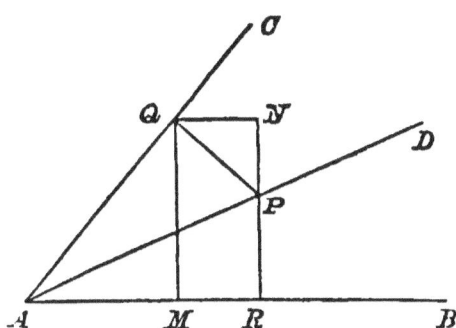

Let the angle BAC be represented by A and CAD by B. Then the angle BAD will be represented by $A-B$.

From P^*, any point in AD, draw PR at right angles to AB and PQ at right angles to AC.

From Q draw QM at right angles to AB and QN at right angles to RP produced.

Then angle $QPN = 90° - PQN = CQN = BAC = A$.

Now $\sin(A-B) = \sin PAR = \dfrac{RP}{AP}$

$= \dfrac{RN - NP}{AP} = \dfrac{QM - NP}{AP} = \dfrac{QM}{AP} - \dfrac{NP}{AP}$

$= \dfrac{QM}{AQ} \cdot \dfrac{AQ}{AP} - \dfrac{NP}{PQ} \cdot \dfrac{PQ}{AP}$

$= \sin A . \cos B - \cos A . \sin B.$

$\cos(A-B) = \cos PAR = \dfrac{AR}{AP}$

$= \dfrac{AM + MR}{AP} = \dfrac{AM + NQ}{AP} = \dfrac{AM}{AP} + \dfrac{NQ}{AP}$

$= \dfrac{AM}{AQ} \cdot \dfrac{AQ}{AP} + \dfrac{NQ}{PQ} \cdot \dfrac{PQ}{AP}$

$= \cos A . \cos B + \sin A . \sin B.$

---

* P is taken in the line bounding the angle under consideration, that is, BAD.

119. We shall now give some important examples of the application of the formulæ which we have established.

Ex. 1. *To find the value of $\sin 75°$.*

$$\sin 75° = \sin(45° + 30°)$$
$$= \sin 45° \cdot \cos 30° + \cos 45° \cdot \sin 30°$$
$$= \frac{1}{\sqrt{2}} \cdot \frac{\sqrt{3}}{2} + \frac{1}{\sqrt{2}} \cdot \frac{1}{2} \quad \text{(Arts. 78, 79)}$$
$$= \frac{\sqrt{3}}{2\sqrt{2}} + \frac{1}{2\sqrt{2}}$$
$$= \frac{\sqrt{3} + 1}{2\sqrt{2}}.$$

Ex. 2. *To find the value of $\cos 15°$.*

$$\cos 15° = \cos(45° - 30°)$$
$$= \cos 45° \cdot \cos 30° + \sin 45° \cdot \sin 30$$
$$= \frac{1}{\sqrt{2}} \cdot \frac{\sqrt{3}}{2} + \frac{1}{\sqrt{2}} \cdot \frac{1}{2}$$
$$= \frac{\sqrt{3}}{2\sqrt{2}} + \frac{1}{2\sqrt{2}}$$
$$= \frac{\sqrt{3} + 1}{2\sqrt{2}},$$

a result identical with the value of $\sin 75°$, in accordance with Art. 99, for

$$\sin 75° = \cos(90° - 75°) = \cos 15°.$$

Ex. 3. *To shew that $\sin(90° + A) = \cos A$.*

Assuming the conclusions of Art. 117 to be true for all values of A and B,

$$\sin(90° + A) = \sin 90° \cdot \cos A + \cos 90° \cdot \sin A$$
$$= 1 \cdot \cos A + 0 \cdot \sin A \quad \text{(Art. 71)}$$
$$= \cos A.$$

And similarly other relations between trigonometrical functions established in Chapter X. may be proved.

Ex. 4. *To find a value of θ which satisfies the equation*

$$\sin \theta + \cos \theta = 0.$$

Multiply both sides by $\frac{1}{\sqrt{2}}$.

Then $\sin \theta \cdot \frac{1}{\sqrt{2}} + \cos \theta \cdot \frac{1}{\sqrt{2}} = 0;$

$\therefore \sin \theta \cdot \cos 45^\circ + \cos \theta \cdot \sin 45^\circ = 0,$

or, $\sin (\theta + 45^\circ) = 0;$

$\therefore (\theta + 45^\circ) = 0;$

$\therefore \theta = -45^\circ.$

EXAMPLES.—XXVII.

Prove the following relations :

(1) $\sin (A+B) \cdot \sin (A-B) = \sin^2 A - \sin^2 B.$

(2) $\sin (a+\beta) \cdot \sin (a-\beta) = \cos^2 \beta - \cos^2 a.$

(3) $\cos (A+B) \cdot \cos (A-B) = \cos^2 A - \sin^2 B.$

(4) $\cos (a+\beta) \cdot \cos (a-\beta) = \cos^2 \beta - \sin^2 a.$

(5) $2 \sin (x+y) \cdot \cos (x-y) = \sin 2x + \sin 2y.$

(6) $2 \cos (x+y) \cdot \sin (x-y) = \sin 2x - \sin 2y.$

(7) $\tan A + \tan B = \dfrac{\sin (A+B)}{\cos A \cdot \cos B}.$

(8) $\tan a - \tan \beta = \dfrac{\sin (a-\beta)}{\cos a \cdot \cos \beta}.$

Examples.—XXVIII.

(1) Show that $\sin 15° = \dfrac{\sqrt{3}-1}{2\sqrt{2}}$.

(2) Show that $\cos 75° = \dfrac{\sqrt{3}-1}{2\sqrt{2}}$.

(3) Show that $\tan 75° = 2+\sqrt{3}$.

(4) Show that $\cot 75° = 2-\sqrt{3}$.

(5) If $\sin \alpha = \dfrac{1}{3}$ and $\sin \beta = \dfrac{2}{3}$ find the value of $\sin(\alpha+\beta)$.

(6) If $\cos \alpha = \dfrac{3}{4}$ and $\cos \beta = \dfrac{2}{5}$ find the value of $\sin(\alpha-\beta)$.

(7) If $\sin \alpha = \cdot 5$ and $\cos \beta = \dfrac{1}{\sqrt{2}}$ find the value of $\cos(\alpha+\beta)$.

(8) If $\cos \alpha = \cdot 03$ and $\sin \beta = \dfrac{1}{2}$ find the value of $\cos(\alpha-\beta)$.

Examples.—XXIX.

Apply the formulæ established in this chapter to shew the following relations between the Trigonometrical Functions of angles.

(1) $\cos(90°+A) = -\sin A$.   (2) $\sin(180°+A) = -\sin A$.

(3) $\cos(\pi+\theta) = -\cos \theta$.   (4) $\sin\left(\dfrac{3\pi}{2}+\theta\right) = -\cos \theta$.

(5) $\operatorname{cosec}\left(\dfrac{\pi}{2}+\alpha\right) = \sec \alpha$.   (6) $\tan(\pi+\alpha) = \tan \alpha$.

(7) $\sin(2\pi-\theta) = -\sin \theta$.   (8) $\tan(2\pi-\theta) = -\tan \theta$.

(9) $\sec(180°-\theta) = -\sec \theta$.   (10) $\operatorname{cosec}(\pi-\theta) = \operatorname{cosec} \theta$.

EXAMPLES.—XXX.

Find a value of θ to satisfy the following equations, by a process similar to that given in Art. 119, Ex. 4.

(1) $\sin\theta - \cos\theta = 0$.　　(2) $\sin\theta + \cos\theta = 1$.

(3) $\sin\theta - \cos\theta = \sqrt{\dfrac{3}{2}}$.　　(4) $\sin\theta + \cos\theta = \dfrac{\sqrt{3}+1}{2}$.

(5) $\sin\theta + \cos\theta = \sqrt{2}$.　　(6) $\sin\theta - \cos\theta = \dfrac{\sqrt{3}-1}{2}$.

120. Collecting the formulæ of Arts. 117, 118, we next arrange them thus:

$$\sin(A+B) = \sin A \cdot \cos B + \cos A \cdot \sin B,$$
$$\sin(A-B) = \sin A \cdot \cos B - \cos A \cdot \sin B,$$
$$\cos(A-B) = \cos A \cdot \cos B + \sin A \cdot \sin B,$$
$$\cos(A+B) = \cos A \cdot \cos B - \sin A \cdot \sin B.$$

Hence, by addition and subtraction, we obtain the following:

$$\sin(A+B) + \sin(A-B) = 2\sin A \cdot \cos B,$$
$$\sin(A+B) - \sin(A-B) = 2\cos A \cdot \sin B,$$
$$\cos(A-B) + \cos(A+B) = 2\cos A \cdot \cos B,$$
$$\cos(A-B) - \cos(A+B) = 2\sin A \cdot \sin B.$$

Now let $A + B = P$,

and $A - B = Q$.

Then $2A = P + Q$, and $2B = P - Q$;

$\therefore A = \dfrac{P+Q}{2}$, and $B = \dfrac{P-Q}{2}$;

So that the formulæ may be put in this form:

$$\sin P + \sin Q = 2 \sin \frac{P+Q}{2} \cdot \cos \frac{P-Q}{2},$$

$$\sin P - \sin Q = 2 \cos \frac{P+Q}{2} \cdot \sin \frac{P-Q}{2},$$

$$\cos Q + \cos P = 2 \cos \frac{P+Q}{2} \cdot \cos \frac{P-Q}{2},$$

$$\cos Q - \cos P = 2 \sin \frac{P+Q}{2} \cdot \sin \frac{P-Q}{2}.$$

121. As these results are of very great importance we shall repeat them separately, explaining each in words.

(1) $\sin P + \sin Q = 2 \sin \frac{P+Q}{2} \cdot \cos \frac{P-Q}{2},$

that is, *the sum of the sines of two angles is equal to twice the product of the sine of half the sum of the angles into the cosine of half their difference.*

Ex. $\sin 10\theta + \sin 6\theta = 2 \sin \frac{10\theta + 6\theta}{2} \cdot \cos \frac{10\theta - 6\theta}{2}$

$$= 2 \sin 8\theta \cdot \cos 2\theta.$$

(2) $\sin P - \sin Q = 2 \cos \frac{P+Q}{2} \cdot \sin \frac{P-Q}{2},$

that is, *the difference of the sines of two angles is equal to twice the product of the cosine of half the sum of the angles into the sine of half their difference.*

Ex. $\sin 8a - \sin 4a = 2 \cos \frac{8a + 4a}{2} \cdot \sin \frac{8a - 4a}{2}$

$$= 2 \cos 6a \cdot \sin 2a.$$

(3) $\cos Q + \cos P = 2 \cos \frac{P+Q}{2} \cdot \cos \frac{P-Q}{2},$

that is, *the sum of the cosines of two angles is equal to twice the product of the cosine of half the sum of the angles into the cosine of half their difference.*

RATIOS OF TWO ANGLES. 91

Ex. $\cos\theta + \cos 3\theta = 2\cos\dfrac{3\theta+\theta}{2} \cdot \cos\dfrac{3\theta-\theta}{2}$

$\qquad\qquad\qquad = 2\cos 2\theta \cdot \cos\theta.$

(4) $\cos Q - \cos P = 2\sin\dfrac{P+Q}{2} \cdot \sin\dfrac{P-Q}{2},$

that is, *the difference of the cosines of two angles is equal to twice the product of the sine of half the sum of the angles into the sine of half their difference.*

Ex. $\cos 3a - \cos 7a = 2\sin\dfrac{7a+3a}{2} \cdot \sin\dfrac{7a-3a}{2}$

$\qquad\qquad\qquad = 2\sin 5a \cdot \sin 2a.$

122. As the formulæ at the end of Art. 120 teach us how to replace the sum or difference of two sines or cosines by the product of two sines or cosines, so the formulæ at the beginning of Art. 120, when read from right to left, thus:

$2\sin A \cdot \cos B = \sin(A+B) + \sin(A-B),$

$2\cos A \cdot \sin B = \sin(A+B) - \sin(A-B),$

$2\cos A \cdot \cos B = \cos(A-B) + \cos(A+B),$

$2\sin A \cdot \sin B = \cos(A-B) - \cos(A+B),$

furnish rules for replacing the product of two sines or cosines by the sum or difference of sines or cosines.

For example,

$\sin 5\theta \cdot \cos 3\theta = \dfrac{1}{2}\{\sin(5\theta+3\theta) + \sin(5\theta-3\theta)\}$

$\qquad\qquad\quad = \dfrac{1}{2}(\sin 8\theta + \sin 2\theta),$

$\sin\theta \cdot \sin 3\theta = \dfrac{1}{2}\{\cos(3\theta-\theta) - \cos(3\theta+\theta)\}$

$\qquad\qquad\quad = \dfrac{1}{2}(\cos 2\theta - \cos 4\theta).$

Examples.—XXXI.

Prove the following relations:

(1) $\sin 6A + \sin 4A = 2 \sin 5A . \cos A$.

(2) $\sin 5A - \sin 3A = 2 \cos 4A . \sin A$.

(3) $\cos 7\theta + \cos 9\theta = 2 \cos 8\theta . \cos \theta$.

(4) $\cos \theta - \cos 5\theta = 2 \sin 3\theta . \sin 2\theta$.

(5) $\sin a + \sin 4a = 2 \sin \dfrac{5a}{2} . \cos \dfrac{3a}{2}$.

(6) $\cos 5a - \cos 8a = 2 \sin \dfrac{13a}{2} . \sin \dfrac{3a}{2}$.

(7) $2 \sin 5\theta . \cos 7\theta = \sin 12\theta - \sin 2\theta$.

(8) $2 \sin 3\theta . \sin 5\theta = \cos 2\theta - \cos 8\theta$.

(9) $2 \cos a . \cos 4a = \cos 5a + \cos 3a$.

(10) $2 \cos a . \sin 2a = \sin 3a + \sin a$.

(11) $\dfrac{\sin A + \sin B}{\cos A + \cos B} = \tan \dfrac{A+B}{2}$.

(12) $\dfrac{\cos A - \cos 3A}{\sin 3A - \sin A} = \tan 2A$.

(13) $\dfrac{\sin 2A + \sin A}{\cos 2A + \cos A} = \tan \dfrac{3A}{2}$.

(14) $\cos (30° - \theta) - \cos (30° + \theta) = \sin \theta$.

(15) $\cos \left(\dfrac{\pi}{3} + \theta\right) + \cos \left(\dfrac{\pi}{3} - \theta\right) = \cos \theta$

(16) $\sin \left(\dfrac{\pi}{3} + a\right) - \sin \left(\dfrac{\pi}{3} - a\right) = \sin a$.

(17) $\dfrac{\sin a - \sin \beta}{\cos \beta - \cos a} = \cot \dfrac{a+\beta}{2}$.

(18) $\dfrac{\sin a - \sin \beta}{\cos \beta + \cos a} = \tan \dfrac{a-\beta}{2}$.

(19) $\dfrac{\sin 5\theta + \sin 3\theta}{\cos 3\theta - \cos 5\theta} = \cot \theta$.

(20) $\dfrac{\cos a + \cos \beta}{\cos \beta - \cos a} = \dfrac{\cot \frac{1}{2}(a+\beta)}{\tan \frac{1}{2}(a-\beta)}$.

123. We can also express the sum or difference of a sine and a cosine as the product of sines or cosines.

For since $\cos \theta = \sin \left(\dfrac{\pi}{2} - \theta\right)$ (Art. 99),

$$\sin a + \cos \theta = \sin a + \sin \left(\dfrac{\pi}{2} - \theta\right)$$

$$= 2 \sin \dfrac{1}{2}\left(a + \dfrac{\pi}{2} - \theta\right) \cdot \cos \dfrac{1}{2}\left(a - \dfrac{\pi}{2} + \theta\right).$$

Again

$$\sin 40^\circ + \cos 60^\circ = \sin 40^\circ + \sin 30^\circ$$

$$= 2 \sin 35^\circ \cdot \cos 5^\circ.$$

EXAMPLES.—XXXII.

Express as the product of sines or cosines:

(1) $\sin a - \cos \beta$, (2) $\sin \left(\dfrac{\pi}{2} + a\right) + \cos \left(\dfrac{\pi}{2} - a\right)$,

(3) $\sin a + \cos a$, (4) $\sin a - \cos a$,

(5) $\sin 30^\circ + \cos 80^\circ$, (6) $\sin 20^\circ - \cos 80^\circ$,

(7) $\sin \dfrac{\pi}{4} + \cos \dfrac{\pi}{6}$, (8) $\sin \dfrac{\pi}{3} - \cos \dfrac{\pi}{5}$.

124. We now proceed to explain how the Tangent of the sum and difference of two angles can be expressed in terms of the tangents of the angles themselves.

$$\tan(A+B) = \frac{\sin(A+B)}{\cos(A+B)}$$

$$= \frac{\sin A \cdot \cos B + \cos A \cdot \sin B}{\cos A \cdot \cos B - \sin A \cdot \sin B},$$

and, dividing each term of the numerator and denominator by $\cos A \cdot \cos B$,

$$= \frac{\dfrac{\sin A \cdot \cos B}{\cos A \cdot \cos B} + \dfrac{\cos A \cdot \sin B}{\cos A \cdot \cos B}}{\dfrac{\cos A \cdot \cos B}{\cos A \cdot \cos B} - \dfrac{\sin A \cdot \sin B}{\cos A \cdot \cos B}}$$

$$= \frac{\tan A + \tan B}{1 - \tan A \cdot \tan B}.$$

$$\tan(A-B) = \frac{\sin(A-B)}{\cos(A-B)}$$

$$= \frac{\sin A \cdot \cos B - \cos A \cdot \sin B}{\cos A \cdot \cos B + \sin A \cdot \sin B}$$

$$= \frac{\dfrac{\sin A \cdot \cos B}{\cos A \cdot \cos B} - \dfrac{\cos A \cdot \sin B}{\cos A \cdot \cos B}}{\dfrac{\cos A \cdot \cos B}{\cos A \cdot \cos B} + \dfrac{\sin A \cdot \sin B}{\cos A \cdot \cos B}}$$

$$= \frac{\tan A - \tan B}{1 + \tan A \cdot \tan B}.$$

COR. We proved in Art. 79 that $\tan 45° = 1$.

Hence

$$\tan(45° + A) = \frac{\tan 45° + \tan A}{1 - \tan 45° \cdot \tan A}$$

$$= \frac{1 + \tan A}{1 - \tan A},$$

$$\tan(45° - A) = \frac{\tan 45° - \tan A}{1 + \tan 45° \cdot \tan A}$$

$$= \frac{1 - \tan A}{1 + \tan A}.$$

125. The results of the preceding article may be obtained without assuming the formulæ for the sine and cosine, thus:

Taking the Diagram of Art. 117, we have

$$\tan(A+B) = \frac{PR}{AR} = \frac{NR+PN}{AM-MR}$$

$$= \frac{QM+PN}{AM-NQ}$$

$$= \frac{\dfrac{QM}{AM} + \dfrac{PN}{AM}}{1 - \dfrac{NQ}{AM}}.$$

Now $\dfrac{QM}{AM} = \tan A$,

and observing that PNQ, MQA are similar triangles,

$$\frac{PN}{AM} = \frac{PQ}{AQ} = \tan B,$$

$$\frac{NQ}{AM} = \frac{NQ}{PN} \cdot \frac{PN}{AM} = \tan A \cdot \tan B;$$

$$\therefore \tan(A+B) = \frac{\tan A + \tan B}{1 - \tan A \cdot \tan B}.$$

Again, taking the diagram of Art. 118, we have

$$\tan(A-B) = \frac{PR}{AR} = \frac{NR-PN}{AM+MR}$$

$$= \frac{QM-PN}{AM+NQ}$$

$$= \frac{\dfrac{QM}{AM} - \dfrac{PN}{AM}}{1 + \dfrac{NQ}{AM}}.$$

Now $\dfrac{QM}{AM} = \tan A$,

and observing that PNQ, MQA are similar triangles,

$$\frac{PN}{AM} = \frac{PQ}{AQ} = \tan B,$$

$$\frac{NQ}{AM} = \frac{NQ}{PN} \cdot \frac{PN}{AM} = \tan A \cdot \tan B;$$

$$\therefore \tan(A-B) = \frac{\tan A - \tan B}{1 + \tan A \cdot \tan B}.$$

Examples.—XXXIII.

Prove the following relations:

(1) $\dfrac{\tan \alpha + \tan \beta}{\cot \alpha + \cot \beta} = \tan \alpha \cdot \tan \beta.$

(2) $\dfrac{\tan \alpha + \tan \beta}{\cot \alpha - \tan \beta} = \tan \alpha \cdot \tan(\alpha + \beta).$

(3) $\dfrac{\tan \alpha - \tan \beta}{\cot \alpha + \tan \beta} = \tan \alpha \cdot \tan(\alpha - \beta).$

(4) $\tan \dfrac{\phi+\psi}{2} + \tan \dfrac{\phi-\psi}{2} = \dfrac{2 \sin \phi}{\cos \phi + \cos \psi}$

(5) $\sin \phi = \sin \psi \cdot \cos(\phi - \psi) + \cos \psi \cdot \sin(\phi - \psi).$

(6) $\cos \phi = \sin \psi \cdot \sin(\phi + \psi) + \cos \psi \cdot \cos(\phi + \psi).$

(7) $(\cos \alpha + \cos \beta)\{1 - \cos(\alpha+\beta)\} = (\sin \alpha + \sin \beta) \cdot \sin(\alpha+\beta).$

(8) $\dfrac{\sin(\alpha+\beta)}{\sin \alpha + \sin \beta} = \dfrac{\cos \dfrac{\alpha+\beta}{2}}{\cos \dfrac{\alpha-\beta}{2}}.$

(9) $\dfrac{\sin(\alpha+\beta)}{\sin \alpha - \sin \beta} = \dfrac{\sin \dfrac{\alpha+\beta}{2}}{\sin \dfrac{\alpha-\beta}{2}}.$

(10) $\cot \dfrac{\alpha+\beta}{2} + \cot \dfrac{\alpha-\beta}{2} = \dfrac{2 \sin \alpha}{\cos \beta - \cos \alpha}.$

(11) $\tan\dfrac{a+\beta}{2} - \tan\dfrac{a-\beta}{2} = \dfrac{2\sin\beta}{\cos a + \cos\beta}$.

(12) $\dfrac{\cos a - \cos\beta}{\sin a + \sin\beta} = \tan\dfrac{\beta-a}{2}$.

(13) $\cot\beta - \tan a = \dfrac{\cos(a+\beta)}{\cos a . \sin\beta}$.

(14) $\cot\theta + \tan\phi = \dfrac{\cos(\phi-\theta)}{\cos\phi . \sin\theta}$.

(15) $\tan^2 a - \tan^2\beta = \dfrac{\sin(a+\beta)\sin(a-\beta)}{\cos^2 a . \cos^2\beta}$.

(16) $1 + \tan a . \tan\beta = \dfrac{\cos(a-\beta)}{\cos a . \cos\beta}$.

(17) $1 - \tan a . \tan\beta = \dfrac{\cos(a+\beta)}{\cos a . \cos\beta}$.

(18) $\dfrac{\cot a + \tan\beta}{\tan a + \cot\beta} = \cot a . \tan\beta$.

(19) $\dfrac{\tan^2 x - \tan^2 y}{1 - \tan^2 x . \tan^2 y} = \tan(x+y) . \tan(x-y)$.

(20) $\cot(\theta + 45^0) = \dfrac{\cot\theta - 1}{\cot\theta + 1}$.

(21) $\sin\theta + \cos\theta = \sqrt{2} . \sin(45^0 + \theta)$.

(22) $\cos\theta - \sin\theta = \sqrt{2} . \sin\left(\dfrac{\pi}{4} - \theta\right)$.

(23) $\dfrac{\tan a - \tan\beta}{\tan a + \tan\beta} = \dfrac{\sin(a-\beta)}{\sin(a+\beta)}$.

(24) $\dfrac{\cot x - \cot y}{\cot x + \cot y} = \dfrac{\sin(y-x)}{\sin(y+x)}$.

(25) $\cos(A-B) + \sin(A+B) = 2\sin(A+45^0) . \cos(B-45^0)$.

(26) $\cos(A-B) - \sin(A+B) = 2\sin(45^0-A) . \cos(45^0+B)$.

(27) $\cos(A+B) + \sin(A-B) = 2\sin(45^0+A) . \cos(45^0+B)$

(28) $\cos(A+B) - \sin(A-B) = 2\sin(45° - A) \cdot \cos(45° - B)$.

✓(29) $\dfrac{\cos\alpha + \cos\beta}{\cos\alpha - \cos\beta} = -\dfrac{\cot\dfrac{\alpha+\beta}{2}}{\tan\dfrac{\alpha-\beta}{2}}$.

(30) $\sec 72° - \sec 36° = \sec 60°$.

(31) $\sin 108° = (\sin 81° + \sin 9°)(\sin 81° - \sin 9°)$.

(32) $\dfrac{\cos 3° - \cos 33°}{\sin 3° + \sin 33°} = \tan 15°$.

✓(33) $\dfrac{\sin 33° + \sin 3°}{\cos 33° + \cos 3°} = \tan 18°$.

✓(34) $\dfrac{\cos 9° + \sin 9°}{\cos 9° - \sin 9°} = \tan 54°$.

✓(35) $\dfrac{\cos 27° - \sin 27°}{\cos 27° + \sin 27°} = \tan 18°$.

(36) $\tan 50° + \cot 50° = 2\sec 10°$.

CHAPTER XIII.

On the Trigonometrical Ratios for multiple and submultiple Angles.

126. THE angles $2A$, $3A$, $4A$ ...... are called Multiples of A, and the angles $\frac{A}{2}$, $\frac{A}{3}$, $\frac{A}{4}$ ...... are called Submultiples of A.

We shall first shew how to express the Trigonometrical Ratios of $2A$ and $\frac{A}{2}$ in terms of the ratios of A.

127. $\sin 2A = \sin(A+A)$
$= \sin A \cdot \cos A + \cos A \cdot \sin A$
$= \sin A \cdot \cos A + \sin A \cdot \cos A$
$= 2 \sin A \cdot \cos A.$

$\cos 2A = \cos(A+A)$
$= \cos A \cdot \cos A - \sin A \cdot \sin A$
$= \cos^2 A - \sin^2 A.$

Now we may put $1 - \sin^2 A$ in the place of $\cos^2 A$ (Art. 90), and we then have

$\cos 2A = 1 - \sin^2 A - \sin^2 A$
$= 1 - 2 \sin^2 A.$

Or we may put $1 - \cos^2 A$ in the place of $\sin^2 A$ (Art. 90), and we then have

$\cos 2A = \cos^2 A - (1 - \cos^2 A)$
$= \cos^2 A - 1 + \cos^2 A$
$= 2 \cos^2 A - 1.$

$$\tan 2A = \tan(A+A)$$
$$= \frac{\tan A + \tan A}{1 - \tan A \cdot \tan A}, \text{ (Art. 124)}$$
$$= \frac{2 \tan A}{1 - \tan^2 A}.$$

128. If we put A in the place of $2A$, and $\dfrac{A}{2}$ in the place of A, we have

$$\sin A = 2 \sin \frac{A}{2} \cdot \cos \frac{A}{2},$$

$$\cos A = \cos^2 \frac{A}{2} - \sin^2 \frac{A}{2}$$

$$= 1 - 2 \sin^2 \frac{A}{2}$$

$$= 2 \cos^2 \frac{A}{2} - 1,$$

$$\tan A = \frac{2 \tan \frac{A}{2}}{1 - \tan^2 \frac{A}{2}}.$$

Hence we can show that $\dfrac{1 - \cos A}{1 + \cos A} = \tan^2 \dfrac{A}{2}$, a formula of great importance.

For $\dfrac{1-\cos A}{1+\cos A} = \dfrac{1 - \left(1 - 2\sin^2\frac{A}{2}\right)}{1 + \left(2\cos^2\frac{A}{2} - 1\right)} = \dfrac{2\sin^2\frac{A}{2}}{2\cos^2\frac{A}{2}} = \tan^2\dfrac{A}{2}.$

Examples.—XXXIV.

Prove the following relations:

✓(1) $\sin 2A = \dfrac{2 \cot A}{1 + \cot^2 A}.$

(2) $\dfrac{\sin 2A}{1+\cos 2A} \cdot \dfrac{\cos A}{1+\cos A} = \tan \dfrac{A}{2}$.

(3) $\operatorname{cosec} A + \cot A = \cot \dfrac{A}{2}$.

(4) $\tan \theta + \cot \theta = \dfrac{2}{\sin 2\theta}$.

(5) $\sin 2\theta = \dfrac{2 \tan \theta}{1 + \tan^2 \theta}$.

(6) $2 \operatorname{cosec} 2A = \sec A \cdot \operatorname{cosec} A$.

(7) $\cos 2\theta = \dfrac{1 - \tan^2 \theta}{1 + \tan^2 \theta}$.

(8) $\sec^2 \theta = \dfrac{2 \sec 2\theta}{1 + \sec 2\theta}$.

(9) $\dfrac{1 - 2\sin^2 A}{1 + \sin 2A} = \dfrac{1 - \tan A}{1 + \tan A}$.

(10) $\cot \theta - 2 \cot 2\theta = \tan \theta$.

(11) $\dfrac{1 - \cos a}{\sin a} = \tan \dfrac{a}{2}$.

(12) $\sin 2\phi = \dfrac{2 \sqrt{(\operatorname{cosec}^2 \phi - 1)}}{\operatorname{cosec}^2 \phi}$.

(13) $\cos 2\phi = \dfrac{2 - \sec^2 \phi}{\sec^2 \phi}$.

(14) $\tan 2\phi = \dfrac{2 \cot \phi}{\cot^2 \phi - 1}$.

(15) $\sin a = \sqrt{\left(\dfrac{\sec 2a - 1}{2 \sec 2a}\right)}$.

(16) $\cos a = \sqrt{\left(\dfrac{\sec 2a + 1}{2 \sec 2a}\right)}$.

MULTIPLE AND SUBMULTIPLE ANGLES.

(17) $\tan a = \csc 2a - \cot 2a$.

(18) $\cot \beta = \csc 2\beta + \cot 2\beta$.

(19) $\tan (45° + A) = \dfrac{\cos 2A}{1 - \sin 2A}$.

(20) $\cot (45° - A) = \sec 2A + \tan 2A$.

(21) $\dfrac{1+\sin a}{1+\cos a} = \dfrac{1}{2}\left(1 + \tan \dfrac{a}{2}\right)^2$.

(22) $\dfrac{1-\sin a}{1-\cos a} = \dfrac{1}{2}\left(\cot \dfrac{a}{2} - 1\right)^2$.

(23) $\tan \theta = \tan \dfrac{\theta}{2} + \dfrac{1}{2} \tan \theta \cdot \sec^2 \dfrac{\theta}{2}$.

(24) $\dfrac{1+\sin \theta}{1-\sin \theta} = (\sec \theta + \tan \theta)^2$.

√(25) $\sin 2A = \dfrac{1 - \tan^2(45° - A)}{1 + \tan^2(45° - A)}$.

√(26) $\sin 2\theta = \dfrac{\tan\left(\dfrac{\pi}{4} + \theta\right) - \tan\left(\dfrac{\pi}{4} - \theta\right)}{\tan\left(\dfrac{\pi}{4} + \theta\right) + \tan\left(\dfrac{\pi}{4} - \theta\right)}$.

129. We shall next show how to express the Ratios of $3A$ in terms of the Ratios of A.

$\sin 3A = \sin (2A + A)$

$\qquad = \sin 2A \cdot \cos A + \cos 2A \cdot \sin A$

$\qquad = (2 \sin A \cdot \cos A) \cdot \cos A + (1 - 2 \sin^2 A) \cdot \sin A$

$\qquad = 2 \sin A \cdot \cos^2 A + \sin A - 2 \sin^3 A$

$\qquad = 2 \sin A \cdot (1 - \sin^2 A) + \sin A - 2 \sin^3 A$

$\qquad = 2 \sin A - 2 \sin^3 A + \sin A - 2 \sin^3 A$

$\qquad = 3 \sin A - 4 \sin^3 A$.

130. $\cos 3A = \cos(2A + A)$

$= \cos 2A \cdot \cos A - \sin 2A \cdot \sin A$

$= (2\cos^2 A - 1) \cdot \cos A - (2\sin A \cdot \cos A) \cdot \sin A$

$= 2\cos^3 A - \cos A - 2\sin^2 A \cdot \cos A$

$= 2\cos^3 A - \cos A - 2\cos A(1 - \cos^2 A)$

$= 2\cos^3 A - \cos A - 2\cos A + 2\cos^3 A$

$= 4\cos^3 A - 3\cos A.$

131. $\tan 3A = \dfrac{\sin 3A}{\cos 3A}$

$= \dfrac{3\sin A - 4\sin^3 A}{4\cos^3 A - 3\cos A}$, and, dividing by $\cos^3 A$,

$= \dfrac{\dfrac{3\sin A}{\cos^3 A} - 4\tan^3 A}{4 - \dfrac{3}{\cos^2 A}}$

$= \dfrac{3\tan A \cdot \sec^2 A - 4\tan^3 A}{4 - 3\sec^2 A}$

$= \dfrac{3\tan A(1 + \tan^2 A) - 4\tan^3 A}{4 - 3(1 + \tan^2 A)}$

$= \dfrac{3\tan A - \tan^3 A}{1 - 3\tan^2 A}.$

Examples.—XXXV.

In some of these Examples the student may employ with advantage the formulæ given in Art. 121.

1. (1) $\dfrac{\cos 3\theta - \sin 3\theta}{\sin \theta + \cos \theta} = 1 - 2\sin 2\theta.$

✓ (2) $\sin 2\theta + \cos \theta = \dfrac{2\tan \theta + \sec \theta}{1 + \tan^2 \theta}.$

(3) $\sin A = \tan \dfrac{A}{2} + 2 \sin^2 \dfrac{A}{2} \cot A.$

(4) $\dfrac{\cot A}{\cot A - \cot 3A} + \dfrac{\tan A}{\tan A - \tan 3A} = 1.$

✓(5) $\cos 4A + \cos 4B = 2\{1 - 2\sin^2(A+B)\}\{1 - 2\sin^2(A-B)\}.$

(6) $\tan(45° + \theta) - \tan(45° - \theta) = 2 \cdot \dfrac{\sec 2\theta - \cos 2\theta}{\sin 2\theta}.$

(7) $\cot^2 \theta - \tan^2 \theta = 8 \dfrac{\cos 2\theta}{1 - \cos 4\theta}.$

(8) $2 \sin A \cdot \cos 2A = \sin 3A - \sin A.$

(9) $\dfrac{\cos nA - \cos(n+2)A}{\sin(n+2)A - \sin nA} = \tan(n+1)A.$

✓(10) $\cos 9A + 3\cos 7A + 3\cos 5A + \cos 3A = 8 \cos^3 A \cdot \cos 6A.$

(11) $\dfrac{\operatorname{cosec} 2A - \cot 2A}{\operatorname{cosec} 2A + \cot 2A} = \tan^2 A.$

(12) $\dfrac{1 - \sin A}{1 + \cos A} = \dfrac{1}{2}\left(1 - \tan \dfrac{A}{2}\right)^2.$

(13) $\dfrac{2 \cos 2A - 3}{2 \cos 2A + 3} = \dfrac{\cos 3A - 2\cos A}{\sin 3A + 2\sin A} \cdot \tan A.$

(14) $\tan(45° - A) + \tan(45° + A) = 2 \sec 2A.$

(15) $\cos a - \tan \dfrac{a}{2} \sin a = \cos 2a + \tan \dfrac{a}{2} \cdot \sin 2a.$

★(16) $\cot^2 A - \tan^2 A = 4 \cot 2A \cdot \operatorname{cosec} 2A.$

(17) $\operatorname{cosec} a \cdot \cot a - \sec a \cdot \tan a = \operatorname{cosec}^2 2a(\cos^3 a - \sin^3 a).$

✓(18) $\cot^2 a - \tan^2 a = \dfrac{4 \cos 2a}{\sin^2 2a}.$

(19) $\csc^2 b - \sec^2 b = 4\cos 2b \cdot \csc^2 2b$.

(20) $\cot^2\left(45° + \dfrac{A}{2}\right) = \dfrac{2\csc 2A - \sec A}{2\csc 2A + \sec A}$.

(21) $\sin\left(\dfrac{5\pi}{2}+\theta\right) - \sin\left(\dfrac{3\pi}{2}-\theta\right) = \sin\left(\dfrac{5\pi}{2}-\theta\right) - \sin\left(\dfrac{3\pi}{2}+\theta\right)$.

(22) $\cot\left(\dfrac{\pi}{2}+\theta\right) - \tan\left(\dfrac{\pi}{2}+\theta\right) = 2\cot 2\theta$.

(23) $\dfrac{(\csc a + \sec a)^2}{\csc^2 a + \sec^2 a} = 1 + \sin 2a$.

(24) $\dfrac{\tan\theta}{\tan 2\theta - \tan\theta} = \cos 2\theta$. (25) $\dfrac{\tan 2\theta \cdot \tan\theta}{\tan 2\theta - \tan\theta} = \sin 2\theta$.

(26) $\tan(\alpha+\beta) = \dfrac{\sin^2\alpha - \sin^2\beta}{\sin\alpha \cdot \cos\alpha - \sin\beta \cdot \cos\beta}$.

(27) $4\sin A \cdot \sin(60°+A) \cdot \sin(60°-A) = \sin 3A$.

(28) $\csc 2\theta + \cot 4\theta + \csc 4\theta = \cot\theta$.

2. Solve the equations:

(1) $\sin 2\theta + \sqrt{3} \cdot \cos 2\theta = 1$. (2) $\sin^2 2\theta - \sin^2\theta = \sin^2\dfrac{\pi}{4}$.

(3) $\sin 5x \cdot \cos 3x = \sin 9x \cdot \cos 7x$. (4) $2\sin^2 3\theta + \sin^2 6\theta = 2$.

(5) $\cos 2A + \sin^2 A = \dfrac{3}{4}$. (6) $\cos 3\theta - \cos 5\theta = \sin\theta$.

(7) $\sin 5\theta - \cos 3\theta = \sin\theta$. (8) $\tan 2\alpha = 3\tan\alpha$.

(9) $2\cos 2\theta = 2\sin\theta + 1$. (10) $\sin 7\alpha - \sin\alpha = \sin 3\alpha$.

(11) $\csc^2\theta - \sec^2\theta = 2\csc^2\theta \div 3$.

(12) $\sin 6\theta = \sin 4\theta - \sin 2\theta$.

132. *To find the Trigonometrical Ratios for an angle of* 18°.*

Let $A = 18°$.

Then $2A = 36°$,

and $3A = 54°$.

Now the sine of an angle is equal to the cosine of the complement of the angle;

$$\therefore \sin 36° = \cos 54°;$$

$$\therefore \sin 2A = \cos 3A;$$

$$\therefore 2 \sin A \cdot \cos A = 4 \cos^3 A - 3 \cos A.$$

Divide by $\cos A$.

Then
$$2 \sin A = 4 \cos^2 A - 3,$$
$$2 \sin A = 4(1 - \sin^2 A) - 3,$$
$$2 \sin A = 4 - 4 \sin^2 A - 3,$$
$$4 \sin^2 A + 2 \sin A = 1,$$
$$\sin^2 A + \frac{1}{2} \sin A = \frac{1}{4},$$
$$\sin^2 A + \frac{1}{2} \sin A + \frac{1}{16} = \frac{5}{16},$$
$$\sin A + \frac{1}{4} = \frac{\sqrt{5}}{4},$$

and taking the upper sign, since $\sin 18°$ must be positive,

$$\sin 18° = \frac{\sqrt{5} - 1}{4}.$$

Hence we can find $\cos 18°$, $\tan 18°$ and the other ratios.

Examples.—XXXVI.

Given $\sin 18° = \frac{\sqrt{5}-1}{4}$, find the value of the following Ratios.

(1) $\sin 36°$.   (2) $\cos 36°$.   (3) $\sin 54°$.   (4) $\cos 54°$.

(5) $\sin 72°$.   (6) $\tan 72°$.   (7) $\sin 90°$.   (8) $\cos 90°$.

* A geometrical proof is given in the Appendix.

Shew that

$$\sin(36°+A)+\sin(72°-A)-\sin(36°-A)-\sin(72°+A)=\sin A,$$

and that

$$\sin(54°+A)+\sin(54°-A)-\sin(18°+A)-\sin(18°-A)=\cos A.$$

133. We now proceed to the formulæ relating to submultiples of angles, and first we shall prove that

$$\sin\frac{A}{2}=\pm\sqrt{\left(\frac{1-\cos A}{2}\right)}.$$

Since $\quad \cos A = 1 - 2\sin^2\frac{A}{2}$ (Art. 128);

$$2\sin^2\frac{A}{2}=1-\cos A\,;$$

$$\therefore \sin^2\frac{A}{2}=\frac{1-\cos A}{2}\,;$$

$$\therefore \sin\frac{A}{2}=\pm\sqrt{\frac{1-\cos A}{2}}.$$

If the value of A be given, we know whether $\sin\frac{A}{2}$ is positive or negative, and hence we know which sign is to be taken. Thus, if A be between $0°$ and $360°$, $\frac{A}{2}$ lies between $0°$ and $180°$, and $\therefore \sin\frac{A}{2}$ is positive: but if A be between $360°$ and $720°$, $\frac{A}{2}$ lies between $180°$ and $360°$, and $\therefore \sin\frac{A}{2}$ is negative.

134. We shall next shew that

$$\cos\frac{A}{2}=\pm\sqrt{\left(\frac{1+\cos A}{2}\right)}.$$

Since $\quad \cos A = 2\cos^2\frac{A}{2}-1$ (Art. 128);

$$\therefore\ -2\cos^2\frac{A}{2}=-1-\cos A\,;$$

$$\therefore 2\cos^2\frac{A}{2} = 1 + \cos A;$$

$$\therefore \cos^2\frac{A}{2} = \frac{1+\cos A}{2};$$

$$\therefore \cos\frac{A}{2} = \pm\sqrt{\frac{1+\cos A}{2}}.$$

If the value of A be given, we know whether $\cos\frac{A}{2}$ is positive or negative, and thus we know which sign is to be taken. For instance, if A lies between $0°$ and $180°$, $\cos\frac{A}{2}$ is positive: but if A lies between $180°$ and $360°$, $\cos\frac{A}{2}$ is negative.

135. *To prove that*

$$2\cos\frac{A}{2} = \pm\sqrt{1+\sin A} \pm \sqrt{1-\sin A},$$

and

$$2\sin\frac{A}{2} = \pm\sqrt{1+\sin A} \mp \sqrt{1-\sin A}$$

Since

$$\cos^2\frac{A}{2} + \sin^2\frac{A}{2} = 1,$$

and

$$2\cos\frac{A}{2} \cdot \sin\frac{A}{2} = \sin A;$$

$$\therefore \cos^2\frac{A}{2} + 2\cos\frac{A}{2} \cdot \sin\frac{A}{2} + \sin^2\frac{A}{2} = 1 + \sin A,$$

and

$$\cos^2\frac{A}{2} - 2\cos\frac{A}{2} \cdot \sin\frac{A}{2} + \sin^2\frac{A}{2} = 1 - \sin A.$$

Hence, taking the square root of each side of both equations,

$$\cos\frac{A}{2} + \sin\frac{A}{2} = \pm\sqrt{1+\sin A},$$

and
$$\cos\frac{A}{2} - \sin\frac{A}{2} = \pm\sqrt{1-\sin A}.$$

Therefore, by addition,

$$2\cos\frac{A}{2} = \pm\sqrt{1+\sin A} \pm \sqrt{1-\sin A},$$

and, by subtraction,

$$2\sin\frac{A}{2} = \pm\sqrt{1+\sin A} \mp \sqrt{1-\sin A}.$$

136. If the value of A be given, we know the *signs* of $\sin\frac{A}{2}$ and $\cos\frac{A}{2}$, as we explained in the preceding articles. We also know whether $\sin\frac{A}{2}$ is greater or less than $\cos\frac{A}{2}$. Hence, if A be known, we can assign with certainty the signs which the root-symbols are to have in the *intermediate* equations

$$\cos\frac{A}{2} + \sin\frac{A}{2} = \pm\sqrt{1+\sin A}, \quad (1)$$

$$\cos\frac{A}{2} - \sin\frac{A}{2} = \pm\sqrt{1-\sin A}, \quad (2)$$

and hence we can select the proper signs in the *final* equations.

For instance, suppose A to lie between $180°$ and $270°$.

Then $\frac{A}{2}$ lies between $90°$ and $135°$.

Therefore $\sin\frac{A}{2}$ is positive and $\cos\frac{A}{2}$ is negative.

Also, for an angle between $90°$ and $135°$ the sine is numerically greater than the cosine.

Hence we must take the positive sign in equation (1), and the negative sign in equation (2).

Examples.—XXXVII.

(1) Affix to the root-symbols the proper signs when A is $15°$.

(2) Affix to the root symbols the proper signs when A is $300°$.

(3) If $\sin 378° = \dfrac{\sqrt{5}-1}{4}$, determine $\cos 189°$ and $\sin 189°$.

(4) If $\sin 19°.29' = \dfrac{1}{3}$, what is the value of $\sin 9°.44'.30''$?

(5) If $\cos 315° = \dfrac{1}{\sqrt{2}}$, find the value of $\cos 157°.30'$.

137. We mentioned in Art. 114 what are called the Inverse Trigonometrical Functions, $\sin^{-1} x$, $\cos^{-1} x$, &c. We shall now give an example to illustrate the method of combining these functions.

To prove that $\tan^{-1}\dfrac{1}{2} + \tan^{-1}\dfrac{1}{3} = 45°$.

Let $\quad a = \tan^{-1}\dfrac{1}{2}$ and $\beta = \tan^{-1}\dfrac{1}{3}$;

then $\quad \tan a = \dfrac{1}{2}$ and $\tan \beta = \dfrac{1}{3}$.

Now $\quad \tan(a+\beta) = \dfrac{\tan a + \tan \beta}{1 - \tan a \cdot \tan \beta}$

$$= \dfrac{\dfrac{1}{2}+\dfrac{1}{3}}{1-\dfrac{1}{2}\cdot\dfrac{1}{3}}$$

$$= \dfrac{5}{5}$$

$$= 1;$$

$\therefore a + \beta = 45°$,

that is, $\quad \tan^{-1}\dfrac{1}{2} + \tan^{-1}\dfrac{1}{3} = 45°$.

Examples.—XXXVIII.

(1) If $A = \sin^{-1}\dfrac{3}{5}$ and $B = \sin^{-1}\dfrac{4}{5}$, shew that $A + B = 90°$.

(2) If $A = \tan^{-1}\dfrac{1}{7}$ and $B = \tan^{-1}\dfrac{1}{3}$, shew that $A + 2B = 45°$.

(3) Shew that $\sin^{-1}\dfrac{1}{\sqrt{5}} + \cot^{-1} 3 = 45°$.

(4) Shew that $\tan^{-1}\dfrac{1}{3} + \tan^{-1}\dfrac{1}{5} + \tan^{-1}\dfrac{1}{7} + \tan^{-1}\dfrac{1}{8} = 45°$.

(5) Shew that $\cot^{-1}\dfrac{3}{4} + \cot^{-1}\dfrac{1}{7} = 135°$.

(6) Shew that $\tan^{-1}\dfrac{3}{5} + \cot^{-1}\dfrac{7}{3} = \cot^{-1}\dfrac{13}{18}$.

(7) Shew that $\tan^{-1} x - \tan^{-1} y = \tan^{-1}\dfrac{x-y}{1+xy}$.

(8) Shew that $\sin^{-1} x + \cos^{-1} x = 90°$.

(9) Shew that $\sin^{-1}\dfrac{4}{5} + \sin^{-1}\dfrac{5}{13} + \sin^{-1}\dfrac{16}{65} = \dfrac{\pi}{2}$.

(10) Shew that $4\tan^{-1}\dfrac{1}{5} - \tan^{-1}\dfrac{1}{239} = \dfrac{\pi}{4}$.

CHAPTER XIV.

On Logarithms.

138. Def. The LOGARITHM of a number to a given base is the index of the power to which the base must be raised to give the number.

Thus if $m = a^x$, x is called the logarithm of m to the base a.

For instance, if the base of a system of Logarithms be 2,

3 is the logarithm of the number 8,

because $8 = 2^3$:

and if the base be 5, then

3 is the logarithm of the number 125,

because $125 = 5^3$.

139. The logarithm of a number m to the base a is written thus, $\log_a m$; and so, if $m = a^x$,

$$x = \log_a m.$$

Hence it follows that $m = a^{\log_a m}$.

140. Since $1 = a^0$, the logarithm of unity to any base is zero.

Since $a = a^1$, the logarithm of the base of any system is unity.

141. We now proceed to describe that which is called the Common System of logarithms.

The base of the system is 10.

By a *system* of logarithms to the base 10, we mean a succession of values of x which satisfy the equation

$$m = 10^x$$

for all positive values of m, integral or fractional.

Such a system is formed by the series of logarithms of the natural numbers from 1 to 100000, which constitute the logarithms registered in our ordinary tables, and which are therefore called *tabular logarithms*.

142. Now
$$1 = 10^0,$$
$$10 = 10^1,$$
$$100 = 10^2,$$
$$1000 = 10^3,$$

and so on.

Hence the logarithm of 1 is 0,
of 10 is 1,
of 100 is 2,
of 1000 is 3,

and so on.

Hence for all numbers between 1 and 10 the logarithm is a decimal less than 1,

between 10 and 100 the logarithm is a decimal between 1 and 2,

between 100 and 1000 .... a decimal between 2 and 3, and so on.

143. The logarithms of the natural numbers from 1 to 12 stand thus in the tables:

No.	Log	No.	Log
1	0·0000000	7	0·8450980
2	0·3010300	8	0·9030900
3	0·4771213	9	0·9542425
4	0·6020600	10	1·0000000
5	0·6989700	11	1·0413927
6	0·7781513	12	1·0791812

The logarithms are calculated to seven places of decimals.

S. T.

144. The integral parts of the logarithms of numbers higher than 10 are called the *characteristics* of those logarithms, and the decimal parts of the logarithms are called the *mantissæ*.

Thus   1 is the characteristic,

·0791812 the mantissa,

of the logarithm of 12.

145. The logarithms for 100 and the numbers that succeed it (and in some tables those that precede 100) have no characteristic prefixed, because it can be supplied by the reader, being 2 for all numbers between 100 and 1000, 3 for all between 1000 and 10000, and so on. Thus in the Tables we shall find

No.	Log
100	0000000
101	0043214
102	0086002
103	0128372
104	0170333
105	0211893

which we read thus:

the logarithm of 100 is 2,

of 101 is 2·0043214,

of 102 is 2·0086002; and so on.

146. Logarithms are of great use in making arithmetical computations more easy, for by means of a Table of Logarithms the operation

of Multiplication is changed into that of Addition,

... Division .... Subtraction,

... Involution .... Multiplication,

... Evolution .... Division,

as we shall shew in the next four Articles.

147. *The logarithm of a product is equal to the sum of the logarithms of its factors.*

Let $m = a^x$,

and $n = a^y$.

Then $mn = a^{x+y}$;

$\therefore \log_a mn = x + y$
$= \log_a m + \log_a n.$

Hence it follows that

$$\log_a mnp = \log_a m + \log_a n + \log_a p,$$

and similarly it may be shewn that the Theorem holds good for any number of factors.

Thus the operation of Multiplication is changed into that of Addition.

Suppose, for instance, we want to find the product of 246 and 357, we add the logarithms of the factors, and the sum is the logarithm of the product: thus

$$\log 246 = 2{\cdot}3909351$$
$$\log 357 = 2{\cdot}5526682$$
their sum $= 4{\cdot}9436033$

which is the logarithm of 87822, the product required.

NOTE. We do not write $\log_{10} 246$, for so long as we are treating of logarithms to the particular base 10, we may omit the suffix.

148. *The logarithm of a quotient is equal to the logarithm of the dividend diminished by the logarithm of the divisor.*

Let $m = a^x$,

and $n = a^y$.

Then $\dfrac{m}{n} = a^{x-y}$;

$\therefore \log_a \dfrac{m}{n} = x - y$
$= \log_a m - \log_a n.$

Thus the operation of Division is changed into that of Subtraction.

If, for example, we are required to divide 371·49 by 52·376, we proceed thus,

$$\log 371\cdot 49 = 2\cdot 5699471$$
$$\log 52\cdot 376 = 1\cdot 7191323$$
$$\text{their difference} = \overline{\cdot 8508148}$$

which is the logarithm of 7·092752, the quotient required.

149. *The logarithm of any power of a number is equal to the product of the logarithm of the number and the index denoting the power.*

Let $\qquad m = a^x.$

Then $\qquad m^r = a^{rx};$

$$\therefore \log_a m^r = rx$$
$$= r \cdot \log_a m.$$

Thus the operation of Involution is changed into Multiplication.

Suppose, for instance, we have to find the fourth power of 13, we may proceed thus,

$$\log 13 = 1\cdot 1139434$$
$$\underline{4}$$
$$4\cdot 4557736$$

which is the logarithm of 28561, the number required.

150. *The logarithm of any root of a number is equal to the quotient arising from the division of the logarithm of the number by the number denoting the root.*

Let $\qquad m = a^x.$

Then $\qquad m^{\frac{1}{r}} = a^{\frac{x}{r}};$

$$\therefore \log_a m^{\frac{1}{r}} = \frac{x}{r}$$
$$= \frac{1}{r} \cdot \log_a m.$$

Thus the operation of Evolution is changed into Division.

If, for example, we have to find the fifth root of 16807, we proceed thus,

$$5 \,\underline{|\, 4{\cdot}2254902}, \text{ the log of } 16807$$
$$\cdot 8450980$$

which is the logarithm of 7, the root required.

151. The common system of Logarithms has this advantage over all others for numerical calculations, that its base is the same as the radix of the common scale of notation.

Hence it is that the same mantissa serves for all numbers which have the same significant digits and differ only in the position of the place of units relatively to those digits.

For, since log 60 = log 10   + log 6 = 1 + log 6,

      log 600 = log 100 + log 6 = 2 + log 6,

      log 6000 = log 1000 + log 6 = 3 + log 6,

it is clear that if we know the logarithm of any number, as 6, we also know the logarithms of the numbers resulting from multiplying that number by the powers of 10.

So again, if we know that

      log 1·7692 is ·247783,

we also know that

      log 17·692 is 1·247783,

      log 176·92 is 2·247783,

      log 1769·2 is 3·247783,

      log 17692 is 4·247783,

      log 176920 is 5·247783.

152. We must now treat of the logarithms of numbers less than unity.

Since $1 = 10^0$,

$$\cdot 1 = \frac{1}{10} = 10^{-1},$$

$$\cdot 01 = \frac{1}{100} = 10^{-2},$$

the logarithm of a number

.... between 1 and ·1 lies between 0 and −1,
.... between ·1 and ·01 .... −1 and −2,
.... between ·01 and ·001 .... −2 and −3,

and so on.

Hence the logarithms of all numbers less than unity are Negative.

We do not require a separate table for these logarithms, for we can deduce them from the logarithms of numbers greater than unity by the following process:

$$\log \cdot 6 = \log \frac{6}{10} = \log 6 - \log 10 = \log 6 - 1,$$

$$\log \cdot 06 = \log \frac{6}{100} = \log 6 - \log 100 = \log 6 - 2,$$

$$\log \cdot 006 = \log \frac{6}{1000} = \log 6 - \log 1000 = \log 6 - 3.$$

Now the logarithm of 6 is ·7781513.

Hence

$\log \cdot 6 \ \ = -1 + \cdot 7781513$, which is written $\overline{1} \cdot 7781513$,

$\log \cdot 06 \ \ = -2 + \cdot 7781513$, which is written $\overline{2} \cdot 7781513$,

$\log \cdot 006 = -3 + \cdot 7781513$, which is written $\overline{3} \cdot 7781513$,

the characteristics only being negative and the mantissæ positive.

153. Thus the same mantissæ serve for the Logarithms of all numbers, *whether greater or less than unity,* which have the same significant digits and differ only in the position of the place of units relatively to those digits.

It is best to regard the Table as a register of the logarithms of numbers which have *one* significant digit before the decimal point.

For instance, when we read in the tables $\begin{array}{c|c}\text{No.} & \text{Log} \\ 144 & 1583625\end{array}$, to interpret the entry thus,

$$\log 1\cdot 44 \text{ is } \cdot 1583625.$$

We then obtain the following rules for the characteristic to be attached in each case.

I. If the decimal point be shifted one, two, three ... n places to the right, prefix as a characteristic 1, 2, 3 ... n.

II. If the decimal point be shifted one, two, three ... n places to the left, prefix as a characteristic $\bar{1}, \bar{2}, \bar{3} \ldots \bar{n}$.

Thus $\log 1\cdot 44$ is $\cdot 1583625$,

$\therefore \log 14\cdot 4$ is $1\cdot 1583625$,

$\log 144$ is $2\cdot 1583625$,

$\log 1440$ is $3\cdot 1583625$,

and $\log \cdot 144$ is $\bar{1}\cdot 1583625$,

$\log \cdot 0144$ is $\bar{2}\cdot 1583625$,

$\log \cdot 00144$ is $\bar{3}\cdot 1583625$.

154. In calculations with negative characteristics we follow the rules of algebra. Thus,

(1) If we have to add the logarithms $\bar{3}\cdot 64628$ and $2\cdot 42367$, we first add the mantissæ, and the result is $1\cdot 06995$, and then add the characteristics, and this result is $\bar{1}$.

The final result is $\bar{1} + 1\cdot 06995$, that is, $\cdot 06995$.

(2) To subtract $\bar{5}\cdot 6249372$ from $\bar{3}\cdot 2456973$, we may arrange the numbers thus,

$$\begin{array}{r} -3 + \cdot 2456973 \\ -5 + \cdot 6249372 \\ \hline 1 + \cdot 6207601 \end{array}$$

the 1 carried on from the last subtraction in decimal places changing -5 into -4, and then -4 subtracted from -3 giving 1 as a result.

Hence the resulting logarithm is $1\cdot 6207601$.

(3) To multiply $\bar{3}\cdot 7482569$ by 5.

$$\bar{3}\cdot 7482569$$
$$5$$
$$\overline{\overline{12}\cdot 7412845}$$

the 3 carried on from the last multiplication of the decimal places being added to -15, and thus giving -12 as a result.

(4) To divide $\overline{14}\cdot 2456736$ by 4.

Increase the negative characteristic so that it may be exactly divisible by 4, making a proper compensation, thus,

$$\overline{14}\cdot 2456736 = \overline{16} + 2\cdot 2456736.$$

Then $\dfrac{\overline{14}\cdot 2456736}{4} = \dfrac{\overline{16} + 2\cdot 2456736}{4} = \bar{4} + \cdot 5614184;$

and so the result is $\bar{4}\cdot 5614184$.

Examples.—XXXIX.

(1) Add $\bar{3}\cdot 1651553$, $\bar{4}\cdot 7505855$, $6\cdot 6879746$, $\bar{2}\cdot 6150026$.

(2) Add $\bar{4}\cdot 6843785$, $\bar{5}\cdot 6650657$, $3\cdot 8905196$, $\bar{3}\cdot 4675284$.

(3) Add $2\cdot 5324716$, $3\cdot 6650657$, $\bar{5}\cdot 8905196$, $\cdot 3156215$.

(4) From $2\cdot 483269$ take $\bar{3}\cdot 742891$.

(5) From $\bar{2}\cdot 352678$ take $\bar{5}\cdot 428619$.

(6) From $\bar{5}\cdot 349162$ take $\bar{3}\cdot 624329$.

(7) Multiply $\bar{2}\cdot 4596721$ by 3.

(8) Multiply $\bar{7}\cdot 429683$ by 6.

(9) Multiply $\bar{9}\cdot 2843617$ by 7.

(10) Divide $\bar{6}\cdot 3725409$ by 3.

(11) Divide $\overline{14}\cdot 432962$ by 6.

(12) Divide $\bar{4}\cdot 53627188$ by 9.

155. We shall now explain how a system of logarithms calculated to a base a may be transformed into another system of which the base is b.

Let m be a number of which the logarithm in the first system is x and in the second y.

Then
$$m = a^x,$$
and
$$m = b^y.$$
Hence
$$b^y = a^x,$$
$$\therefore b = a^{\frac{x}{y}};$$
$$\therefore \frac{x}{y} = \log_a b;$$
$$\therefore \frac{y}{x} = \frac{1}{\log_a b};$$
$$\therefore y = \frac{1}{\log_a b} x.$$

Hence if we multiply the logarithm of any number in the system of which the base is a by $\dfrac{1}{\log_a b}$ we shall obtain the logarithm of the same number in the system of which the base is b.

This constant multiplier $\dfrac{1}{\log_a b}$ is called THE MODULUS *of the system of which the base is b* with reference to the system of which the base is a.

156. The common system of logarithms is used in all numerical calculations, but there is another system, which we must notice, employed by the discoverer of logarithms, Baron Napier, and hence called The Napierian System.

The base of this system, denoted by the symbol e, is the number which is the sum of the series

$$2 + \frac{1}{2} + \frac{1}{2.3} + \frac{1}{2.3.4} + \dots ad\ inf.,$$

of which sum the first eight digits are 2·7182818.

157. Our common logarithms are formed from the Logarithms of the Napierian System by multiplying each of the

latter by a common multiplier called The Modulus of the Common System.

This modulus is, in accordance with the conclusion of Art. 155, $\dfrac{1}{\log_e 10}$.

That is, if l and N be the logarithms of the same number in the common and Napierian systems respectively,

$$l = \dfrac{1}{\log_e 10} \cdot N.$$

Now $\log_e 10$ is $2\cdot30258509$;

$$\therefore \dfrac{1}{\log_e 10} \text{ is } \dfrac{1}{2\cdot30258509} \text{ or } \cdot43429448,$$

and so the modulus of the common system is $\cdot43429448$.

158. To prove that $\log_a b \times \log_b a = 1$.

Let $\qquad x = \log_a b$.

Then $\qquad b = a^x$;

$$\therefore b^{\frac{1}{x}} = a;$$

$$\therefore \dfrac{1}{x} = \log_b a.$$

Thus $\quad \log_a b \times \log_b a = x \times \dfrac{1}{x}$

$$= 1.$$

159. The following are simple examples of the method of applying the principles explained in this Chapter.

Ex. (1) Given $\log 2 = \cdot3010300$, $\log 3 = \cdot4771213$

and $\log 7 = \cdot8450980$, find $\log 42$.

Since $\qquad 42 = 2 \times 3 \times 7$

$\log 42 = \log 2 + \log 3 + \log 7$

$\qquad = \cdot3010300 + \cdot4771213 + \cdot8450980$

$\qquad = 1\cdot6232493$.

ON LOGARITHMS.

Ex. (2) Given $\log 2 = \cdot 3010300$ and $\log 3 = \cdot 4771213$, find the logarithms of 64, 81 and 96.

$$\log 64 = \log 2^6 = 6 \log 2$$
$$\log 2 = \cdot 3010300$$
$$6$$
$$\therefore \log 64 = \overline{1 \cdot 8061800}$$

$$\log 81 = \log 3^4 = 4 \log 3$$
$$\log 3 = \cdot 4771213$$
$$4$$
$$\therefore \log 81 = \overline{1 \cdot 9084852}$$

$$\log 96 = \log (32 \times 3) = \log 32 + \log 3,$$

and $$\log 32 = \log 2^5 = 5 \log 2;$$

$$\therefore \log 96 = 5 \log 2 + \log 3 = 1 \cdot 5051500 + \cdot 4771213 = 1 \cdot 9822713.$$

Ex. (3) Given $\log 5 = \cdot 6989700$, find the logarithm of $\sqrt[7]{(6 \cdot 25)}$.

$$\log (6 \cdot 25)^{\frac{1}{7}} = \frac{1}{7} \log 6 \cdot 25 = \frac{1}{7} \log \frac{625}{100} = \frac{1}{7} (\log 625 - \log 100)$$

$$= \frac{1}{7} (\log 5^4 - 2) = \frac{1}{7} (4 \log 5 - 2)$$

$$= \frac{1}{7} (2 \cdot 7958800 - 2) = \cdot 1136971.$$

Examples.—XL.

1. Given $\log 2 = \cdot 3010300$, find $\log 128$, $\log 125$ and $\log 2500$.

2. Given $\log 2 = \cdot 3010300$ and $\log 7 = \cdot 8450980$, find the logarithms of 50, ·005 and 196.

3. Given $\log 2 = \cdot 3010300$, and $\log 3 = \cdot 4771213$, find the logarithms of 6, 27, 54 and 576.

4. Given $\log 2 = \cdot 3010300$, $\log 3 = \cdot 4771213$, $\log 7 = \cdot 8450980$, find $\log 60$, $\log \cdot 03$, $\log 1 \cdot 05$, and $\log \cdot 0000432$.

5. Given $\log 2 = \cdot 3010300$, $\log 18 = 1\cdot 2552725$ and $\log 21 = 1\cdot 3222193$, find $\log \cdot 00075$ and $\log 31\cdot 5$.

6. Given $\log 5 = \cdot 6989700$, find the logarithms of 2, $\cdot 064$, and $\left(\dfrac{2^{60}}{5^{30}}\right)^{\frac{1}{14}}$.

7. Given $\log 2 = \cdot 3010300$, find the logarithms of 5, $\cdot 125$ and $\left(\dfrac{5^{90}}{2^{40}}\right)^{\frac{1}{15}}$.

8. What are the logarithms of $\cdot 01$, 1 and 100 to the base 10? What to the base $\cdot 01$?

9. What is the characteristic of $\log 1593$, (1) to base 10, (2) to base 12?

10. Given $\dfrac{4^x}{2^{x+y}} = 8$, and $x = 3y$, find x and y.

11. Given $\log 4 = \cdot 6020600$, $\log 1\cdot 04 = \cdot 0170333$:

(a) Find the logarithms of 2, 25, 83·2, $(\cdot 625)^{\frac{1}{100}}$.

(b) How many digits are there in the integral part of $(1\cdot 04)^{6000}$?

12. Given $\log 25 = 1\cdot 3979400$, $\log 1\cdot 03 = \cdot 0128372$:

(a) Find the logarithms of 5, 4, 51·5, $(\cdot 064)^{\frac{1}{100}}$.

(b) How many digits are there in the integral part of $(1\cdot 03)^{600}$?

13. Having given $\log 3 = \cdot 4771213$, $\log 7 = \cdot 8450980$,
$$\log 11 = 1\cdot 0413927:$$
find the logarithms of 7623, $\dfrac{77}{300}$ and $\dfrac{3}{539}$.

14. Solve the equations:

(1) $4096^x = \dfrac{8}{64^x}$.

(2) $\left(\dfrac{1}{\cdot 4}\right)^x = 6\cdot 25$.

(3) $a^x \cdot b^x = m$.

(4) $a^{mx} b^{2x} = c$.

(5) $a^{3x} \cdot b^{4-x} = c^{2x-1}$.

(6) $a^x b^{mx} = c^{1-3x}$.

CHAPTER XV.

On Trigonometrical and Logarithmic Tables.

160. WE shall give in this Chapter a short description of the Tables which have been constructed for the purpose of facilitating Trigonometrical calculations.

The methods by which these Tables are formed do not fall within the range of this treatise: we have merely to explain how they are applied to the solution of such simple examples as we shall hereafter give.

We shall arrange our remarks in the following order:

I. On Tables of Logarithms of Numbers.

II. On Tables of Trigonometrical Ratios.

III. On Tables of Logarithms of Trigonometrical Ratios.

I. *On Tables of Logarithms of Numbers.*

161. These Tables are arranged so as to give the mantissæ of the logarithms of the natural numbers from 1 to 100000, that is of numbers containing from one to five digits.

We shall now show how by aid of these tables, first, to find the logarithm of any given number, and, secondly, how to determine the number which corresponds to a given logarithm.

162. *When a number is given to find its logarithm.*

When the given number has not more than five digits we can take its logarithm at once from the tables.

When the given number has more than five digits we can determine its logarithm by a process, which will be best explained by an example.

Suppose we require to find the logarithm of 6276153.

We find from the tables

$$\log 62761 \text{ is } 4\cdot7976899,$$

and

$$\log 62762 \text{ is } 4\cdot7976988.$$

Hence

$$\log 6276200 \text{ is } 6\cdot7976988.$$

and

$$\log 6276100 \text{ is } 6\cdot7976899.$$

Thus for a difference of 100 in the numbers the difference of the logarithms is $\cdot0000089$.

We then reason thus: If we have to add $\cdot0000089$ to the logarithm of 6276100 to obtain the logarithm of 6276200, what must we add to the logarithm of 6276100 to obtain the logarithm of 6276153?

Assuming that the increase of the logarithm is proportional to the increase of the number (which is nearly but not quite true), we shall have

$$100 : 53 = \cdot0000089 : \text{that which we have to add};$$

$$\therefore \text{ number to be added} = \frac{53 \times \cdot0000089}{100} = \cdot000004717,$$

and therefore, omitting the last two figures,

$$\log 6276153 = 6\cdot7976899 + \cdot0000047$$

$$= 6\cdot7976946.$$

If the first of the figures omitted be 5 or a digit higher than 5, it is usual to increase the figure immediately preceding it by 1: thus if the number to be added had been $\cdot000004757$ we should have added $\cdot0000048$.

163. We took in the last article an *integral* number, but the same process will apply to numbers containing decimals.

For suppose we have to find the logarithm of 627·6153: we can find log 6276153 as before, and the only difference to be made in the final result is to change the characteristic from 6 to 2, that is,

$$\log 627\cdot 6153 = 2\cdot 7976946.$$

So again, in accordance with Art. 153,

$$\log \cdot 00006276153 = \bar{5}\cdot 7976946.$$

Examples.—XLI.

(1) Given
$$\log 52502 = 4\cdot 7201758,$$
$$\log 52503 = 4\cdot 7201841,$$
find
$$\log 52502\cdot 5.$$

(2) Given
$$\log 3\cdot 0042 = \cdot 4777288,$$
$$\log 3\cdot 0043 = \cdot 4777433,$$
find
$$\log 300\cdot 425.$$

(3) Given
$$\log 3202\cdot 5 = 3\cdot 5054891,$$
$$\log 3202\cdot 6 = 3\cdot 5055027,$$
find
$$\log 32\cdot 025613.$$

(4) Given
$$\log 23660 = 4\cdot 3740147,$$
$$\log 23661 = 4\cdot 3740331,$$
find
$$\log 236\cdot 601.$$

(5) Given
$$\log 67502 = 4\cdot 8293166,$$
$$\log 67503 = 4\cdot 8293231,$$
find
$$\log 67\cdot 5021.$$

(6) Given
$$\log 73335 = 4\cdot 8653113,$$
$$\log 73336 = 4\cdot 8653172,$$
find
$$\log \cdot 007333533.$$

(7) Given log 65931 = 4·8190897,
log 65932 = 4·8190962,
find log ·000006593171.

(8) Given log 34·077 = 1·5324614,
log 34·078 = 1·5324741,
find log 3407·78.

(9) Given log 39097 = 4·5921434,
log 39098 = 4·5921545,
find log 390974.

(10) Given log 25819 = 4·4119394,
log 25820 = 4·4119562,
find log 2·581926.

164. *When a logarithm is given, to find the number to which it corresponds.*

If the decimal part of the logarithm is found exactly in the tables, we can take out the corresponding number.

Thus if we have to find the number corresponding to the logarithm 2·8598645, we look in the tables for the mantissa ·8598645, and we find it set down opposite the number 72421, hence

2·8598645 is the logarithm of 724·21.

Next, suppose that the decimal part of the logarithm is not found exactly in the tables, and that we have to find the number corresponding to the logarithm 3·9212074.

We find from the tables

log 8340·8 = 3·9212077,
and log 8340·7 = 3·9212025.

Hence a difference of ·1 in the numbers gives a difference of ·0000052 in the logarithms.

Then we reason thus: If we must add ·1 to 8340·7 for an excess of ·0000052 above the logarithm of 8340·7, what must we add for an excess of (3·9212074 − 3·9212025) or ·0000049 ?

Assuming that the increase of the number is proportional to the increase of the logarithm, we have

·0000052 : ·0000049 = ·1 : what is to be added to 8340·7;

therefore we must add

$$\frac{·0000049 \times ·1}{·0000052}, \text{ or, } \frac{49 \times ·1}{52} \text{ or } ·094;$$

therefore number required is 8340·794.

If the given logarithm be negative, as −(2·1401355), we can change it into another of which the characteristic only is negative, thus $\bar{3}$·8598645, and we can find the number corresponding to this logarithm, as before. The number required is ·008340794.

Examples.—XLII.

(1) Given   log 12954 = 4·1124039,

   log 12955 = 4·1124374,

find the number whose logarithm is 4·112431.

(2) Given   log 462·45 = 2·6650648,

   log 462·46 = 2·6650742,

find the number whose logarithm is 3·6650657.

(3) Given   log 34572 = 4·5387245,

   log 34573 = 4·5387371,

find the number whose logarithm is 2·5387359.

(4) Given   log 39375 = 4·5952206,

   log 39376 = 4·5952316,

find the number whose logarithm is 5·5952282.

(5) Given log 3·7159 = ·5700640,

log 3·7160 = ·5700757,

find the number whose logarithm is 3·5700702.

(6) Given log 96461 = 4·9843518,

log 96462 = 4·9843563,

find the number whose logarithm is $\bar{3}$·9843542.

(7) Given log 25725 = 4·4103554,

log 25726 = 4·4103723,

find the number whose logarithm is $\bar{7}$·4103720.

(8) Given log 60195 = 4·7795532,

log 60196 = 4·7795604,

find the number whose logarithm is 2·7795561.

(9) Given log 10905 = 4·0376257,

log 10906 = 4·0376655,

find the number whose logarithm is 3·0376371.

(10) Given log 26201 = 4·4183179,

log 26202 = 4·4183344,

find the number whose logarithm is 2·4183314.

II. *On Tables of the Trigonometrical Ratios.*

165. We have explained in earlier parts of this treatise how to find the values of certain Trigonometrical Ratios **exactly** or **approximately**.

Thus we showed that $\sin 30° = \dfrac{1}{2}$, that is, ·5 exactly.

Again, $\tan 60° = \sqrt{3}$, that is, 1·73205 approximately.

Now the values of all the Trigonometrical Ratios for a **regular succession of angles in the first quadrant have been** calculated and registered in tables. In some tables the angles succeed each other at intervals of 1″, in others at intervals of 10″, but in ordinary tables at intervals of 1′, and to the last-mentioned we shall refer.

These tables are commonly called Tables of *Natural* Sines, Cosines, &c. so as to distinguish them from the Tables of the *Logarithms* of the Sines, Cosines, &c. of which we shall hereafter treat.

We intend to explain, first, how we can determine the value of a Ratio that lies between the Ratios of two consecutive angles given in the tables, and secondly, how to determine the angle to which a given Ratio corresponds.

166. *To find the sine of a given angle.*

Suppose we want to determine the sine of $25°.14′.20″$, having given

$\sin 25°.14′ = \cdot 4263056$ and $\sin 25°.15′ = \cdot 4265687$.

From $\sin 25°.15′ = \cdot 4265687$
Take $\sin 25°.14′ = \cdot 4263056$
$\qquad\qquad\overline{\cdot 0002631}$ is the difference for 1′.

Now if we have to add $\cdot 0002631$ to the sine of $25°.14′$ to obtain the sine of $25°.15′$, what must we add to the sine of $25°.14′$ to obtain the sine of $25°.14′.20″$?

Assuming that an increase in the angle is proportional to an increase in the sine, we have

$1′ : 20″ = \cdot 0002631$: that which we have to add;

therefore we must add

$$\frac{20 \times \cdot 0002631}{60}, \text{ or, } \cdot 0000877;$$

$\therefore$ sine $25°.14′.20″ = \cdot 4263056 + \cdot 0000877$

$$= \cdot 4263933.$$

167. *To find the cosine of a given angle.*

If we have to determine the cosine of 74°. 45'. 40", having given

$$\cos 74°. 46' = ·4263056 \text{ and } \cos 74°. 45' = ·4265687,$$

we proceed thus:

$$\cos 74°. 45' = ·4265687$$
$$\cos 74°. 46' = ·4263056$$
$$\overline{·0002631} \text{ is the } \textit{decrease} \text{ corresponding to } 1',$$

observing that the cosine *decreases* as the angle increases from 0° to 90°.

Hence

1' : 40" = ·0002631 : what we have to take from ·4265687;

therefore we must take away

$$\frac{40 \times ·0002631}{60} = ·0001754;$$

$$\therefore \cos 74°. 45'. 40" = ·4265687 - ·0001754$$
$$= ·4263933.$$

Similar methods are to be taken to find the values of the other ratios, observing that the tangents and secants increase and the cotangents and cosecants decrease as the angle increases from 0° to 90°.

EXAMPLES.—XLIII.

(1) Given $\sin 42°. 15' = ·6723668,$
$\sin 42°. 16' = ·6725821,$

find $\sin 42°. 15'. 16".$

(2) Given $\sin 72°. 14' = ·9523071,$
$\sin 72°. 15' = ·9523958,$

find $\sin 72°. 14'. 6".$

(3) Given $\sin 54°.35' = \cdot 8149593$,
                $\sin 54°.36' = \cdot 8151278$,
find $\sin 54°.35'.45''$.

(4) Given $\sin 87°.26' = \cdot 9989968$,
                $\sin 87°.27' = \cdot 9990098$,
find $\sin 87°.26'.15''$.

(5) Given $\sin 43°.14' = \cdot 6849711$,
                $\sin 43°.15' = \cdot 6851830$,
find $\sin 43°.14'.20''$.

(6) Given $\cos 41°.13' = \cdot 7522233$,
                $\cos 41°.14' = \cdot 7520316$,
find $\cos 41°.13'.26''$.

(7) Given $\tan 1°.22' = \cdot 0238573$,
                $\tan 1°.23' = \cdot 0241484$,
find $\tan 1°.22'.30''$.

(8) Given $\cot 35°.6' = 1\cdot 4228561$,
                $\cot 35°.7' = 1\cdot 4219766$,
find $\cot 35°.6'.23''$.

(9) Given $\sin 67°.22' = \cdot 9229865$,
                $\sin 67°.23' = \cdot 9230984$,
find $\sin 67°.22'.48''\cdot 5$.

(10) Given $\cos 34°.12' = \cdot 8270806$,
                 $\cos 34°.13' = \cdot 8269170$,
find $\cos 34°.12'.19''\cdot 6$.

168. *To find the angle which corresponds to a given sine.*

Suppose the given sine to be ·5082784.

We find from the Tables

$$\text{sine } 30°.\,33' = ·5082901$$
$$\text{sine } 30°.\,32' = ·5080396$$
$$\overline{·0002505 \text{ difference for } 1'.}$$

$$\text{given sine} = ·5082784$$
$$\text{sine } 30°.\,32' = ·5080396$$
$$\overline{·0002388}$$

Hence if x be the number of seconds to be added to $30°.\,32'$,

$$·0002505 : ·0002388 = 60 : x;$$

$$\therefore x = \frac{2388 \times 60}{2505} = \frac{9552}{167} = 57·2 \text{ nearly};$$

$\therefore$ the required angle is $30°.\,32'.\,57''·2$.

169. *To find the angle which corresponds to a given cosine.*

Suppose the given cosine to be ·5082784.

We find from the Tables

$$\cos 59°.\,27' = ·5082901$$
$$\cos 59°.\,28'' = ·5080396$$
$$\overline{·0002505 \text{ difference for } 1'.}$$

$$\cos 59°.\,27' = ·5082901$$
$$\text{given cosine} = ·5082784$$
$$\overline{·0000117}$$

Hence if x be the number of seconds to be added to $59°.\,27'$,

$$·0002505 : ·0000117 = 60 : x;$$

$$\therefore x = \frac{117 \times 60}{2505} = 2·8 \text{ nearly};$$

$\therefore$ required angle is $59°.\,27'.\,2'''·8$.

Examples.—XLIV.

(1) Given sin 48°. 47′ = ·7522233,
           sin 48°. 46′ = ·7520316,
find the angle of which the sine is ·752140.

(2) Given cos 2°. 34′ = ·9989968,
           cos 2°. 33′ = ·9990098,
find the angle of which the cosine is ·999000.

(3) Given sin 43°. 14′ = ·6849711,
           sin 43°. 15′ = ·6851830,
find the angle of which the sine is ·685.

(4) Given cos 32°. 31′ = ·8432351,
           cos 32°. 32′ = ·8430787,
find the angle of which the cosine is ·8432.

(5) Given sin 24°. 11′ = ·4096577,
           sin 24°. 12′ = ·4099230,
find the angle of which the sine is ·4097559.

(6) Given sec 82°. 22′ = 7·528249,
           sec 82°. 23′ = 7·552169,
find the angle of which the secant is 7·53.

(7) Given cos 53°. 7′ = ·6001876,
           cos 53°. 8′ = ·5999549,
find the angle of which the cosine is ·6.

(8) Given cosec 25°. 3′ = 2·36179,
           cosec 25°. 4′ = 2·36029,
find the angle of which the cosecant is 2·361.

(9) Given $\quad \sin 73^\circ.44' = \cdot 9599684,$

$\quad\quad\quad\quad\quad \sin 73^\circ.45' = \cdot 9600499,$

find the angle of which the sine is $\cdot 96$.

(10) Given $\quad \tan 77^\circ.19' = 4\cdot 44338,$

$\quad\quad\quad\quad\quad \tan 77^\circ.20' = 4\cdot 44942,$

find the angle of which the tangent is 4.4.

III. *On Tables of Logarithms of Trigonometrical Ratios.*

170. The Trigonometrical Ratios being numbers have logarithms that correspond to them, and these logarithms are in practice much more useful than the numbers themselves.

Now since the sines and cosines of all angles and the tangents of angles less than 45° are *less than unity*, the logarithms of these sines, cosines and tangents are negative. In order to avoid the inconvenience of printing negative characteristics, the logarithms of all the Ratios given in the tables are *increased by* 10. The numbers thus registered are called *The Tabular Logarithms* of the sine, cosine, &c., and they are denoted by the symbol L, that is, $L \sin A$ denotes the tabular logarithm of the sine of A.

When the value of any one of these Tabular Logarithms is given we must take away 10 from it to obtain the true value of the logarithm in question: thus

$\quad L \sin 25^\circ$ is set down in the tables as $9\cdot 6259483$,

and the true value of the logarithm of the sine of 25° is therefore

$\quad\quad 9\cdot 6259483 - 10,$ that is, $-\cdot 3740517,$

or we might adopt the usual logarithmic notation of Art. 152, and say

$\quad\quad \log . \sin 25^\circ = \bar{1}\cdot 6259483.$

The Tables to which we refer are calculated for all angles in the first quadrant at intervals of $1'$.

171. *To find the logarithmic sine of an angle not exactly given in the tables.*

Suppose we have to find $L \sin 6°.32'.37''$.

$L \sin 6°.33' = 9\cdot0571723$

$L \sin 6°.32' = 9\cdot0560706$

$\overline{\cdot0011017}$ difference for 1.

Then if x be the number to be *added* to $9\cdot0560706$ to give us $L \sin 6°.32'.37''$, we have

$$60 : 37 = \cdot0011017 : x;$$

$$\therefore x = \frac{\cdot0011017 \times 37}{60} = \cdot0006794, \text{ nearly};$$

$$\therefore L \sin 6°.32'.37'' = 9\cdot0560706 + \cdot0006794$$

$$= 9\cdot05675.$$

172. *To find the logarithmic cosine of an angle not exactly given in the tables.*

Suppose we have to find $L \cos 83°.27'.23''$.

$L \cos 83°.27' = 9\cdot0571723$

$L \cos 83°.28' = 9\cdot0560706$

$\overline{\cdot0011017}$ difference for $1'$.

Then, if x be the number to be *subtracted* from $9\cdot0571723$ to give us $L \cos 83°.27'.23''$, we have

$$60 : 23 = \cdot0011017 : x;$$

$$\therefore x = \frac{\cdot0011017 \times 23}{60} = \cdot0004223 \text{ nearly};$$

$$\therefore L \cos 83°.27'.23'' = 9\cdot0571723 - \cdot0004223$$

$$= 9\cdot05675.$$

Similar methods must be taken to find the Tabular Logarithms of the other Trigonometrical Ratios : it being remembered that the tangent and secant *increase*, and the cotangent and cosecant *decrease*, as we pass from 0° to 90°.

Examples.—XLV.

(1) Given $L \sin 55°.33' = 9·9162539$,
$L \sin 55°.34' = 9·9163406$,
find $L \sin 55°.33'.54''$.

(2) Given $L \sin 29°.25' = 9·6912205$,
$L \sin 29°.26' = 9·6914445$,
find $L \sin 29°.25'.2''$.

(3) Given $L \cos 37°.28' = 9·8996604$,
$L \cos 37°.29' = 9·8995636$,
find $L \cos 37°.28'.36''$.

(4) Given $L \sin 54°.13' = 9·9091461$,
$L \sin 54°.14' = 9·9092371$,
find $L \sin 54°.13'.19''$.

(5) Given $L \tan 27°.42' = 9·7201690$,
$L \tan 27°.43' = 9·7204759$,
find $L \tan 27°.42'.34''$.

(6) Given $L \tan 5°.13' = 8·9604728$,
$L \tan 5°.14' = 8·9618659$,
find $L \tan 5°.13'.23''$.

(7) Given $L \cot 3°.37' = 11·1992368$,
$L \cot 3°.38' = 11·1972347$,
find $L \cot 3°.37'\ 50''$.

(8) Given $L \sin 39°.25' = 9·8027431$,
$L \sin 39°.26' = 9·8028968$,
find $L \sin 39°.25'.10''$.

(9) Given $L \sin 70°. 34' = 9·9745252$,

$L \sin 70°. 35' = 9·9745697$,

find $L \sin 70°. 34'. 17''$.

(10) Given $L \cos 88°. 54' = 8·2832434$,

$L \cos 88°. 55' = 8·2766136$,

find $L \cos 88°. 54'. 16''$.

173. *To find the angle which corresponds to a given Tabular Logarithmic Sine.*

Let the given L sine be $8·878594$.

We find from the tables

$L \sin 4°. 21' = 8·8799493$

$L \sin 4°. 20' = 8·8782854$

$\overline{·0016639}$ difference for $1'$.

given $L \sin = 8·8789540$

$L \sin 4°. 20' = 8·8782854$

$\overline{·0006686}$

Hence if x be the number of seconds to be added to $4°. 20'$,

$$·0016639 : ·0006686 = 60 : x;$$

$$\therefore x = \frac{6686 \times 60}{16639} = 24 \text{ nearly};$$

$\therefore$ required angle is $4°. 20'. 24''$.

174. *To find the angle which corresponds to a given Tabular Logarithmic Cosine.*

Let the given L cosine be $8·878954$.

We find from the tables

$L \cos 85°. 39' = 8·8799493$

$L \cos 85°. 40' = 8·8782854$

$\overline{·0016639}$ difference for $1'$.

$$L \cos 85°. 39' = 8\cdot 8799493$$
$$\text{given } L \cosine = 8\cdot 8789540$$
$$\overline{\cdot 0009953}$$

Hence if x be the number of seconds to be added to 85°. 39',
$$\cdot 0016639 : \cdot 0009953 = 60 : x;$$
$$\therefore x = \frac{9953 \times 60}{16639} = 35\cdot 8 \text{ nearly};$$
$$\therefore \text{ required angle is } 85°. 39'. 35'''\cdot 8.$$

EXAMPLES.—XLVI.

(1) Given $L \sin 14°. 24' = 9\cdot 3956581,$
$L \sin 14°. 25' = 9\cdot 3961499,$
find the angle whose $L \sin$ is $9\cdot 3959449$.

(2) Given $L \sin 54°. 13' = 9\cdot 9091461,$
$L \sin 54°. 14' = 9\cdot 9092371,$
find the angle whose $L \sin$ is $9\cdot 9091760$.

(3) Given $L \sin 71°. 40' = 9\cdot 9773772,$
$L \sin 71°. 41' = 9\cdot 9774191,$
find the angle whose $L \sin$ is $9\cdot 9773897$.

(4) Given $L \cos 29°. 25' = 9\cdot 9400535,$
$L \cos 29°. 26' = 9\cdot 9399823,$
find the angle whose $L \cos$ is $9\cdot 9400512$.

(5) Given $L \tan 30°. 50' = 9\cdot 7759077,$
$L \tan 30°. 51' = 9\cdot 7761947,$
find the angle whose $L \tan$ is $9\cdot 7760397$.

(6) Given $L \cot 86°. 32' = 8\cdot 7823199,$
$L \cot 86°. 33' = 8\cdot 7802218,$
find the angle whose $L \cot$ is $8\cdot 7814643$.

(7) Given L sin 24°. 8′ = 9·6115762,

L sin 24°. 9′ = 9·6118580,

find the angle whose L sin is 9·6117876.

(8) Given L tan 11°. 39′ = 9·3142468,

L tan 11°. 40′ = 9·3148851,

find the angle whose L tan is 9·3148011.

(9) Given L cosec 46 . 23′ = 10·1402787,

L cosec 46°. 24′ = 10·1401584,

find the angle whose L cosec is 10·1402367.

(10) Given L sec 29°. 54′ = 10·0620326,

L sec 29°. 55′ = 10·0621053,

find the angle whose L sec is 10·0620G8557.

CHAPTER XVI.

On the Relations between the Sides of a Triangle and the Trigonometrical Ratios of the Angles of the Triangle.

175. A TRIANGLE is composed of six parts, three sides and three angles.

Three of these parts being given, one at least of the three being a side, we can generally determine the other three parts.

If only the three angles be given, we cannot determine the sides, because an infinite number of triangles may be constructed with the three angles of the one equal to the three angles of the other, each to each.

176. We shall denote the angles of a triangle by the letters A, B, C; the sides respectively opposite to them by the letters a, b, c.

The student must remember the results established in Art. 101,
$$\sin(180^\circ - A) = \sin A,$$
$$\cos(180^\circ - A) = -\cos A.$$

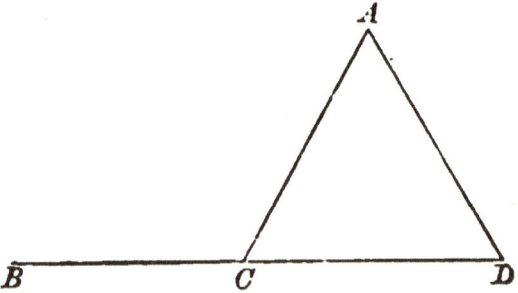

Thus, if ACB be an exterior angle of the triangle ACD,
$$\sin ACB = \sin ACD,$$
$$\cos ACB = -\cos ACD.$$

The results of Examples xiii. (2), on page 36 are also frequently employed in this and the next Chapters.

177. *To shew that in any triangle*

$$c = a \cdot \cos B + b \cdot \cos A.$$

Fig. 1.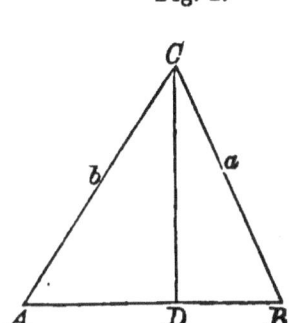

Fig. 2.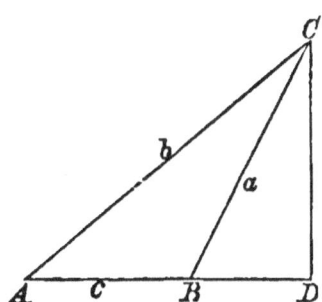

Let A, B be any two angles of the triangle ABC, and as one of them must be acute, let it be A.

Then according as B is acute or obtuse, draw CD at right angles to AB or to AB produced.

Then, in fig. 1,

$$c = AD + DB$$
$$= AC \cdot \cos A + BC \cdot \cos B$$
$$= b \cdot \cos A + a \cdot \cos B;$$

and in fig. 2,

$$c = AD - DB$$
$$= AC \cdot \cos A - CB \cdot \cos CBD$$
$$= b \cdot \cos A + a \cdot \cos B, \text{ since } \cos CBD = -\cos ABC.$$

If the angle at B be a right angle, the theorem holds good, for then $\cos B = \cos 90° = 0$, and $\therefore a \cdot \cos B = 0$, and we have

$$c = b \cdot \cos A.$$

178. *To shew that in every triangle the sides are proportional to the sines of the opposite angles.*

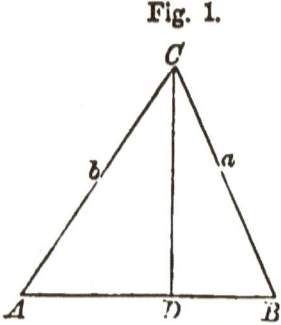
Fig. 1.

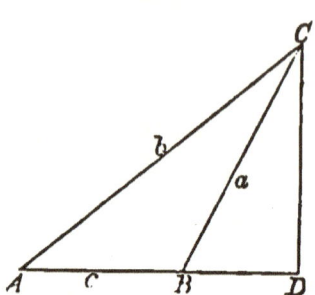
Fig. 2.

Let A, B be any two angles of the triangle ABC, and as one of them must be an acute angle, let it be A.

Then, according as B is acute or obtuse, draw CD at right angles to AB or to AB produced.

Then in fig. 1,
$$\sin A = \frac{CD}{b},$$
$$\sin B = \frac{CD}{a};$$
$$\therefore \frac{\sin A}{\sin B} = \frac{CD}{b} \div \frac{CD}{a} = \frac{CD}{b} \times \frac{a}{CD} = \frac{a}{b};$$

and in fig. 2,
$$\sin A = \frac{CD}{b},$$
$$\sin B = \sin(180° - B) = \sin CBD = \frac{CD}{a};$$
$$\therefore \frac{\sin A}{\sin B} = \frac{CD}{b} \div \frac{CD}{a} = \frac{CD}{b} \times \frac{a}{CD} = \frac{a}{b}.$$

If the angle at B be a right angle, the theorem still holds good, for then
$$\sin A = \frac{a}{b},$$
$$\sin B = 1;$$
$$\therefore \frac{\sin A}{\sin B} = \frac{a}{b}.$$

Similarly it may be shown that in any triangle

$$\frac{\sin A}{\sin C} = \frac{a}{c} \text{ and } \frac{\sin B}{\sin C} = \frac{b}{c},$$

and therefore we conclude that

$$\frac{\sin A}{a} = \frac{\sin B}{b} = \frac{\sin C}{c}.^*$$

179. *To express the cosine of an angle of a triangle in terms of the sides.*

Fig. 1. 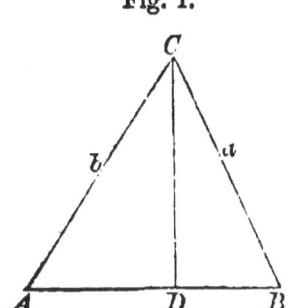   Fig. 2.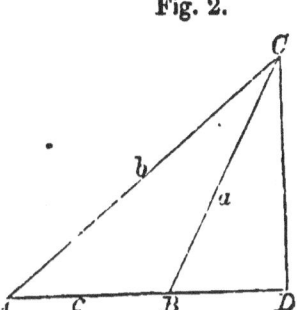

Let A, B be any two angles of the triangle ABC, and as one of them must be acute, let it be A.

Then, according as B is acute or obtuse, draw CD at right angles to AB or to AB produced.

Now, in fig. 1, by Euclid II. 13,

$$AC^2 = AB^2 + BC^2 - 2AB \cdot BD,$$

or

$$b^2 = c^2 + a^2 - 2c \cdot BD.$$

Now, from the right-angled triangle BCD,

$$\frac{BD}{BC} = \cos B, \text{ or } \frac{BD}{a} = \cos B, \text{ or } BD = a \cdot \cos B;$$

$$\therefore b^2 = c^2 + a^2 - 2ac \cdot \cos B.$$

Again, in fig. 2, by Euclid II. 12,

$$AC^2 = AB^2 + BC^2 + 2AB \cdot BD,$$

or

$$b^2 = c^2 + a^2 + 2c \cdot BD.$$

---

* For another proof of this proposition, see Art. 221.

Now $\dfrac{BD}{BC} = \cos CBD = -\cos(180° - CBD) = -\cos B$;

$\therefore BD = -BC \cdot \cos B$, or $BD = -a \cdot \cos B$;

$\therefore b^2 = c^2 + a^2 - 2ac \cdot \cos B$.

Hence, in each case,
$$2ac \cdot \cos B = c^2 + a^2 - b^2,$$
or
$$\cos B = \frac{c^2 + a^2 - b^2}{2ac}.$$

So also
$$\cos A = \frac{b^2 + c^2 - a^2}{2bc},$$

and
$$\cos C = \frac{a^2 + b^2 - c^2}{2ab}.$$

If B is a right angle, $\cos B = 0$, and the theorem still holds true, for then
$$b^2 = a^2 + c^2.$$

180. *To shew that*
$$\tan\frac{A-B}{2} = \frac{a-b}{a+b} \cdot \cot\frac{C}{2}.$$

Since
$$\frac{a}{b} = \frac{\sin A}{\sin B},$$

$$\frac{a-b}{a+b} = \frac{\sin A - \sin B}{\sin A + \sin B}$$

$$= \frac{2\cos\dfrac{A+B}{2} \cdot \sin\dfrac{A-B}{2}}{2\sin\dfrac{A+B}{2} \cdot \cos\dfrac{A-B}{2}} \quad \text{(Art. 120)}$$

$$= \frac{\tan\dfrac{A-B}{2}}{\tan\dfrac{A+B}{2}}$$

$$= \frac{\tan\dfrac{A-B}{2}}{\cot\dfrac{C}{2}}, \text{ since } \frac{A+B}{2} = 90° - \frac{C}{2};$$

$$\therefore \tan\frac{A-B}{2} = \frac{a-b}{a+b} \cdot \cot\frac{C}{2}.$$

181. If $s = \dfrac{a+b+c}{2}$, we can prove the following results:

(1) $\sin \dfrac{A}{2} = \sqrt{\dfrac{(s-b)(s-c)}{bc}}$.

(2) $\cos \dfrac{A}{2} = \sqrt{\dfrac{s \cdot (s-a)}{bc}}$.

The method of proof will be given in the next two articles.

182. First, *to shew that*

$$\sin \dfrac{A}{2} = \sqrt{\dfrac{(s-b)(s-c)}{bc}}.$$

Since $\cos A = 1 - 2\sin^2 \dfrac{A}{2}$,

$$2\sin^2 \dfrac{A}{2} = 1 - \cos A$$

$$= 1 - \dfrac{b^2 + c^2 - a^2}{2bc} \text{ (Art. 179)}$$

$$= \dfrac{2bc - b^2 - c^2 + a^2}{2bc}$$

$$= \dfrac{a^2 - (b^2 - 2bc + c^2)}{2bc}$$

$$= \dfrac{(a+b-c)(a-b+c)}{2bc}.$$

Now if $s = \dfrac{a+b+c}{2}$, $2s = a+b+c$;

∴ $a+b-c = 2s-2c$ and $a-b+c = 2s-2b$;

$$\therefore 2\sin^2\frac{A}{2} = \frac{2(s-c).2(s-b)}{2bc};$$

$$\therefore \sin\frac{A}{2} = \sqrt{\frac{(s-b).(s-c)}{bc}}.$$

We must take the positive sign with the root-symbol, because A being an angle of a triangle must be less than $180°$, and therefore $\frac{A}{2}$ less than $90°$, and consequently $\sin\frac{A}{2}$ is positive.

183. Next, *to shew that*
$$\cos\frac{A}{2} = \sqrt{\frac{s.(s-a)}{bc}}.$$

Since $\qquad \cos A = 2\cos^2\frac{A}{2} - 1;$

$$\therefore 2\cos^2\frac{A}{2} = 1 + \cos A$$

$$= 1 + \frac{b^2 + c^2 - a^2}{2bc}$$

$$= \frac{2bc + b^2 + c^2 - a^2}{2bc}$$

$$= \frac{(b+c+a)(b+c-a)}{2bc}.$$

Now, if $\qquad s = \frac{b+c+a}{2},$

$b+c+a = 2s$ and $b+c-a = 2s - 2a;$

$$\therefore 2\cos^2\frac{A}{2} = \frac{2s.2(s-a)}{2bc};$$

$$\therefore \cos^2\frac{A}{2} = \frac{s.(s-a)}{bc};$$

$$\therefore \cos\frac{A}{2} = \sqrt{\frac{s.(s-a)}{bc}}.$$

184. From the preceding articles we may at once derive two other formulæ:

(1) $\sin A = 2\sin\dfrac{A}{2}\cdot\cos\dfrac{A}{2}$

$= 2\sqrt{\dfrac{(s-b)(s-c)}{bc}}\cdot\sqrt{\dfrac{s\cdot(s-a)}{bc}}$

$= \dfrac{2}{bc}\cdot\sqrt{s\cdot(s-a)(s-b)(s-c)},$

(2) $\tan\dfrac{A}{2} = \sin\dfrac{A}{2} \div \cos\dfrac{A}{2}$

$= \sqrt{\dfrac{(s-b)(s-c)}{bc}} \div \sqrt{\dfrac{s\cdot(s-a)}{bc}}$

$= \sqrt{\dfrac{(s-b)(s-c)}{s\cdot(s-a)}}.$

Examples.—XLVII.

Prove the following relations when A, B, C are the angles of a triangle:

(1) $\sin(A+B) = \sin C.$

(2) $\cos(A+B) = -\cos C.$

(3) $\sin\dfrac{A+B}{2} = \cos\dfrac{C}{2}.$

(4) $\cos\dfrac{A+B}{2} = \sin\dfrac{C}{2}.$

(5) $\tan\dfrac{A+B}{2} = \cot\dfrac{C}{2}.$

(6) $\cot\dfrac{A+B}{2} = \tan\dfrac{C}{2}.$

185. Many other relations may be established by the use of the important formulæ explained in Art. 120 and the set of examples just given.

Thus, to show that, if $A+B+C = 180°$,

$$\sin A + \sin B + \sin C = 4\cos\dfrac{A}{2}\cdot\cos\dfrac{B}{2}\cdot\cos\dfrac{C}{2},$$

we proceed thus,

$$\sin A + \sin B = 2 \sin \frac{A+B}{2} \cdot \cos \frac{A-B}{2} \quad \text{(Art. 120)}$$

$$= 2 \cos \frac{C}{2} \cdot \cos \frac{A-B}{2};$$

$$\therefore \sin A + \sin B + \sin C = 2 \cos \frac{C}{2} \cdot \cos \frac{A-B}{2} + 2 \sin \frac{C}{2} \cdot \cos \frac{C}{2}$$

$$= 2 \cos \frac{C}{2} \left(\cos \frac{A-B}{2} + \cos \frac{A+B}{2} \right)$$

$$= 2 \cos \frac{C}{2} \left(2 \cos \frac{A}{2} \cdot \cos \frac{B}{2} \right) \quad \text{(Art. 120)}$$

$$= 4 \cos \frac{A}{2} \cdot \cos \frac{B}{2} \cdot \cos \frac{C}{2}.$$

EXAMPLES.—XLVIII.

1. If A, B, C be the angles of a triangle, prove the following relations:

(1) $\sin 2A + \sin 2B + \sin 2C = 4 \sin A \sin B \sin C$.

(2) $4 \sin A \cdot \sin B \cdot \sin C = \sin(-A+B+C)$
$\qquad + \sin(A-B+C) + \sin(A+B-C)$.

(3) $\dfrac{\cot \dfrac{A}{2} + \cot \dfrac{C}{2}}{\cot \dfrac{B}{2} + \cot \dfrac{C}{2}} = \dfrac{\sin B}{\sin A}$.

(4) $\tan A + \tan B + \tan C = \tan A \cdot \tan B \cdot \tan C$.

(5) $\cot A \cdot \cot B + \cot A \cdot \cot C + \cot B \cdot \cot C = 1$.

(6) $\cot \dfrac{A}{2} + \cot \dfrac{B}{2} + \cot \dfrac{C}{2} = \cot \dfrac{A}{2} \cdot \cot \dfrac{B}{2} \cdot \cot \dfrac{C}{2}$.

(7) $4 \cos A \cdot \cos B \cdot \cos C = -(1 + \cos 2A + \cos 2B + \cos 2C)$.

(8) $\cos A + \cos B + \cos C = 4 \sin \dfrac{A}{2} \cdot \sin \dfrac{B}{2} \cdot \sin \dfrac{C}{2} + 1$.

(9) $4 \sin A \cdot \cos B \cdot \cos C = -\sin 2A + \sin 2B + \sin 2C$.

(10) $\sin A + \sin B - \sin C = 4 \sin \dfrac{A}{2} \cdot \sin \dfrac{B}{2} \cdot \cos \dfrac{C}{2}$.

(11) $\sin 2A + \sin 2B - \sin 2C = 4 \sin C \cdot \cos A \cdot \cos B$.

(12) $\cos A + \cos B - \cos C = 4 \cos \dfrac{A}{2} \cdot \cos \dfrac{B}{2} \cdot \sin \dfrac{C}{2} - 1$.

(13) $\cos^2 \dfrac{A}{2} + \cos^2 \dfrac{B}{2} + \cos^2 \dfrac{C}{2} = 2 + 2 \sin \dfrac{A}{2} \cdot \sin \dfrac{B}{2} \cdot \sin \dfrac{C}{2}$.

(14) $\sin^2 \dfrac{A}{2} + \sin^2 \dfrac{B}{2} + \sin^2 \dfrac{C}{2} = 1 - 2 \sin \dfrac{A}{2} \cdot \sin \dfrac{B}{2} \cdot \sin \dfrac{C}{2}$.

2. In a right-angled triangle where C is the right angle, prove that

(1) $b + c = a \cdot \cot \dfrac{A}{2}$.

(2) $2 \operatorname{cosec} 2A \cdot \cot B = \dfrac{c^2}{b^2}$.

(3) $\sin \dfrac{B}{2} = \sqrt{\left(\dfrac{c-a}{2c}\right)}$.

(4) $\cos \dfrac{B}{2} = \sqrt{\left(\dfrac{a+c}{2c}\right)}$.

(5) $\dfrac{\cos 2B - \cos 2A}{\sin 2A} = \tan A - \tan B$.

(6) $\tan 2A - \sec 2B = \dfrac{b+a}{b-a}$.

(7) $(\sin A - \sin B)^2 + (\cos A + \cos B)^2 = 4 \sin^2 \dfrac{C}{2}$.

(8) $\sec 2A = \dfrac{c^2}{b^2 - a^2}$.

(9) $abc = a^3 \cdot \cos A + b^3 \cdot \cos B$.

(10) $\cot (B - A) + \cot 2 \left(A + \dfrac{C}{2}\right) = 0$.

3. In any triangle prove the following relations:

(1) $\dfrac{\sin A - \sin B}{a - b} = \dfrac{\sin C}{c}$.

(2) $\dfrac{\sin (A - B)}{\sin C} = \dfrac{a^2 - b^2}{c^2}$.

(3) $\tan A = \dfrac{a \cdot \sin C}{b - a \cos C}$.

(4) $\cot A = \dfrac{c}{a} \cdot \operatorname{cosec} B - \cot B$.

(5) $a+b+c = (a+b)\cos C + (a+c)\cos B + (b+c)\cos A.$

(6) $(a+b)\sin\dfrac{C}{2} = c.\cos\dfrac{A-B}{2}.$

(7) $(a-b)\cos\dfrac{C}{2} = c.\sin\dfrac{A-B}{2}.$

(8) $\dfrac{\tan B}{\tan C} = \dfrac{a^2+b^2-c^2}{a^2-b^2+c^2}.$ (9) $c = a(\cos B + \sin B.\cot A).$

(10) $a^2+b^2+c^2 = 2(ab.\cos C + ac.\cos B + bc.\cos A).$

(11) $\cos^2 A + \cos^2 B + \cos^2 C + 2\cos A.\cos B.\cos C = 1.$

(12) $\sin\dfrac{A-B}{2} = \dfrac{a-b}{c}.\cos\dfrac{C}{2}.$

(13) $\cos A + \cos B = \dfrac{a+b}{c}.2\sin^2\dfrac{C}{2}.$

(14) $a^2\sin A + ab.\sin B + ac.\sin C = (a^2+b^2+c^2)\sin A.$

(15) $\cot\dfrac{A}{2} : \cot\dfrac{B}{2} = b+c-a : a+c-b.$

(16) $\cot\dfrac{A}{2}.\cot\dfrac{B}{2} = \dfrac{a+b+c}{a+b-c}.$

(17) $a.\sin(B-C) + b.\sin(C-A) + c.\sin(A-B) = 0.$

4. If a, b, c be in arithmetical progression, shew that
$$\sin\left(A+\dfrac{B}{2}\right) = 2\sin\dfrac{B}{2}.$$

5. If ABC be a triangle and AD be drawn at right angles to BC, shew that
$$AD = \dfrac{b^2\sin C + c^2\sin B}{b+c}.$$

6. The sides of a triangle being 4, 9, 12, shew that the length of the line bisecting the angle between the two shorter sides is $2\frac{4}{13}$.

7. If $\sin A = 2 \cos B \cdot \sin C$, shew that the triangle is isosceles.

8. If $\cos A \cdot \cos B \cdot \sin C = \dfrac{\sin A + \sin B}{\sec A + \sec B}$, shew that $C = 90°$.

9. If $\sin^2 A = \sin^2 B + \sin^2 C$, shew that $A = 90°$.

10. If $\dfrac{a^3 + b^3 + c^3}{a + b + c} = c^2$ and also $\sin A \cdot \sin B = \sin^2 C$, shew that the triangle is equilateral.

11. If $C = 120°$, shew that $c^2 = a^2 + ab + b^2$.

12. If CD bisect the angle C and meet AB in D, shew that
$$\tan ADC = \frac{a+b}{a-b} \tan \frac{C}{2}.$$

13. If CD bisect AB, shew that
$$CD^2 = \frac{a^2}{2} + \frac{b^2}{2} - \frac{c^2}{4}.$$

CHAPTER XVII.

On the solution of right-angled Triangles.

186. Let a, b, c be the sides of a triangle and A, B, C the angles opposite to them. Of these *six* elements which present themselves in every triangle *three* must be known in order that we may determine the others, and one of these three must be *a side*.

187. The three angles of every triangle are together equal to two right angles: that is,

$$A + B + C = 180°.$$

Hence, if two of the angles be known, the third will be known also.

188. Several of the results obtained in Chap. XVI. are to be carefully remembered, and especial attention must be given to the following formulæ, established in Arts. 178, 179, 180.

I. The Sine-rule, $\dfrac{\sin A}{a} = \dfrac{\sin B}{b} = \dfrac{\sin C}{c}$.

II. The Cosine-rule, $\cos A = \dfrac{b^2 + c^2 - a^2}{2bc}$.

III. The Tangent-rule, $\tan \dfrac{A-B}{2} = \dfrac{a-b}{a+b} \cdot \cot \dfrac{C}{2}$.

189. We may now proceed to explain the method of solving right-angled triangles.

We shall denote the right angle by C. Then we may have the following data:

(1) Two sides and an angle,

(2) Two angles and a side.

190. First, *when two sides and an angle are given as* b, c, C.

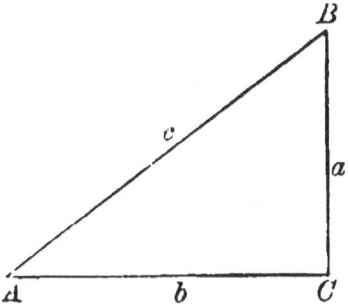

When two sides of a right-angled triangle are known, we can determine the third side; thus, in this case,

$$a = \sqrt{c^2 - b^2},$$

and so a is determined.

Next, $\sin A = \dfrac{a}{c}$, from which we can find A.

Lastly, $B = 90° - A$, and so B is determined.

191. Next, *when two angles and a side are given*, as c, A, C.

First, $\dfrac{a}{c} = \sin A$, from which we can find a.

Next, $\dfrac{b}{c} = \cos A$, from which we can find b

Lastly, $B = 90° - A$, from which we can find B.

192. If A be one of the angles of a triangle and the value of $\sin A$ be given, we cannot determine the value of A without previously knowing whether A is an *acute* or an *obtuse* angle.

Thus, suppose we know that $\sin A = \dfrac{1}{2}$, one value of A which satisfies this equation is $30°$, but another value of A which satisfies the equation is $150°$, for since the sine of an angle is equal to the sine of the supplement of the angle,

$$\sin 150° = \sin(180° - 150°) = \sin 30°.$$

In a right-angled triangle A, when not the right angle, *must* be acute, and so in the cases we have considered no ambiguity can occur.

In triangles other than right-angled we shall find only one case in which we cannot determine with certainty the value of A from the known value of $\sin A$.

193. We shall now give some Examples of the practical application of the methods of solution described in the preceding Articles.

To take the first of the two cases, suppose we have the following data:

$$b = 5, \quad c = 13, \quad C = 90°.$$

Then $\quad a = \sqrt{c^2 - b^2} = \sqrt{169 - 25} = \sqrt{144} = 12.$

and $\quad \sin A = \dfrac{a}{c} = \dfrac{12}{13} = \cdot 9230769.$

Now from the tables we find

$$\sin 67° . 22' = \cdot 9229865,$$

$$\sin 67° . 23' = \cdot 9230984.$$

And hence, by the method explained in Art. 168, we find the value of A to be $67° . 22' . 48'''\cdot 5$.

194. Again, to take the second case, suppose we have given

$$c = 25, \quad A = 60°, \quad C = 90°.$$

OF RIGHT-ANGLED TRIANGLES:

$$\therefore \frac{a}{25} = \frac{\sqrt{3}}{2}, \therefore a = \frac{25\sqrt{3}}{2}.$$

$$\frac{b}{c} = \cos A;$$

$$\therefore \frac{b}{25} = \frac{1}{2}; \therefore b = \frac{25}{2}.$$

Also, $B = 180° - (A + C) = 180° - 150° = 30°.$

Examples.—XLIX.

Solve the triangles referred to in the following examples by the use of natural sines, cosines, &c, C being a right angle.

(1) Given $b=3$, $c=5$, sin 53°. 7' = ·7998593,
sin 53°. 8' = ·8000338.

(2) Given $b=15$, $c=17$, sin 28°. 4' = ·4704986,
sin 28°. 5' = ·4707553.

(3) Given $b=21$, $c=29$, sin 43°. 36' = ·6896195,
sin 43°. 37' = ·6898302.

(4) Given $b=7$, $c=25$, cos 73°. 44' = ·2801083,
cos 73°. 45' = ·2798290.

(5) Given $b=33$, $c=65$, cos 59°. 29' = ·5077890,
cos 59°. 30' = ·5075384.

(6) Given $c=13$, $A=67°. 22'. 48''·5$, sin 67°. 22' = ·9229865,
sin 67°. 23' = ·9230984.

(7) Given $c=41$, $A=77°. 19'. 10'''·6$, sin 77°.19' = ·9755985,
sin 77°. 20' = ·9756623.

(8) Given $c=73$, $B=48°. 53'. 16'''·5$, cos 48°. 53' = ·6575944,
cos 48°. 54' = ·6573752.

(9) Given $c=89$, $B=64°.0'.38''\cdot8$, $\cos 64° = \cdot 4383711$,

$\cos 64°.1' = \cdot 4381097$.

(10) Given $a=40$, $A=77°.19'.10''\cdot 6$, $\tan 77°.19' = 4\cdot 4433769$,

$\tan 77°.20' = 4\cdot 4494186$.

195. The process of solution by means of natural sines, cosines, &c. can only be applied with advantage to cases in which the measures of the sides are small numbers.

We proceed to show how the use of logarithmic calculations assists us in the solution of triangles.

196. It must be observed that a formula is adapted to Logarithmic calculation only when it consists of the product or quotient of two or more numbers.

For instance, we derive no advantage from logarithms in finding c from the equation $c^2 = a^2 + b^2$, when a and b are given.

But if a and c be given, we can apply logarithms with advantage to find b from the equation

$$b^2 = c^2 - a^2;$$

for instance, if $a = 644$ and $c = 725$,

$$b^2 = c^2 - a^2$$
$$= (c+a)(c-a)$$
$$= 1369 \times 81;$$
$$\therefore \log b^2 = \log(1369 \times 81);$$
$$\therefore 2\log b = \log 1369 + \log 81$$
$$= 3\cdot 1364034 + 1\cdot 9084850$$
$$= 5\cdot 0448884;$$
$$\therefore \log b = 2\cdot 5224442;$$
$$\therefore b = 333.$$

197. Let $a = 644$, $c = 725$, $C = 90°$.

We first find $b = 333$, as explained in the preceding Article.

Then $$\sin A = \frac{a}{c};$$

$\therefore \log \sin A = \log a - \log c$.

Now $L \sin A$ is the true log sin A increased by 10, Art. 170, hence we put here and in all similar cases $L \sin A - 10$ in place of $\log \sin A$.

Thus $L \sin A - 10 = \log a - \log c$,

$L \sin A = 10 + 2\cdot8088859 - 2\cdot8603380$

$\qquad = 9\cdot9485479$.

Now from the tables

$L \sin 62°. 39' = 9\cdot9485189$,

$L \sin 62°. 40' = 9\cdot9485842$.

Hence, by the method of Art. 168, we may find $A = 62°. 39'. 27''$ nearly; and therefore $B = 27°. 20'. 33''$.

Examples.—L.

Solve the triangles referred to in the following Examples by Logarithmic calculations, C being a right angle:

(1) Given $a = 104$, $c = 185$, $\log a = 2\cdot0170333$,

$\log c = 2\cdot2671717$, $\log 153 = 2\cdot1846914$,

$\log 289 = 2\cdot4608978$, $\log 81 = 1\cdot9084850$,

$L \sin 34°. 12' = 9\cdot7498007$, $L \sin 34°. 13' = 9\cdot7499866$.

(2) Given $a = 304$, $c = 425$, $\log a = 2\cdot4828736$,

$\log c = 2\cdot6283889$, $\log 297 = 2\cdot4727564$,

$\log 729 = 2\cdot8627275$, $\log 121 = 2\cdot0827854$,

$L \sin 45°. 40' = 9\cdot8544799$, $L \sin 45°. 41' = 9\cdot8546033$.

(3) Given $a=840$, $c=841$, $\log a = 2\cdot 9242793$,
$\log c = 2\cdot 9247960$, $\log 41 = 1\cdot 6127839$,
$\log 1681 = 3\cdot 2255677$,
$L \sin 87°. 12' = 9\cdot 9994812$, $L \sin 87°. 13' = 9\cdot 9994874$.

(4) Given $a=336$, $c=625$, $\log a = 2\cdot 5263393$,
$\log c = 2\cdot 7958800$, $\log 527 = 2\cdot 7218106$,
$\log 961 = 2\cdot 9827234$, $\log 289 = 2\cdot 4608978$,
$L \sin 32°. 31' = 9\cdot 7304148$, $L \sin 32°. 32' = 9\cdot 7306129$.

(5) Given $a=1100$, $c=1109$, $\log a = 3\cdot 0413927$,
$\log c = 3\cdot 0449315$, $\log 141 = 2\cdot 1492191$,
$\log 2209 = 3\cdot 3441957$, $\log 3 = \cdot 4771213$,
$L \sin 82°. 41' = 9\cdot 9964493$, $L \sin 82°. 42' = 9\cdot 9964655$.

(6) Given $b=195$, $c=773$, $\log b = 2\cdot 2900346$,
$\log c = 2\cdot 8881795$, $\log 748 = 2\cdot 8739016$,
$\log 968 = 2\cdot 9858754$, $\log 578 = 2\cdot 7619278$,
$L \cos 75°. 23' = 9\cdot 4020048$, $L \cos 75°. 24' = 9\cdot 4015201$.

(7) Given $b=273$, $c=785$, $\log b = 2\cdot 4361626$,
$\log c = 2\cdot 8948697$, $\log 736 = 2\cdot 8668778$,
$\log 1058 = 3\cdot 0244857$, $\log 2 = \cdot 3010300$,
$L \cos 69°. 38' = 9\cdot 5416126$, $L \cos 69°. 39' = 9\cdot 5412721$.

(8) Given $b=609$, $c=641$, $\log b = 2\cdot 7846173$,
$\log c = 2\cdot 8068580$,
$\log 1250 = 3\cdot 0969100$, $\log 2 = \cdot 3010300$,
$L \cos 18°. 10' = 9\cdot 9777938$, $L \cos 18°. 11' = 9\cdot 9777523$.

(9) Given $a=276$, $b=493$, $\log a = 2\cdot 4409091$,
$\log b = 2\cdot 6928469$,
$L \tan 29°. 14' = 9\cdot 7479125$, $L \tan 29°. 15' = 9\cdot 7482089$.

(10) Given $a = 396$, $b = 403$, $\log a = 2·5976952$,

$\log b = 2·6053050$,

$L \tan 44°. 29' = 9·9921670$, $L \tan 44°. 30' = 9·9924197$.

198. We shall now give a few Problems to illustrate the practical use of the methods of solution of triangles explained in this Chapter.

EXAMPLES.—LI.

(1) Having measured a distance of 220 feet in a direct horizontal line from the bottom of a steeple, the angle of elevation of its top was found to be 46°. 30'. Required the height of the steeple.

Given $\log 220 = 2·3424227$, $L \tan 46°. 30' = 10·0227500$,

$\log 2·31835 = ·3651727$.

(2) A river AC whose breadth is 200 feet runs at the foot of a tower CB, which subtends an angle BAC of 25°.10' at the edge of the bank.

Required the height of the tower, given

$\log 5 = ·6989700$, $L \tan 25°. 10' = 9·6719628$,

$\log 9397 = 3·9729928$.

(3) A person on the top of a tower, whose height is 50 feet, observes the angles of depression of two objects on the horizontal plane which are in the same straight line with the tower to be 30° and 45°. Find their distances from each other and from the observer.

(4) At 140 feet from the base of a tower, and on a level with the base the angle of elevation of the top was found to be 54°. 27'. Find the height of the tower, having given

$\tan 54°.27' = 1·399364$.

(5) A person observes the angle of elevation of a hill to be 32°. 14′, and on approaching 500 yards nearer, he observes it to be 63°. 26′. Find the height of the hill, having given

$$\tan 32°.\ 14' = \cdot 63, \quad \tan 63°.\ 26' = 1 \cdot 998.$$

(6) A tower 150 feet high throws a shadow 75 feet long upon the horizontal plane on which it stands. Find the sun's altitude, having given $\log 2 = \cdot 3010300$,

$$L \tan 63°.\ 26' = 10 \cdot 3009994, \quad L \tan 63°.\ 27' = 10 \cdot 3013153.$$

(7) A tower stands by a river. A person on the opposite bank finds its elevation to be 60°: he recedes 40 yards in a direct line from the tower, and then finds the elevation to be 50°. Find the breadth of the river, having given $\tan 50° = 1 \cdot 19$.

(8) A rope is fastened to the top of a building 60 feet high. The length of the rope is 109 feet. Find the angle at which it is inclined to the horizon.

Given $\quad \sin 33°.\ 23' = \cdot 5502, \quad \sin 33°.\ 24' = \cdot 55048.$

(9) A tower is 140 feet in height. At what angle must a rope be inclined to the horizon which reaches from the top of the tower to the ground, and is 221 feet in length?

Given $\quad \sin 39°.\ 5' = \cdot 63045, \quad \sin 39°.\ 6' = \cdot 6306758.$

(10) A person standing at the edge of a river observes that the top of a tower on the edge of the opposite side subtends an angle of 55° with a line drawn from his eye parallel to the horizon; receding backwards 30 feet, he then finds it to subtend an angle of 48°. Find the breadth of the river.

Given $\quad L \sin 7° = 9 \cdot 08589, \quad L \sin 35° = 9 \cdot 75859.$

$L \sin 48° = 9 \cdot 87107, \quad \log 3 = \cdot 47712, \quad \log 1 \cdot 0493 = \cdot 02089.$

(11) Standing straight in front of the corner of a house which is 150 feet long, I observe that the length subtends an angle whose cosine is $\dfrac{1}{\sqrt{5}}$, and its height subtends an angle whose sine is $\dfrac{3}{\sqrt{34}}$; determine the height.

(12) Standing straight in front of one corner of a house, I find that its length subtends an angle whose tangent is 2, while its height subtends an angle whose tangent is $\dfrac{3}{5}$: the height of the house is 45 feet, find its length.

CHAPTER XVIII.

On the solution of Triangles other than right-angled.

199. IN the solution of triangles other than right-angled, usually called Oblique-angled Triangles, we meet with four distinct cases, the following being the data.

(1) The three sides a, b, c.

(2) Two angles and a side, as A, C, b.

(3) Two sides and the angle between them, as a, b, C.

(4) Two sides and an angle opposite one of them, as a, b, A.

These cases we shall discuss in order.

CASE I.

200. *Given the three sides* a, b, c.

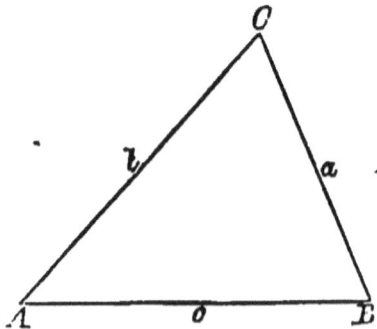

We first find A from one of the formulæ

$$\cos A = \frac{b^2 + c^2 - a^2}{2bc},$$

$$\tan \frac{A}{2} = \sqrt{\frac{(s-b)\cdot(s-c)}{s\cdot(s-a)}}.$$

The formula $\cos A = \dfrac{b^2+c^2-a^2}{2bc}$ is not adapted to logarithmic calculation; but if a, b, c contain less than three digits we may use it to find A by aid of the table of natural cosines.

Thus, if $a=6$, $b=5$, $c=10$,

$$\cos A = \frac{25+100-36}{100} = \cdot 89.$$

And hence we find $A = 27°. 7'. 36''$.

201. When a, b, c, contain three or more digits, we may employ with advantage the formula

$$\tan \frac{A}{2} = \sqrt{\frac{(s-b)(s-c)}{s \cdot (s-a)}},$$

from which we have

$$L \tan \frac{A}{2} - 10 = \frac{1}{2}\{\log(s-b) + \log(s-c) - \log s - \log(s-a)\},$$

and then we may find $\tan \dfrac{B}{2}$ or $\tan \dfrac{C}{2}$ *by means of the same logarithms*, thus

$$L \tan \frac{B}{2} - 10 = \frac{1}{2}\{\log(s-a) + \log(s-c) - \log s - \log(s-b)\}.$$

For example, let $a = 9459\cdot31$, $b = 8032\cdot29$, $c = 8242\cdot58$.

Then $s = 12867\cdot09$, $s-a = 3407\cdot78$,

$s-b = 8434\cdot80$, $s-c = 4624\cdot51$.

$$L \tan \frac{A}{2} - 10 = \frac{1}{2}\{\log(s-b) + \log(s-c) - \log s - \log(s-a)\}$$

$$= \frac{1}{2}\{3\cdot 6843785 + 3\cdot 6650657 - 4\cdot 1094804 - 3\cdot 5324716\}$$

$$= -\cdot 1462539;$$

$\therefore L \tan \dfrac{A}{2} = 9\cdot 8537461$.

Whence $\dfrac{A}{2} = 35°.31'.47''\cdot 5$,

and $A = 71°.3'.35''$.

Similarly we may find $B = 53°.26'$ and $C = 55°.30'.25''$.

202. When A has been found we can find B from the relation

$$\dfrac{\sin B}{\sin A} = \dfrac{b}{a},$$

and then C may be found from the relation

$$C = 180° - (A + B).$$

203. If we are required to find only one angle, as A, we may take the formula

$$\sin \dfrac{A}{2} = \sqrt{\dfrac{(s-b)(s-c)}{bc}},$$

where

$$s = \dfrac{a+b+c}{2}.$$

Taking the example given in Art. 200 we have

$$\sin \dfrac{A}{2} = \sqrt{\left\{\dfrac{\frac{11}{2} \times \frac{1}{2}}{5 \times 10}\right\}} = \sqrt{\dfrac{11}{200}};$$

$$\therefore L \sin \dfrac{A}{2} - 10 = \dfrac{1}{2} \{\log 11 - \log 200\}$$

$$= \dfrac{1}{2} \cdot \{1\cdot0413927 - 2\cdot3010300\};$$

$$\therefore L \sin \dfrac{A}{2} = 10 - \cdot 6298186$$

$$= 9\cdot3701814.$$

And hence we find from the tables $\dfrac{A}{2} = 13°.33'.48''$, and thus we know that the value of A is $27°.7'.36''$.

Case II.

204. *Given two angles and a side,* A, C, b.

First, $B = 180° - (A + C)$, from which we can find B.

Next, $\dfrac{a}{b} = \dfrac{\sin A}{\sin B}$, from which we can find a.

Lastly, $\dfrac{c}{b} = \dfrac{\sin C}{\sin B}$, from which we can find c.

205. Here we have no difficulty, and we shall merely give an example to illustrate the method of finding a from the formula

$$\dfrac{a}{b} = \dfrac{\sin A}{\sin B}, \text{ when } b, A, B \text{ are known.}$$

Let $b = 40$, $A = 12°.40'$, $B = 77°.10'$.

Then $\log a = \log b + L \sin A - L \sin B$

$\qquad = 1{\cdot}6020600 + 9{\cdot}3409963 - 9{\cdot}9890137$

$\qquad = {\cdot}9540426,$

whence $a = 9$ nearly.

206. It is in practice an easier method to write the equation thus,

$$a = b \cdot \sin A \cdot \operatorname{cosec} B,$$

so as to save a subtraction of decimals.

Thus, taking the same Example, we have

$\log a = \log b + L \sin A + L \operatorname{cosec} B - 20$

$\qquad = 1{\cdot}6020600 + 9{\cdot}3409963 + 10{\cdot}0109863 - 20$

$\qquad = {\cdot}9540426.$

Case III.

207. *Given two sides and the angle between them,* a, b, C.

We may find c from the formula

$$c^2 = a^2 + b^2 - 2ab \cdot \cos C.$$

Then from $\dfrac{\sin A}{\sin C} = \dfrac{a}{c}$ we can find A.

Lastly, from $B = 180° - (A + C)$, we can find B.

Or we may proceed to find A and B before we find c, thus: by the formula established in Art. 180,

$$\tan \frac{A-B}{2} = \frac{a-b}{a+b} \cdot \cot \frac{C}{2},$$

and from this we can find $\dfrac{A-B}{2}$.

Then, as we know that $\dfrac{A+B}{2} = 90° - \dfrac{C}{2}$, we shall have two equations by which we may determine A and B.

Then we can find c from the equation $\dfrac{c}{a} = \dfrac{\sin C}{\sin A}$.

208. The first formula given,

$$c^2 = a^2 + b^2 - 2ab \cdot \cos C,$$

is not adapted to logarithmic calculation.

We must take then, in all cases where a and b are not small integers, the formula

$$\tan \frac{A-B}{2} = \frac{a-b}{a+b} \cdot \cot \frac{C}{2},$$

for finding the values of A and B.

SOLUTION OF TRIANGLES. 169

Suppose then we have given

$$a = 12{\cdot}96, \quad b = 9{\cdot}78, \quad C = 57°.48'.32'',$$

we proceed thus:

$$a-b = 3{\cdot}18, \quad a+b = 22{\cdot}74, \quad \frac{C}{2} = 28°.54'.16''.$$

Then

$$L \tan \frac{A-B}{2} - 10 = \log(a-b) - \log(a+b) + L \cot \frac{C}{2} - 10,$$

$$\therefore L \tan \frac{A-B}{2} = \log 3{\cdot}18 - \log 22{\cdot}74 + L \cot 28°.54'.16''$$

$$= {\cdot}5024271 - 1{\cdot}3567905 + 10{\cdot}2579579$$

$$= 9{\cdot}4035945.$$

Whence $\dfrac{A-B}{2} = 14°.12'.46''.$

Also $\dfrac{A+B}{2} = 61°.5'.44''$ (the complement of $\dfrac{C}{2}$);

$$\therefore A = 75°.18'.30'',$$

$$B = 46°.52'.58''.$$

The other formulæ of this case require no special remark.

209. Though the formula $c^2 = a^2 + b^2 - 2ab \cdot \cos C$ is not adapted to logarithmic calculation, we can find c from it (in any case where we do not require the values of A and B also) by the following process:

$$c^2 = a^2 + b^2 - 2ab \cdot \cos C$$

$$= a^2 + b^2 - 2ab \cdot \left(1 - 2\sin^2 \frac{C}{2}\right)$$

$$= a^2 + b^2 - 2ab + 4ab \cdot \sin^2 \frac{C}{2}$$

$$= (a-b)^2 \cdot \left\{1 + \frac{4ab}{(a-b)^2} \cdot \sin^2 \frac{C}{2}\right\}.$$

Now, since the tangent of an angle may be of any magnitude, there is some angle (suppose θ) such that

$$\tan^2 \theta = \frac{4ab}{(a-b)^2} \cdot \sin^2 \frac{C}{2}.$$

Knowing a, b, C we can apply logarithms to find θ from this equation.

Then, from the equation

$$c^2 = (a-b)^2 \{1 + \tan^2 \theta\},$$

that is, $\qquad c^2 = (a-b)^2 \cdot \sec^2 \theta,$

we can apply logarithms to find c.

An angle introduced, as in this case, to assist the solution of an equation, by breaking it up into two or more equations, is called a *Subsidiary Angle*.

CASE IV.

210. *Given two sides and an angle opposite one of them, a, b, A.*

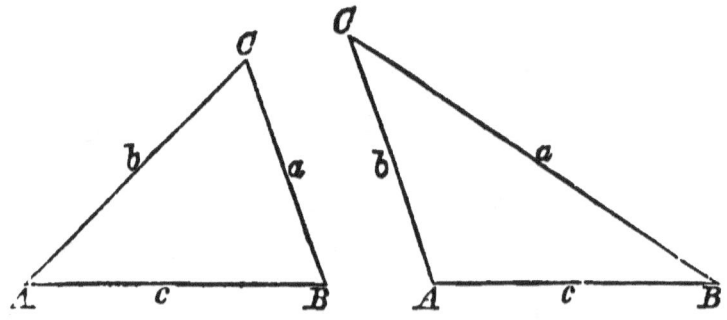

$\dfrac{\sin B}{\sin A} = \dfrac{b}{a}$, from which we have to determine B.

If we can find B, we have

$C = 180° - (A + B)$, from which we can find C,

and $\qquad \dfrac{c}{a} = \dfrac{\sin C}{\sin A}$, from which we can find c.

211. Thus the solution of this case depends on the possibility of determining B from the equation

$$\frac{\sin B}{\sin A} = \frac{b}{a} \quad (1).$$

Now since we know a, b, A, we obtain from this equation

$$\sin B = \text{a known numerical quantity} \quad (2).$$

But, as has been explained in Art. 74, we cannot determine the value of B from a given value of $\sin B$, unless we know whether B is greater or less than $90°$.

The only way in which we can tell whether the greater or the smaller value of B which satisfies equation (2) is to be taken, is by knowing *that a is greater than b*. In that case A is also greater than B, and therefore B must be less than $90°$ otherwise $A + B$ would not be less than $180°$, which is impossible.

212. This, which is called *The Ambiguous Case*, may be shewn geometrically in the following manner.

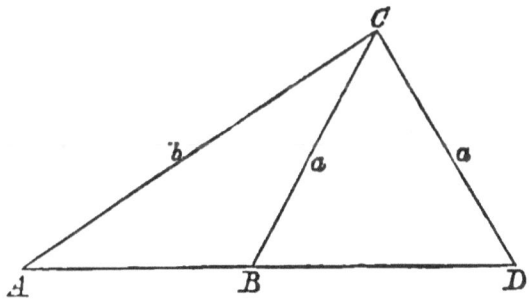

If from C we can draw a line CD equal to CB, to meet AB produced on the side of B, both the triangles ABC, ADC have the given parts a, b, A.

We can always draw $CD = CB$, *so long as AC is greater than BC*, for then a circle described with centre C and radius CB will cut AB produced in two points both on the same side of A.

SOLUTION OF TRIANGLES.

213. The following is a more complete discussion of *the Ambiguous Case*,

$$\sin B = \frac{b \cdot \sin A}{a}$$ a known numerical quantity.

Now, provided $b \sin A$ be not $> a$,

$$\frac{b \sin A}{a} \text{ is not } > 1,$$

and this numerical quantity is a possible value to be the sine of an angle.

We have now two cases.

I. If $b \sin A < a$, $\dfrac{b \sin A}{a} < 1$, and there are two angles which have this value for their sine, supplementary to one another, and therefore one acute and one obtuse.

Now when a is $> b$, A is $> B$, and therefore we cannot take this obtuse value for B, for then A and B would be together $>$ two right angles.

But when a is $< b$, A is $< B$, and we can take both the acute and the obtuse value for B, and then we shall have two corresponding values for C, and two for c, and thus we get two triangles having the given parts the same.

II. If $b \sin A = a$, $\sin B = 1$, and B has only one value viz. $90°$.

Of course, if $a = b$, $B = A$ at once without using the equation $\sin B = \dfrac{b \sin A}{a}$ at all.

This ambiguity can be exhibited geometrically as follows:

Fig. 1.   Fig. 2.

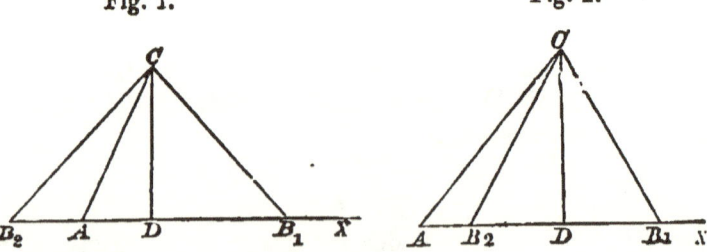

Let $CAX = A$, $AC = b$.

Draw CD perpendicular to AX, then $CD = b \sin A$. With centre C and radius equal to a describe a circle.

Now provided CD be not $> a$, this circle will meet AX.

I. If $CD < a$, this circle will meet AX in two points, B_1 and B_2.

Now when a is $> b$, B_1 and B_2 will fall on opposite sides of A as in fig. 1, and we have only one triangle, viz. CAB_1, having the given angle A, and the sides CA, CB_1, equal to b and a.

But when a is $< b$, B_1 and B_2 will fall on the same side of A as in fig. 2, and we have two triangles, viz. CAB_1, CAB_2 having the given angle A and the sides CB_1 and CB_2 equal to a, and the side AC equal to b, and in this case CB_2A is supplementary to CB_2X and therefore to its equal CB_1A.

II. If $CD = a$, the circle will meet AX in one point only, viz. at D, and CAD will be the required triangle.

Of course, if $b = a$, B_2 will coincide with A and we have only one triangle CAB_1.

214. The formulæ to be used in this case are simple, and we have only to give instances of cases (1) ambiguous, (2) in which no ambiguity exists.

(1) To take a very simple case, suppose

$$a = 5,\ b = 6,\ A = 30°.$$

Then
$$\frac{\sin B}{\sin A} = \frac{b}{a};$$

$$\therefore \sin B = \frac{b}{a} \cdot \sin A = \frac{6}{5} \times \frac{1}{2} = \frac{6}{10} = \cdot 6.$$

Now from the tables we find $\cdot 6$ to be the value of the sine of $36°.52'.12''$, and since $143°.7'.48''$ is the supplement of $36°.52'.12''$, it also has $\cdot 6$ for the value of its sine. Thus there is an ambiguity in the result.

Next, suppose $a = 178\cdot3$, $b = 145$, $B = 41°. 10'$.

Then $\sin A = \dfrac{a}{b} \sin B$;

$\therefore L \sin A = \log a - \log b + L \sin B$

$\qquad = 2\cdot2511513 - 2\cdot1613680 + 9\cdot8183919$

$\qquad = 9\cdot9081752.$

Hence $A = 54°. 2'. 22''$ or $125°. 57'. 38''$.

(2) Now if we change the values of the sides a and b we shall get

$$L \sin A = 9\cdot7286086;$$

$$\therefore A = 32°. 21'. 54'',$$

and the supplement of A cannot belong to the proposed triangle, because if A were $147°. 38'. 6''$, then, since B is greater than A, A and B would be together greater than $180°$, which is impossible. So in this case there is no ambiguity.

215. The following are applications of the principles laid down in this chapter.

Examples.—LII.

1. Find A from the following data:

(1) Given $a = 37$, $b = 13$, $c = 40$, $\sin 67°. 22' = \cdot9229865$,
$\sin 67°. 23' = \cdot9230984$.

(2) Given $a = 101$, $b = 29$, $c = 120$, $\sin 43°. 36' = \cdot6896195$,
$\sin 43°. 37' = \cdot6898302$.

(3) Given $a = 37$, $b = 13$, $c = 30$, $\log 9 = \cdot9542425$,
$\log 13 = 1\cdot1139434$,
$L \sin 56°. 18' = 9\cdot9200994$, $L \sin 56°. 19' = 9\cdot9201836$.

(4) Given $a = 409$, $b = 241$, $c = 600$, $\log 723 = 2\cdot8591383$,
$\log 360 = 2\cdot5563025$,
$L \sin 29°. 51' = 9\cdot6969947$, $L \sin 29°. 52' = 9\cdot6972148$.

2. If $a = 5780$, $c = 7639$, $B = 43°.8'$, find A and C, having given

$$\log 185\cdot9 = 2\cdot26928,\ \log 13\cdot419 = 1\cdot12772,$$

$$L \cot 21°.34' = 10\cdot40312,\ L \tan 19°.18'.50'' = 9\cdot54468.$$

3. If $A = 41°.13'.22''$, $B = 71°.19'.5''$, $a = 55$, find b, having given

$$\log 55 = 1\cdot7403627,\ L \sin B = 9\cdot9764927,\ L \sin A = 9\cdot8188779,$$

$$\log 79\cdot063 = 1\cdot8979775.$$

4. If $B = 84°.47'.38''$, $C = 41°.10'$, $c = 145$, find b, having given

$$\log 145 = 2\cdot1613680,\ L \sin 41°.10' = 9\cdot8183919,$$

$$L \sin 84°.47'.38'' = 9\cdot9982047,\ \log 219\cdot37 = 2\cdot3411808.$$

5. If $a = 567\cdot2341$, $b = 351\cdot9872$, $B = 31°.27'.18''$, find A, having given

$$\log a = 2\cdot7537623,\ \log b = 2\cdot5465269,$$

$$L \sin B = 9\cdot7175280,\ L \sin 57°.14' = 9\cdot9247349,$$

$$L \sin 57°.15' = 9\cdot9248161.$$

6. When $C = 30°$, $b = 16$, $c = 8$, is the triangle ambiguous or not?

7. Simplify the expression $\cos A = \dfrac{b^2 + c^2 - a^2}{2bc}$ in the case of an equilateral triangle.

8. Given $\log 3 = \cdot 4771213$ and $L \tan 57°.19'.11'' = 10\cdot1928032$, show that, if one angle be $60°$ and the two sides containing it as 19 to 1, the other two angles are $117°.19'.11''$, and $2°.40'.49''$.

9. The sides of a triangle are 2, $\sqrt{6}$ and $1 + \sqrt{3}$: find the angles.

10. If a, b, B had been given to solve a triangle, where b is less than a, and if c_1, c_2 be the two values found for determining the third side, prove that $b^2 + c_1 c_2 = a^2$.

11. Two sides of a triangle are to each other as 9 : 7 and the included angle is 64°. 12′; determine the other angles.

Given log 2 = ·30103, L tan 57°. 54′ = 10·2025255, L tan 11°. 16′ = 9·2993216 ; L tan 11°. 17′ = 9·2999804.

12. The sides a, b, c of a triangle are as the numbers 4, 5, 6. Find the angle B.

Given log 2 = ·3010299. L cos 27°. 53′ = 9·9464040,

log 5 = ·6989700, L cos 27°. 54′ = 9·9463371.

13. If in a triangle ABC, $BC = 70$, $AC = 35$, and $\angle ACB = 36°. 52′. 12″$ find the remaining angles.

Given log 3 = ·4771213 and L cot 18°. 26′. 6″ = 10·4771213.

216. Up to this point we have supplied the student with all the materials required for the solution of each example. But as he ought to have some practice in making extracts from the tables we shall suppose him to be in possession of a set of tables, and we shall now give a series of examples by which he may test his ability to apply the formulæ for the solution of Triangles.

Examples.—LIII.

Solve the triangles for which the following parts are given :

(1) $a = 4$, $b = 3$, $C = 90°$.

(2) $b = 55$, $c = 73$, $C = 90°$.

(3) $a = 272$, $b = 225$, $C = 90°$.

(4) $b = 399$, $c = 401$, $C = 90°$.

(5) $c = 445$, $A = 10°. 52′. 50‴·4$, $C = 90°$.

(6) $c = 629$, $A = 46°. 59′. 49‴·7$, $C = 90°$.

(7) $c = 449$, $B = 51°. 25′. 11‴·7$, $C = 90$.

(8) $c = 349$, $B = 58°. 57′. 6‴·4$, $C = 90°$.

(9) $a = 520$, $A = 66°. 2′. 52″$, $C = 90°$.

(10) $b = 31$, $A = 88°. 18′. 17″$, $C = 90°$.

Examples.—LIV.

Solve the triangles, not right-angled, for which the following parts are given:

(1) $a=197$, $b=53$, $c=240$.

(2) $a=509$, $b=221$, $c=480$.

(3) $a=533$, $b=317$, $c=510$.

(4) $a=565$, $b=445$, $c=606$.

(5) $a=409$, $b=241$, $c=182$.

(6) $b=29$, $a=43°.36'.10'''\!\cdot\!1$, $C=124°.58'.33''\!\cdot\!6$.

(7) $b=149$, $A=69°.59'.2''\!\cdot\!5$, $C=70°.42'.30''$.

(8) $a=101$, $b=29$, $C=32°.10'.53''\!\cdot\!8$.

(9) $a=401$, $b=41$, $C=96°.57'.20''\!\cdot\!1$.

(10) $a=221$, $b=149$, $C=30°.40'.35''$.

(11) $a=109$, $b=61$, $C=66°.59'.25'''\!\cdot\!4$.

(12) $a=445$, $b=83$, $C=87°.55'$.

(13) $a=229$, $b=109$, $C=131°.24'.44''$.

(14) $a=241$, $b=169$, $C=104°.3'.51''$.

(15) $a=241$, $b=169$, $C=15°.22'.37''$.

(16) $a=13$, $b=37$, $A=18°.55'.28''\!\cdot\!7$, find B.

(17) $a=445$, $b=565$, $A=44°.29'.53''$, find B.

(18) $a=212\!\cdot\!5$, $b=836\!\cdot\!4$, $A=14°.24'.25''$, find B.

(19) $a=379\!\cdot\!5$, $b=564\!\cdot\!8$, $A=40°.32'.16''$, find B.

(20) $a=9459\!\cdot\!31$, $b=8032\!\cdot\!29$, $A=71°.3'.34''\!\cdot\!7$, find B.

CHAPTER XIX.

Measurement of Heights and Distances.

217. IN this chapter we shall give examples of the application of Trigonometry in determining heights and distances.

The problems which occur most frequently in practice, in addition to those given in Chap. VIII., are the following:

(1) *To find the height of an object standing on a horizontal plane, when the base of the object is inaccessible.*

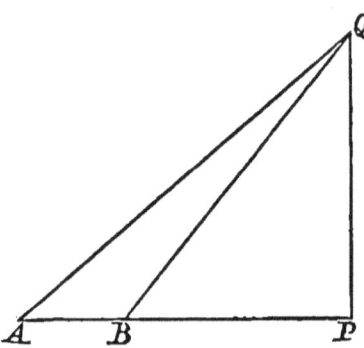

Let PQ be a tower, of which the base P is inaccessible.

Measure a distance AB in the same horizontal plane with P. Observe the angles of elevation QBP and QAP.

Then we can determine the height of the tower, for

$$QP = QB \cdot \sin QBP,$$

and
$$QB = AB \cdot \frac{\sin QAB}{\sin BQA}$$

$$= AB \cdot \frac{\sin QAP}{\sin (QBP - QAP)};$$

$$\therefore QP = AB \cdot \sin QBP \cdot \frac{\sin QAP}{\sin (QBP - QAP)}.$$

HEIGHTS AND DISTANCES. 179

(2) *To find the height of an object whose foot is inaccessible, when a direct line between the observer and the base cannot be measured.*

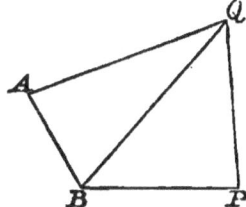

Suppose PQ to be a tower standing on the bank of a river, and B to be a point on the opposite bank. Suppose the ground to rise suddenly from B, so that no distance in a *direct* line with BP can be measured.

Measure a line AB up the rising ground.

Observe the angles QAB and QBA.

Then in the triangle QAB two angles and the side AB are known, and therefore we can find QB.

Then if we observe the angle QBP we may determine QP.

(3) *To find the distance between two inaccessible objects.*

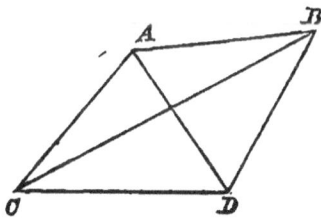

Let A and B be the objects.

Measure a line CD, and suppose A, B, C, D to be in one plane.

Then if we observe the angles ACD and ADC we can determine AC, because we know two angles and a side in the triangle ACD.

12—2

Again, if we observe the angles BCD, BDC we can determine BC, because we know two angles and a side in the triangle BCD.

Thus knowing AC and BC and the included angle ACB (which is the difference between the known angles ACD BCD), we can determine AB.

(4) *To find the distance of a ship from the shore.*

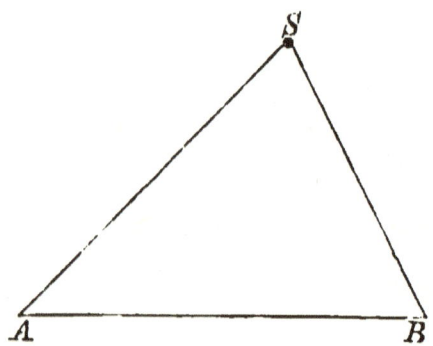

Let S be the position of the ship.

Measure AB, a straight line between two points on the shore.

Observe the angles SAB and SBA.

Then we can determine the distance of S from A, for

$$AS = AB \cdot \frac{\sin SBA}{\sin ASB}$$

$$= AB \cdot \frac{\sin SBA}{\sin (180° - ASB)}$$

$$= AB \cdot \frac{\sin SBA}{\sin (SAB + SBA)}.$$

218. In the first twenty-one of the Examples that we shall now give the results may be obtained without the aid of Tables.

Examples.—LV.

(1) Wishing to know the height of an inaccessible hill I took the angle of elevation of its top to be 60°, I then measured 100 feet away from the hill and found the angle of elevation to be 45°. What is the height of the hill?

(2) Each of two ships, which are a mile apart, finds the angles subtended by the other ship and a fort to be respectively 35°. 14′ and 42°. 12′. Find the distance of each from the fort. Given $\sin 35°. 14' = ·577$, $\sin 42°. 12' = ·671$, $\sin 77°. 26' = ·976$.

(3) Each of two ships, half a mile apart, finds the angles subtended by the other ship and a fort to be respectively 85°. 15′ and 83°. 45′. Find the distance of each from the fort. Given $\sin 85°. 15' = ·9965$, $\sin 83°. 45' = ·9940$, $\sin 11° = ·1908$.

(4) Find the angle which a flag-staff 5 yards long and standing on the top of a tower two hundred yards high subtends at a point in the horizontal plane 100 yards from the base of the tower.

Given $L \tan 34' = 7·9952192$, $L \tan 35' = 8·0078092$.

(5) The angle of elevation of the top of a steeple is 60° from a point on the ground. That of the top of the tower on which the steeple rests is 45° from the same point. What proportion does the height of the steeple bear to that of the tower?

(6) On the bank of a river there is a column 200 feet high supporting a statue 30 feet high. The statue to an observer on the opposite bank subtends the same angle as a man 6 feet high standing at the base of the column. Find the breadth of the river.

(7) A pole is fixed on the top of a mound and the angles of elevation of the top and bottom of the pole are 60° and 30°, shew that the length of the pole is twice the height of the mound.

(8) A person at a distance a from a tower which stands on a horizontal plane, observes that the angle of elevation a of its highest point is the complement of that of a flag-staff on the top of it. Shew that the length of the flag-staff is $2a \cdot \cot 2a$.

(9) If the distance of the person from the tower is unknown, and if, when he recedes a distance c, the angle of elevation of the tower is half of what it was before, shew that the length of the flag-staff is $c \cdot \operatorname{cosec} a \cdot \cos 2a$.

(10) Two spectators at two given stations observe at the same time the altitude of a kite, and find it to subtend the same angle a at each place. The angle which the line joining one station and the kite subtends at the other station is β, and the distance between the two stations is a: find the height of the kite.

(11) Two towers stand on a horizontal plane and their distance from each other is 120 feet. A person standing successively at their bases observes that the angular elevation of one is double that of the other; but when he is half-way between them their elevations appear complementary to each other. Shew that the heights of the towers are 90 and 40 feet respectively.

(12) A, B are two inaccessible points in a horizontal plane, and C, D are two stations, at each of which AB is observed to subtend the angle $30°$. AD subtends at C $19°.15'$, and AC subtends at D $40°.45'$. Shew that $AB = \dfrac{CD}{\sqrt{3}}$.

(13) The length of a road in which the ascent is 1 foot in 5, from the foot of a hill to the top is $1\tfrac{2}{3}$ miles. What will be the length of a zigzag road in which the ascent is one foot in 12?

(14) Two objects, A and B, were observed to be at the same instant in a line inclined at an angle $15°$ to the east of a ship's course, which was at the time due north. The ship's course was then altered, and after sailing 5 miles in a N.W. direction, the same objects were observed to bear E. and N.E. respectively. Required the distance of A from B.

HEIGHTS AND DISTANCES. 183

(15) The elevation of a tower at a place A due south of it is $30°$; and at a place B, due west of A, and at a distance a from it, the elevation is $18°$: show that the height of the tower is

$$\frac{a}{\sqrt{(2\sqrt{5}+2)}}.$$

(16) A circular ring is placed in a vertical plane through the sun's centre, on the top of a vertical staff whose height is eight times its radius; and the extremity of the shadow of the ring is observed to be at a distance from the foot of the staff equal to the staff's height. Determine the altitude of the sun.

(17) The hypotenuse C of a right-angled triangle ABC is trisected in the points D, E: prove that if CD, CE be joined, the sum of the squares of the sides of the triangle CDE

$$= 2c^2.$$

(18) A person stands in the diagonal produced of the square base of St Mary's Church tower, at a distance a from it, and observes the angles of elevation of the two outer corners of the top of the tower to be each $30°$, and of the other $45°$. Show that the breadth of the tower is $a\sqrt{(3-\sqrt{5})}$.

(19) A tower standing on a horizontal plane is surrounded by a moat which is just as wide as the tower is high. A person on the top of another tower whose height is a and whose distance from the moat is c, observes that the first tower subtends an angle of $45°$. Show that the height of the first tower is $\dfrac{a^2+c^2}{a-c}$.

(20) A and B are two points 100 feet apart, and C is a point equally distant from A and B; what must be the distance of C from A and B that the angle ACB may be $150°$?

(21) A headland C bore due north of a ship at A: and after the ship had sailed 10 miles due east to B, the headland bore N.W. Required the distance of the headland from A and B.

(22) The aspect of a wall 18 feet high is due south, and the length of the shadow cast on the north side at noon is 16 feet. Find the sun's altitude.

(23) At a distance of 200 yards from the foot of a church tower, the angle of elevation of the top of the tower was observed to be 30°, and of the top of the spire of the tower 32°. Find the height of the tower and of the spire.

(24) The distances of three objects, ABC, in the same horizontal plane, are $AB = 3$ miles, $BC = 1\cdot8$ mile, $AC = 2$ miles; from a station D in CA produced the angle $ADB = 17°.\ 47'.\ 20''$ is observed: find the distance of D from B.

(25) In an oblique triangle A, B, C, given $\angle ACB = 139°.\ 58'$, $\angle ABC = 22°.\ 18'$, $BC = 840\cdot5$ yards, find by how much AB differs from a mile.

(26) In an oblique-angled triangle ABC, given $AB = 2700$ ft., $\angle A = 50°.\ 20'$, and $\angle B = 110°.\ 12'$, find BC.

To determine the height of the top C of a mountain, a base AB of 2700 feet was measured in the horizontal plane, the angle subtended by CB at A was observed to be 50°. 20′, the angle subtended by AC at B was observed to be 110°. 12′, and the angle of elevation of C from B was observed to be 10°. 7′; find the height of the mountain.

(27) A flag-staff 20 feet high stands on a wall 40 feet high. At a point E on a level with the bottom of the wall the flag-staff subtends an angle of 10°. Find the distance of E from the wall.

(28) From the top of a hill the angles of depression of two consecutive mile-stones on a straight level road are found to be 12°. 13′ and 2°. 45′. Find the height of the hill.

(29) From the top of a tower by the sea-side 150 ft. high, it was found that the angle of depression of a ship's hull was 36°. 18′. Find the distance of the ship from the foot of the tower.

(30) Given $a = 6383\cdot53$, $b = 3157\cdot76$ and $C = 37°.26'$, find the other parts of the triangle.

(31) From each of two ships a mile apart the angle which is subtended by the other ship and a beacon on shore is observed: these angles are $55°$ and $62°.30'$. Determine the distances of the ships from the beacon.

(32) From the lower window of a house the angle of elevation of a church tower is observed to be $45°$, and from a window 20 feet above the former $40°$. How far is the house from the church?

(33) A line AB in length 400 yards is measured close by the side of a river, and a point C close to the bank on the other side is observed from A and B. The angle CAB is $50°$, and CBA $65°$, find the perpendicular breadth of the river.

(34) Two railways intersect at an angle of $35°.20'$: from the point of intersection two trains start together, one at the rate of 30 miles an hour; find the rate of the other train, so that after $2\frac{1}{2}$ hours the trains may be 50 miles apart. Shew that there are two velocities that will satisfy this condition and calculate approximately either of them.

(35) A base line of 600 yards was measured in a straight line close to the bank of a river, and at each end of the line the angles were observed between the other end and a tree close to the edge of the river on the opposite side of it: these angles were found to be $52°.14'$ and $68°.32'$. Find the breadth of the river.

(36) The angle of elevation of a tower 100 feet high, due north of an observer, was $50°$; what will be its angle of elevation after the observer has walked due east 300 feet?

(37) A flag-staff, 12 feet high, on the top of a tower, subtends an angle of $48'.20''$ to an observer at the distance of 100 yards from the foot of the tower: required the height of the tower.

(38) At the foot of a hill a visible object has an elevation of $29°.12'.40''$, and when the observer has walked 300 yards up the hill away from the object, he finds himself on a level with it. The slope of the hill being $16°$ and the places of observation in a vertical plane with the object, find the distance of the object from the first place of observation.

(39) AB, AC are two railroads inclined at an angle of $50°.20'$; a locomotive engine starts from A along AB at the rate of 30 miles an hour: after an interval of one hour, another locomotive engine starts from A along AC at the rate of 45 miles an hour: find the distance of the engines from each other, three hours after the first started.

(40) A church tower stands on the bank of a river which is 150 feet wide and on the top of the tower is a spire 30 feet high. To an observer on the opposite bank of the river the spire subtends the same angle that a pole six feet high subtends placed upright from the ground at the base of the tower. Show that the approximate height of the tower is 285 feet.

CHAPTER XX.

Propositions relating to the Areas of Triangles, Polygons, and Circles.

219. *Expressions for the area of a triangle.*

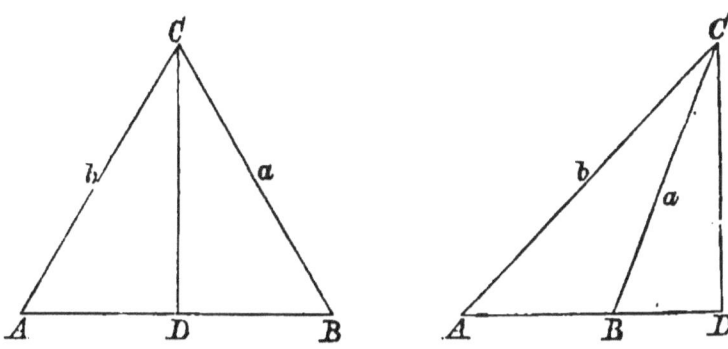

The area of a triangle is equal to half the rectangle contained by one of the sides and the perpendicular drawn to meet that side from the opposite angle.

Let ABC be the triangle, and as one of the angles A, B must be acute, let it be A. Draw a perpendicular from C to meet AB or AB produced in D.

Then, area of triangle $ABC = \frac{1}{2}.AB.CD$

$$= \frac{1}{2}.AB.AC.\sin A$$

$$= \frac{1}{2} cb.\sin A\,;$$

that is, the area of a triangle is equal to *half the product of two sides and the sine of the angle between them.*

Also, since $\sin A = \dfrac{2}{bc} \cdot \sqrt{s \cdot (s-a)(s-b)(s-c)}$, by Art. 184,

area of triangle $ABC = \dfrac{1}{2} cb \cdot \dfrac{2}{bc} \cdot \sqrt{s \cdot (s-a)(s-b)(s-c)}$

$$= \sqrt{s \cdot (s-a)(s-b)(s-c)},$$

which gives an expression for the area in terms of the sides.

For this expression the symbol used is S.

220. *To find the area of a regular polygon in terms of its side.*

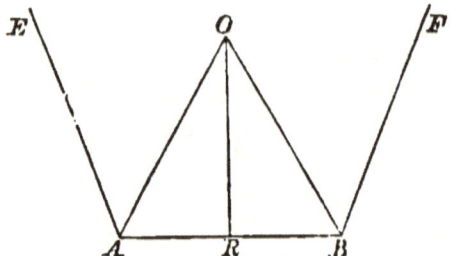

Let EA, AB, BF be three consecutive sides of a regular polygon of n sides and let each of them $= a$.

Bisect the angles EAB, ABF by the lines OA, OB meeting in O.

Draw OR at right angles to AB.

Now angle $AOR = \dfrac{AOB}{2}$,

and angle $AOB = \dfrac{2\pi}{n}$ (Eucl. I. 15, Cor.);

∴ angle $AOR = \dfrac{\pi}{n}$.

Hence area of polygon = n times area of triangle AOB

$$= n \cdot AR \cdot RO$$
$$= n \cdot AR \cdot AR \cdot \cot AOR$$
$$= n \cdot \frac{a}{2} \cdot \frac{a}{2} \cdot \cot \frac{\pi}{n}$$
$$= \frac{na^2}{4} \cdot \cot \frac{\pi}{n}.$$

221. *To find the radius of a circle described about a triangle in terms of the sides of the triangle.*

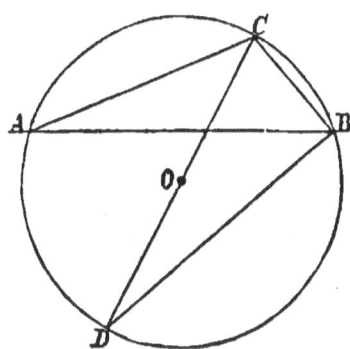

Let O be the centre of the circle described about the triangle ABC, and R its radius.

Through O draw the diameter CD and join BD.

Then CBD, being the angle in a semicircle, is a right angle.

And BDC = angle CAB in the same segment = A.

Now
$$\frac{CB}{CD} = \sin BDC,$$

that is,
$$\frac{a}{2R} = \sin A;$$

$$\therefore a = 2R \cdot \sin A;$$

$$\therefore R = \frac{a}{2 \sin A}.$$

But, by Art. 184, $\sin A = \dfrac{2}{bc} \cdot S$;

$$\therefore R = \frac{abc}{4S}.$$

Note. Since $\frac{a}{2R} = \sin A$, and similarly $\frac{b}{2R} = \sin B$, and $\frac{c}{2R} = \sin C$, we derive another proof of the Theorem

$$\frac{\sin A}{a} = \frac{\sin B}{b} = \frac{\sin C}{c}.$$

222. *To find the radius of a circle inscribed in a triangle in terms of the sides of a triangle.*

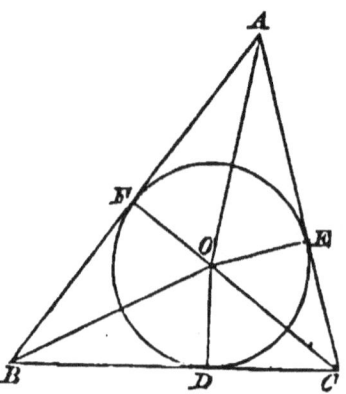

Let O be the centre of the inscribed circle, and r its radius.

Then $S = $ area of ABC

$\quad\quad = $ area of $BOC + $ area of $COA + $ area of AOB

$$= \frac{OD \cdot BC}{2} + \frac{OE \cdot AC}{2} + \frac{OF \cdot AB}{2}$$

$$= \frac{ra}{2} + \frac{rb}{2} + \frac{rc}{2}$$

$$= r \cdot \frac{a+b+c}{2}$$

$$= rs;$$

$$\therefore r = \frac{S}{s}.$$

POLYGONS AND CIRCLES.

223. *To find the radii of the circles escribed, that is which touch one of the sides of a triangle and the other sides produced.*

Let O be the centre of the escribed circle that touches the side BC and the other sides produced, and let the radius of this circle be r_1.

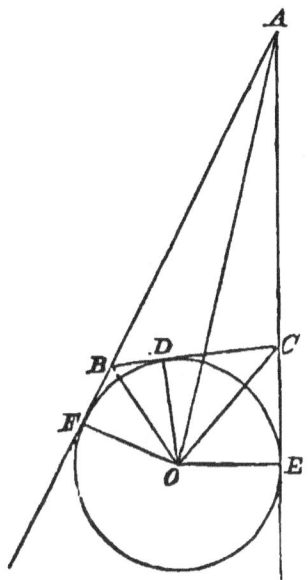

Then quadrilateral $ABOC =$ triangle $AOC +$ triangle AOB

and quadrilateral $ABOC =$ triangle $ABC +$ triangle BOC;

$$\therefore AOC + AOB = ABC + BOC,$$

$$\therefore \frac{AC \cdot OE}{2} + \frac{AB \cdot OF}{2} = S + \frac{BC \cdot OD}{2},$$

$$\therefore \frac{br_1}{2} + \frac{cr_1}{2} = S + \frac{ar}{2};$$

$$\therefore \frac{b+c-a}{2} \cdot r_1 = S;$$

$$\therefore (s-a) r_1 = S;$$

$$\therefore r_1 = \frac{S}{s-a}.$$

Similarly it may be shewn that if r_2, r_3 are the radii of the circles touching AC and AB respectively,

$$r_2 = \frac{S}{s-b},$$

$$r_3 = \frac{S}{s-c}.$$

224. *To find the area of a regular polygon inscribed in a circle.*

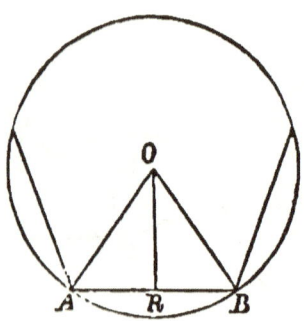

Let O be the centre of the circle, r the radius of the circle, AB a side of the polygon.

Join OA, OB.

Then area of polygon $= n$ times area of triangle AOB

$$= n \cdot \frac{1}{2} AO \cdot OB \cdot \sin AOB \quad \text{(Art. 219)}$$

$$= n \cdot \frac{1}{2} \cdot r \cdot r \cdot \sin \frac{2\pi}{n}$$

$$= \frac{nr^2}{2} \cdot \sin \frac{2\pi}{n}.$$

225. *To find the area of a regular polygon described about a circle.*

Let O be the centre of the circle, r the radius, AB a side of the circumscribing polygon.

Draw the radius OR at right angles to AB.

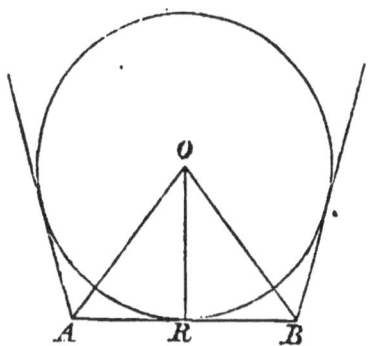

Then area of polygon $= n$ times area of triangle AOB

$$= n \cdot OR \cdot AR$$
$$= n \cdot OR \cdot OR \tan AOR$$
$$= n \cdot r \cdot r \cdot \tan \frac{\pi}{n}$$
$$= nr^2 \cdot \tan \frac{\pi}{n}.$$

226. *To find the area of a circle.*

Taking the figure and notation of the preceding Article, area of circumscribing polygon $= n$ times area of triangle AOB

$$= n \cdot \frac{1}{2} \cdot AB \cdot OR$$
$$= \frac{1}{2} OR \times n \cdot AB$$
$$= \frac{1}{2} OR \times \text{perimeter of polygon}.$$

Now if the number of sides of the polygon be indefinitely increased and the length of each side indefinitely diminished,

S. T.

the perimeter of the polygon coincides with the circumference of the circle, and the area of the polygon is the same as the area of the circle;

$$\therefore \text{ area of circle} = \tfrac{1}{2} OR \times \text{circumference of circle}$$

$$= \tfrac{1}{2} r \times 2\pi r$$

$$= \pi r^2.$$

227. *To find the area of a quadrilateral which can be inscribed in a circle in terms of its sides.*

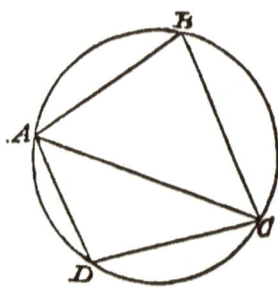

Let $ABCD$ be the quadrilateral. Join AC.

Let $AB = a$, $BC = b$, $CD = c$, $DA = d$.

Then, area of figure = area of $\triangle ABC$ + area of $\triangle ADC$

$$= \tfrac{1}{2} ab \cdot \sin B + \tfrac{1}{2} cd \cdot \sin D.$$

Now angles at B and D are supplementary (Eucl. III. 22);

$$\therefore \sin B = \sin D \text{ (Art. 101);}$$

$$\therefore \text{ area of figure} = \tfrac{1}{2}(ab + cd) \cdot \sin B.$$

We have now to express $\sin B$ in terms of the sides of the figure.

Now, in $\triangle ABC$, $AC^2 = a^2 + b^2 - 2ab \cdot \cos B$,

and, in $\triangle ADC$, $AC^2 = c^2 + d^2 - 2cd \cdot \cos D.$

Hence, observing that
$$\cos D = -\cos B \text{ (Art. 101)},$$
$$a^2 + b^2 - 2ab \cdot \cos B = c^2 + d^2 + 2cd \cdot \cos B;$$

$$\therefore \cos B = \frac{a^2 + b^2 - c^2 - d^2}{2(ab+cd)};$$

$$\therefore \sin^2 B = 1 - \frac{(a^2 + b^2 - c^2 - d^2)^2}{\{2(ab+cd)\}^2}$$

$$= \frac{(2ab + 2cd)^2 - (a^2 + b^2 - c^2 - d^2)^2}{4(ab+cd)^2};$$

$$\therefore \text{(area of figure)}^2 = \frac{1}{4} \cdot (ab+cd)^2 \cdot \sin^2 B$$

$$= \frac{1}{4} \cdot (ab+cd)^2 \cdot \frac{(2ab+2cd)^2 - (a^2+b^2-c^2-d^2)^2}{4(ab+cd)^2}$$

$$= \frac{1}{16} \cdot \{(2ab+2cd)^2 - (a^2+b^2-c^2-d^2)^2\}$$

$$= \frac{1}{16} \cdot \{(2ab+2cd+a^2+b^2-c^2-d^2)(2ab+2cd-a^2-b^2+c^2+d^2)\}$$

$$= \frac{1}{16} \cdot \{(a+b)^2 - (c-d)^2\} \cdot \{(c+d)^2 - (a-b)^2\}$$

$$= \frac{1}{16} \cdot \{(a+b+c-d)(a+b-c+d)(c+d+a-b)(c+d-a+b)\};$$

and if
$$s = \frac{a+b+c+d}{2},$$

$$\text{(area of figure)}^2 = \frac{1}{16} \cdot \{(2s-2d)(2s-2c)(2s-2b)(2s-2a)\}$$

$$= (s-d)(s-c)(s-b)(s-a);$$

$\therefore$ area of figure $= \sqrt{\{(s-a)(s-b)(s-c)(s-d)\}}$.

228. *On the Dip of the Horizon.*

Suppose the earth to be represented by the circle ABC, with centre O.

Let EB be a tangent from the eye of an observer, looking from a height AE, to the earth's surface at B, and let EAC be a straight line through the earth's centre.

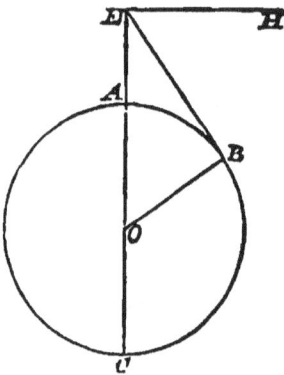

If we draw a horizontal line EH, the angle HEB is called "*The Dip of the Horizon.*"

Then, since EA is very small as compared with AO, and therefore the arc AB very small as compared with the circumference of the earth, $\angle AOB$ is a very small angle.

Hence at spots of small elevation the Dip of the Horizon, which is equal to $\angle AOB$, is very small.

The distance of the horizon at sea may be approximately found by the following rule:

Three times the height of the place of observation in feet is equal to twice the square of the distance seen in miles.

This rule may be proved thus:

Let AE be an object whose height in feet is f, $=\dfrac{f}{5280}$ miles,

EB a tangent to the earth's surface whose length in miles is m,

AC the diameter of the earth $= d = 8000$ miles nearly.

Then sq. on BE = rect. CE, EA (Eucl. III. 36);

$$\therefore m^2 = \left(d + \frac{f}{5280}\right)\frac{f}{5280}$$

$$= \frac{df}{5280} \text{ nearly}$$

$$= \frac{8000 f}{5280} \text{ nearly} = \frac{3f}{2} \text{ nearly.}$$

229. *To shew that if θ be the circular measure of a positive angle less than a right angle, $\sin \theta$, θ, and $\tan \theta$ are in ascending order of magnitude.*

Let Q be the centre of a circle, QE a radius cutting the chord PP' at right angles, TT' a tangent to the circle at E.

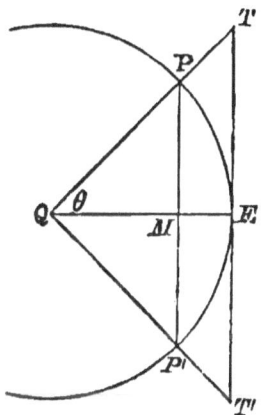

Let the circular measure of the angle EQP be θ.

Then $\qquad \sin \theta = \dfrac{PM}{QP},$

$\qquad\qquad\quad \theta = \dfrac{PE}{QP};$

$\qquad\qquad \tan \theta = \dfrac{TE}{QE} = \dfrac{TE}{QP}.$

Now assuming that PE is greater than PM but less than TE, PM, PE, TE are in ascending order of magnitude.

Therefore $\sin \theta$, θ, $\tan \theta$ are in ascending order of magnitude.

The assumption which we here make that PE is intermediate in magnitude between PM and TE requires some explanation.

Suppose PP' to be a side of a regular polygon of n sides inscribed in the circle.

Then TT' will be the side of a regular polygon of n sides described about the circle, and QE will bisect PP' and TT'.

Now the perimeter of the inscribed polygon is always *less* than the circumference of the circle, as we explained in Art. 10, and we might shew by a similar process that the perimeter of the circumscribed polygon is always *greater* than the circumference of the circle.

Now $PM =$ the $2n$th part of the inscribed polygon,

$TE = $ .... circumscribed ......

$PE = $ .... circumference;

$\therefore PE$ is in magnitude intermediate between PM and TE.

230. *To shew that when θ is indefinitely diminished,*

$$\frac{\theta}{\sin \theta} = 1.$$

Since $\sin \theta$, θ, $\tan \theta$ are in ascending order of magnitude,

$\sin \theta$, θ, $\dfrac{\sin \theta}{\cos \theta}$ are in ascending order of magnitude.

Divide each by $\sin \theta$, then

1, $\dfrac{\theta}{\sin \theta}$, $\dfrac{1}{\cos \theta}$ are in ascending order of magnitude;

$\therefore \dfrac{\theta}{\sin \theta}$ lies between 1 and $\dfrac{1}{\cos \theta}$.

Now when $\theta = 0$, $\cos \theta = 1$,

and therefore $\dfrac{1}{\cos \theta} = 1$;

therefore when $\theta = 0$,

$$\dfrac{\theta}{\sin \theta} = 1.$$

EXAMPLES.—LVI.

1. The angle included between two sides of a triangle whose lengths are 10 inches and 12 inches is 60°: find the area of the triangle.

2. Two sides of a triangle are 40 and 60 feet, and they contain an angle of 30°: find the area of the triangle.

3. What is the area of a triangle whose base is 4 feet, and altitude 1¼ yards?

4. What is the area of a triangle whose sides are 5, 6, 5 inches respectively?

5. If $a = 625$, $b = 505$, $c = 904$, what is the measure of the area of the triangle?

6. If $a = 409$, $b = 169$, $c = 510$, what is the measure of the area of the triangle?

7. If $a = 577$, $b = 73$, $c = 520$, what is the measure of the area of the triangle?

8. In a right-angled triangle area $= s \cdot (s - c)$, C being the right angle.

9. If $a = 52\cdot53$, $b = 48\cdot76$, $c = 44\cdot98$, $\log 146\cdot27 = 2\cdot1651553$,

   $\log 56\cdot31 = 1\cdot7505855$, $\log 48\cdot75 = 1\cdot6879746$,

   $\log 41\cdot21 = 1\cdot6150026$, $\log 2 = \cdot3010300$,

   $\log 1\cdot0169487 = \cdot0072990$, find the measure of area.

10. The sides of a triangle are in arithmetical progression, and its area is to that of an equilateral triangle of the same perimeter as 3 : 5. Shew that its largest angle is 120°.

11. In the rectangular sheet of paper $ABCD$, the angular point A is turned down so as to lie in the side CD, while the crease of the paper passes through the angular point B; show that the area of the part turned down is

$$\frac{1}{2} \cdot \frac{AB^2}{BC} \{AB - \sqrt{(AB^2 - BC^2)}\}.$$

12. Shew that the area of a triangle

$$= \frac{a^2 \cdot \sin B \cdot \sin C}{2 \sin (B+C)}.$$

13. In any triangle the area

$$= \sin \frac{A}{2} \cdot \sin \frac{B}{2} \cdot \sin \frac{C}{2} \left(\frac{a^2}{\sin A} + \frac{b^2}{\sin B} + \frac{c^2}{\sin C} \right).$$

14. If the radius of the inscribed circle be equal to half that of the circumscribed circle, the triangle is equilateral.

15. In any triangle

$$(b-c) \cos \frac{A}{2} = a \cdot \sin \frac{B-C}{2}.$$

16. If the points of contact of a circle inscribed in a triangle with the sides be joined, shew that the area of the triangle so formed

$$= \frac{2}{abc} s^{\frac{1}{2}} \{(s-a)(s-b)(s-c)\}^{\frac{3}{2}}.$$

17. The diagonals of a quadrilateral are in length a, b respectively, and intersect at an angle A. Shew that the area of the quadrilateral

$$= \frac{1}{2} ab \sin A.$$

18. The area of any triangle

$$= \frac{a^2 - b^2}{2} \cdot \frac{\sin A \cdot \sin B}{\sin (A-B)}.$$

19. In an isosceles right-angled triangle, shew that the radius of one of the equal escribed circles is equal to the radius of the circumscribed circle.

20. In any right-angled triangle, C being the right angle,
$$\cot(B-A) + \cot 2\left(A + \frac{C}{2}\right) = 0.$$

21. The area of any triangle
$$= \frac{2abc}{a+b+c} \cdot \cos\frac{A}{2} \cdot \cos\frac{B}{2} \cdot \cos\frac{C}{2}.$$

22. In any isosceles triangle, C being the vertical angle,
$$\text{area} \times 32 \cos^4\frac{A}{2} = \sin 2A\,(2a+c)^2.$$

23. The length of a perpendicular from A to BC
$$= \frac{b^2 \sin C + c^2 \sin B}{b+c}.$$

24. Taking the notation adopted in this Chapter, prove the following relations:

(1) $r = \dfrac{a}{\cot\dfrac{B}{2} + \cot\dfrac{C}{2}}.$

(2) $r = \dfrac{2R \cdot \sin A \cdot \sin\frac{1}{2}B \cdot \sin\frac{1}{2}C}{\cos\frac{1}{2}A}.$

(3) $r_1 = \dfrac{a}{\tan\dfrac{B}{2} + \tan\dfrac{C}{2}}.$

(4) $r_1 = 4R \cdot \sin\dfrac{A}{2} \cos\dfrac{B}{2} \cdot \cos\dfrac{C}{2}.$

(5) $r_1 + r_2 + r_3 = R(3 + \cos A + \cos B + \cos C).$

(6) $R + r = R(\cos A + \cos B + \cos C).$

25. Shew that the area of a regular polygon inscribed in a circle is a mean proportional between the areas of an inscribed and a circumscribed regular polygon of half the number of sides.

26. The distances between the centre of the inscribed and those of the escribed circles of a triangle ABC are

$$4R \cdot \sin\frac{A}{2}, \quad 4R\sin\frac{B}{2}, \quad 4R\sin\frac{C}{2},$$

R being the radius of the circumscribing circle.

27. The points at which the lines bisecting the angles A, B, C of a triangle cut the opposite sides are joined. Shew that the area of the triangle so formed bears to that of the triangle ABC the ratio

$$\frac{2\sin\frac{A}{2}\sin\frac{B}{2}\sin\frac{C}{2}}{\cos\frac{B-C}{2} \cdot \cos\frac{C-A}{2} \cdot \cos\frac{A-B}{2}}.$$

28. If r_1, r_2, r_3 be the radii of the escribed circles and s the semi-perimeter of the triangle, shew that

$$s^2 = r_1 r_2 + r_2 r_3 + r_3 r_1.$$

29. Prove that the lines drawn from the intersection of the perpendiculars to the centres of the escribed circles are each equal to twice the radius of the circumscribed circle.

30. Shew that the distances from the centre of the inscribed circle to the centres of the escribed circles are respectively equal to

$$\frac{a}{\cos\frac{A}{2}}, \quad \frac{b}{\cos\frac{B}{2}}, \quad \frac{c}{\cos\frac{C}{2}}.$$

31. r is the radius of a circle inscribed in a triangle ABC; shew that

$$a = r \cos \frac{A}{2} \operatorname{cosec} \frac{B}{2} \operatorname{cosec} \frac{C}{2}.$$

32. If R, r be the radii of the circles described about and inscribed in the triangle ABC, and s the semi-perimeter of the triangle, prove that

$$\tan \frac{A}{2} + \tan \frac{B}{2} + \tan \frac{C}{2} + \frac{s}{r} = 4R \left(\frac{1}{a} + \frac{1}{b} + \frac{1}{c} \right).$$

33. ABC is a triangle inscribed in a circle, and a point P is taken on the arc BC: shew that

$$PA \cdot \sin A = PB \cdot \sin B + PC \cdot \sin C.$$

34. Given the distances d_1, d_2, d_3 from the angles of the point at which the sides of a plane triangle subtend equal angles, find the sides and area.

35. If the lengths of three lines drawn from any point within a square to three of its angular points be a, b, c, find a side of the square.

36. The areas of all triangles described about the same circle are as their perimeters.

37. If a, b, c be the sides of a triangle and α, β, γ the perpendiculars upon them from the opposite angles, shew that

$$\frac{a^2}{\beta\gamma} + \frac{\beta^2}{\alpha\gamma} + \frac{\gamma^2}{\alpha\beta} = \frac{bc}{a^2} + \frac{ac}{b^2} + \frac{ab}{c^2}.$$

38. A person standing on the sea-shore can just see the top of a mountain whose height he knows to be 1284·80 yards. After ascending vertically to the height of 3 miles in a balloon, he observes the angle of depression of the mountain's summit to be $2° . 15'$. Find the earth's radius.

Given $\log 3 = \cdot 4771213$, $\cot 2° . 15' = 11 \cdot 4057168$,

$\log \cdot 73 = \overline{1} \cdot 863229$, $\log 7986 \cdot 4 = 3 \cdot 9023533$,

$\log 76 \cdot 3551 = 1 \cdot 8828381$.

39. If an equilateral triangle have its angular points in three parallel straight lines of which the middle one is distant from the outside ones by a and b, shew that its side

$$= 2\sqrt{\left(\frac{a^2 + ab + b^2}{3}\right)}.$$

40. In a triangle ABC, $AC = 2BC$. If CD, CE respectively bisect the angle C and the exterior angle formed by producing AC, prove that the triangles CBD, ACD, ABC, CDE have their areas as $1 : 2 : 3 : 4$.

41. If R, r be the radii of the circles described about and in the triangle ABC, the area of the triangle

$$= Rr (\sin A + \sin B + \sin C).$$

42. In the ambiguous case prove that the circles circumscribing the triangles will have the same radius. If the data be $a = 605$, $b = 564$, $B = 50° . 15'$, find the radius of the circumscribing circle.

43. The angles of a quadrilateral inscribed in a circle taken in order, when multiplied by 1, 2, 2, 3, respectively, are in Arithmetical Progression; find their values.

44. If from any point P in a circle lines are drawn to the extremities A, B, and to the point of contact C of a side of the circumscribing square, shew that

$$\frac{(1 + \cot PCA)^2}{\cot PBA} = \frac{(1 + \cot PCB)^2}{\cot PAB}.$$

45. If R, r, r_a, r_b, r_c are the radii of the circumscribed, inscribed and escribed circles respectively of a triangle, and C one of the angles, then $4R \cos C = r + r_a + r_b - r_c$.

46. If r be the radius of the circle inscribed between the base of a right-angled triangle and the other two sides produced, and r' the radius of the circle inscribed between the altitude of the triangle and the other two sides produced, shew that the area of the triangle $= r . r'$.

47. From the top of the peak of Teneriffe the dip of the horizon is found to be $1°.58'.10''$. If the radius of the earth be 4000 miles, what is the height of the mountain?

48. What is the dip of the horizon from the top of a mountain $1\frac{1}{4}$ miles high, the radius of the earth being 4000 miles?

49. A lamp on the top of a pole 32 feet high is just seen by a man 6 feet in height, at a distance of 10 miles; find the earth's radius.

50. A ship, of which the height from the water to the summit of the top-mast is 90 feet, is sailing directly towards an observer at the rate of 10 miles an hour. From the time of its first appearance in the offing till its arrival at the station of the observer is 1 hour 12 minutes. Find approximately the earth's radius.

51. If the diameter of the earth be 7912 miles, what is the dip of the sea-horizon as seen from a mountain 3 miles in height?

52. The angle subtended at the sun by the earth's radius being $8''\cdot868$ and the earth's radius being 4000 miles, shew that the distance of the sun from the earth is approximately 93000000 miles.

53. If the distance of the moon from the earth be 241118 miles, shew that if the earth's radius is 4000 miles it subtends an angle of $57'.1''\cdot48$ at the moon.

54. The tops of two vertical rods on the earth's surface, each of which is 10 feet high, cease to be visible from each other when 8 miles distant. Prove that the earth's radius is nearly 4224 miles.

55. What is the limit of deviation in order that a circular target of 4 feet diameter may be struck at a distance of 200 yards?

56. Explain how it is that a shilling can be placed before the eye so as to hide the moon.

ANSWERS.

I. (Page 1.)

(1) 54.   (2) 26.   (3) 4 inches.   (4) 5 inches.

(5) 3 inches.   (6) 5 inches.   (7) $\dfrac{b}{3a}$.   (8) 7½ inches.

(9) 1 inch and 3 inches.   (10) 13 : 504.   (11) $\dfrac{cn}{3m}$.

II. (Page 3.)

(1) 45 yds.   (2) 10 ft.   (3) 255 yds.   (4) 360·5 ...

(5) 163·25 yds. nearly.   (6) 12 ft., 16 ft.   (8) 63 ft., 45 ft.

(9) $6\sqrt{2}$ ft.   (10) $5\sqrt{2}$ inches.   (11) $625\sqrt{2}$ ft.

(12) $\dfrac{13\sqrt{3}}{2}$.   (13) $10\sqrt{3}$.   (14) 12 inches.

(15) 38 inches.   (16) 634 ft.

III. (Page 9.)

(1) $15\dfrac{5}{7}$ ft.   (2) 86·30681 ft.   (3) 25·714285 miles.

(4) $7954\dfrac{6}{11}$ miles.   (5) $2775834\dfrac{2}{7}$ miles.   (6) $1089\dfrac{17}{22}$ miles.

(7) 6 ft. $6\dfrac{4}{7}$ in.   (8) $47\dfrac{1}{7}$ ft.   (9) $\dfrac{525\sqrt{2}}{22}$ ft.

(10) $\dfrac{350\sqrt{2}}{11}$ ft.   (11) $12\dfrac{6}{7}$ miles.   (12) $22\dfrac{1}{2}$ miles.

IV. (Page 12.)

(1) 24·2680̇5̇. (2) 37·04527̇. (3) 175·0038̇.
(4) ·091̇. (5) 375·06̇. (6) 78·201.

V. (Page 13.)

(1) 25·1425. (2) 38·0415. (3) 214·0307.
(4) ·150745. (5) 425·130554. (6) 2·020222.

VI. (Page 19.)

(1) 30^g. 29'. 19"·75... (2) 174^g. 52'. 12"·96... (3) 45'.
(4) 21^g. 11'. 66"·6̇. (5) 159^g. 5'. 55"·5̇. (6) 31^g. 11'. 11"·1̇.
(7) 11^g. 58'. 88"·8. (8) 30^g. 70'. 74"·07̇4̇.
(9) 333^g. 62'. 90"·1̇234567890̇. (10) 469^g. 2'. 53"·0̇86419753̇.

VII. (Page 20.)

(1) 17⁰. 30'. 48"·78. (2) 111⁰. 38'. 44"'·592.
(3) 26⁰. 46'. 30". (4) 13⁰. 30'. 4"·86. (5) 138⁰. 39'. 54"·576.
(6) 38⁰. 42'. (7) 34⁰. 50'. 26"·9772. (8) 45⁰. 41'. 32"·9532.
(9) 153⁰. 34'. 9"·948. (10) 201⁰. 43'. 29"·9388.

VIII. (Page 21.)

(1) $\frac{\pi}{3}$. (2) $\frac{\pi}{8}$. (3) $\frac{\pi}{16}$. (4) $\frac{3\pi}{2}$.

(5) $\frac{7\pi}{4}$. (6) $\frac{1453\pi}{10800}$. (7) $\frac{143\pi}{270}$. (8) $\frac{2719\pi}{40500}$.

(9) $\frac{\pi}{3}$. (10) $\frac{\pi}{2}, \frac{\pi}{4}, \frac{\pi}{4}$.

IX. (Page 22.)

(1) 90°. (2) 60°. (3) 45°. (4) 30°. (5) 120°.

(6) $\frac{90}{\pi}$ degrees. (7) $\frac{60}{\pi}$ degrees. (8) $\frac{45}{\pi}$ degrees.

(9) $\frac{30}{\pi}$ degrees. (10) $\frac{120}{\pi}$ degrees.

X. (Page 22.)

(1) $\frac{\pi}{4}$. (2) $\frac{\pi}{8}$. (3) $\frac{\pi}{32}$. (4) $\frac{5\pi}{4}$. (5) $\frac{5\pi}{2}$.

(6) $\cdot 0652525\pi$. (7) $\cdot 120751075\pi$. (8) $\cdot 6250065\pi$.

(9) $\cdot 00015\pi$. (10) $\cdot 0000025\pi$.

XI. (Page 22.)

(1) $66\cdot\dot{6}$ grades. (2) 40^g. (3) $33\cdot\dot{3}$ grades.

(4) $133\cdot\dot{3}$ grades. (5) 120^g. (6) $\frac{200}{3\pi}$ grades.

(7) $\frac{40}{\pi}$ grades. (8) $\frac{25}{\pi}$ grades. (9) $\frac{120}{\pi}$ grades.

(10) $\frac{460}{\pi}$ grades.

XII. (Page 23.)

1. $4\cdot 5$. 2. $4\cdot 25$ degrees. 3. $3\frac{1^\circ}{5}, \frac{5}{8}, \frac{6}{6}$

4. $3\frac{1^\circ}{2}, \frac{6}{7}, \frac{7}{6}$. 5. $\frac{14}{15}$. 6. $70 : 67$.

8. $90°, 60°, 30°$; $100^g, 66\frac{2^g}{3}, 33\frac{1^g}{3}$. 10. $35°.6'.38''\cdot 88$.

ANSWERS. 209

11. $\dfrac{5000m}{27}$. 12. $\dfrac{1}{81}$. 13. $1\cdot 9^0$. 16. $20^0, 60^0, 100^0$.

17. $3\cdot 14159$. 18. $36^0, 54^0, 90^0$; $40^g, 60^g, 100^g$; $\dfrac{\pi}{5}, \dfrac{3\pi}{10}, \dfrac{\pi}{2}$.

19. $173\dfrac{1^0}{3}$. 20. $125\cdot 925$ grades. 21. $\dfrac{800}{3\pi}$ grades.

22. $\dfrac{1600\pi - 3600}{9\pi}$ grades. 23. $54^0. 46'. 54''\cdot 5$. 24. $\cdot 1775$.

25. 20π degrees. 26. $\dfrac{1}{144000}$th part. 27. $\dfrac{1}{360}, \dfrac{1}{400}, \dfrac{1}{2\pi}$.

28. $\dfrac{133\pi}{6}$ miles. 29. $67\dfrac{1^0}{2}$, $180^0, 45\pi^0, (n\cdot 180+15)^0$;

$\dfrac{3\pi}{8}, \pi, \left(\dfrac{\pi}{2}\right)^2, n\pi+\dfrac{\pi}{12}$. 30. $\dfrac{\pi}{12}$. 31. $120^0, 108^0$.

32. $120^g, 150^g$. 33. $\dfrac{\pi}{3}, \dfrac{2\pi}{3}$. 34. $\pi - \dfrac{2\pi}{n}$.

35. π feet. 36. 8 and 4.

XIII. (Page 36.)

(1) $\dfrac{BD}{AB}, \dfrac{AD}{AB}, \dfrac{BD}{AD}; \dfrac{AD}{AB}, \dfrac{BD}{AD}, \dfrac{AB}{AD}; \dfrac{BD}{BC}, \dfrac{CD}{BC}, \dfrac{DB}{DC}$.

XIV. (Page 49.)

(1) $\dfrac{1}{2\sqrt{2}}$. (2) $\sqrt{\dfrac{2}{3}}$. (3) $\dfrac{\sqrt{3}}{2}$. (4) $\sqrt{3}$.

(5) $3\sqrt{2}+\sqrt{3}$.

XV. (Page 50.)

(1) $346\cdot 4101600$ feet. (2) $85\cdot 82765$ feet. (3) 60^0. (4) $173\cdot 2$ feet.

(5) $424\cdot 35$ feet from foot of rock. (6) $1\cdot 366$ miles.

(7) 42·25 ft. above the tower. (8) 72 feet. (9) $50\sqrt{3}$ feet
(10) 25°. (11) 139·25 feet. (12) 125 yards.
(13) $92\frac{4}{13}$ feet. (14) $342\frac{6}{7}$ feet. (15) 8·053 feet.

XVII. (Page 60.)

(1) $\sin A = \sqrt{1-\cos^2 A}$, $\tan A = \dfrac{\sqrt{1-\cos^2 A}}{\cos A}$, $\sec A = \dfrac{1}{\cos A}$

$\operatorname{cosec} A = \dfrac{1}{\sqrt{1-\cos^2 A}}$, $\cot A = \dfrac{\cos A}{\sqrt{1-\cos^2 A}}$.

(2) $\sin A = \dfrac{1}{\operatorname{cosec} A}$, $\cos A = \dfrac{\sqrt{\operatorname{cosec}^2 A - 1}}{\operatorname{cosec} A}$,

$\tan A = \dfrac{1}{\sqrt{\operatorname{cosec}^2 A - 1}}$, $\sec A = \dfrac{\operatorname{cosec} A}{\sqrt{\operatorname{cosec}^2 A - 1}}$,

$\cot A = \sqrt{\operatorname{cosec}^2 A - 1}$.

(3) $\sin A = \dfrac{\sqrt{\sec^2 A - 1}}{\sec A}$, $\cos A = \dfrac{1}{\sec A}$, $\tan A = \sqrt{\sec^2 A - 1}$

$\operatorname{cosec} A = \dfrac{\sec A}{\sqrt{\sec^2 A - 1}}$, $\cot A = \dfrac{1}{\sqrt{\sec^2 A - 1}}$.

(4) $\sin A = \dfrac{1}{\sqrt{1+\cot^2 A}}$, $\cos A = \dfrac{\cot A}{\sqrt{1+\cot^2 A}}$, $\tan A = \dfrac{1}{\cot A}$

$\operatorname{cosec} A = \sqrt{1+\cot^2 A}$, $\sec A = \dfrac{\sqrt{1+\cot^2 A}}{\cot A}$.

XVIII. (Page 61.)

(1) $\dfrac{\sqrt{5}}{3}$, $\dfrac{2}{\sqrt{5}}$. (2) $\dfrac{3}{5}$, $\dfrac{3}{4}$. (3) $\dfrac{\sqrt{7}}{4}$, $\dfrac{3}{\sqrt{7}}$.

(4) $\sqrt{\dfrac{2}{3}}$, $\dfrac{1}{\sqrt{2}}$. (5) $\dfrac{\sqrt{(a^4+b^4)}}{a^2}$, $\dfrac{\sqrt{(a^4+b^4)}}{b^2}$.

(6) $\dfrac{\sqrt{(b^2-a^2)}}{a}$, $\dfrac{b}{\sqrt{(b^2-a^2)}}$. (7) $\dfrac{a}{\sqrt{(1-a^2)}}$, $\dfrac{1}{\sqrt{(1-a^2)}}$.

(8) $\dfrac{\sqrt{(1-b^2)}}{b}$, $\dfrac{1}{\sqrt{(1-b^2)}}$. (9) $\dfrac{4}{5}$, $\dfrac{4}{3}$.

(10) $\dfrac{5}{2\sqrt{14}}$, $\dfrac{9}{2\sqrt{14}}$. (11) $\dfrac{\sqrt{403}}{22}$, $\dfrac{\sqrt{403}}{9}$.

(12) $\dfrac{\sqrt{61}}{31}$, $\dfrac{\sqrt{61}}{30}$. (13) $\dfrac{20}{101}$, $\dfrac{20}{99}$.

(14) $\dfrac{99}{101}$, $\dfrac{99}{20}$. (15) $\dfrac{5}{13}$, $\dfrac{13}{12}$.

XX. (Page 65.)

1. (1) $65^0. 45'. 18''$. (2) $46^0. 57'. 3''$. (3) $25^0. 59'. 46''$.
   (4) $7^0. 55'. 45''$. (5) $-(35^0. 15'. 42'')$. (6) $-(88^0. 27'. 34'')$.
   (7) -105^0. (8) -164^0. (9) 115^0. (10) 335^0.

2. (1) $67^g. 76'. 76''$. (2) $4^g. 96'. 25''$. (3) $53^g. 99'. 16''$.
   (4) $97^g. 94'. 96''$. (5) $-(35^g. 2'. 5'')$. (6) $-(69^g. 0'. 3'')$.
   (7) -143^g. (8) -257^g. (9) 135^g. (10) 345^g.

3. (1) $\dfrac{\pi}{4}$. (2) $\dfrac{\pi}{6}$. (3) $-\dfrac{\pi}{10}$. (4) $\dfrac{3\pi}{4}$. (5) $\dfrac{5\pi}{4}$.

XXI. (Page 68.)

1. (1) $145^0. 47'. 11''$. (2) $47^0. 35'. 13''$. (3) $33^0. 59'. 19''$.
   (4) $151^0. 44'. 56''$. (5) $1''$. (6) $79^0. 10'. 7''$.
   (7) -65^0. (8) $-(257^0. 3'. 4'')$. (9) 229^0. (10) 535^0.

2. (1) $67^g. 67'. 58''$. (2) $4^g. 97'. 43''$. (3) $196^g. 2'. 2''$.
   (4) $134^g. 87'. 92''$. (5) $45^g. 96'. 94''$. (6) $25^g. 99'. 96''$.
   (7) -75^g. (8) $-(327^g. 2'. 14'')$. (9) 235^g. (10) 525^g.

3. (1) $\dfrac{\pi}{2}$. (2) $\dfrac{2\pi}{3}$. (3) $\dfrac{\pi}{5}$. (4) $\dfrac{5\pi}{4}$. (5) $\dfrac{7\pi}{4}$.

4. π.

XXIII. (Page 72.)

(1) $\dfrac{\sqrt{3}}{2}$. (2) $-\dfrac{1}{2}$. (3) $\dfrac{1}{\sqrt{2}}$. (4) $-\dfrac{1}{\sqrt{2}}$.

(5) $\dfrac{1}{2}$. (6) $-\dfrac{\sqrt{3}}{2}$. (7) $-\dfrac{1}{\sqrt{2}}$. (8) $-\dfrac{\sqrt{3}}{2}$.

(9) $-\sqrt{3}$. (10) $-\dfrac{2}{\sqrt{3}}$. (11) $\sqrt{2}$. (12) $-\sqrt{3}$.

XXIV. (Page 75.)

(1) $-45°$. (2) $45°$. (3) $0°$. (4) $90°$.
(5) $0°$ or $60°$. (6) $30°$. (7) $30°$. (8) $45°$.
(9) $30°$. (10) $60°$ or $30°$. (11) $30°$ or $60°$. (12) $30°$ or $60°$.
(13) $45°$. (14) $45°$. (15) $30°$. (16) $45°$.
(17) $135°$. (18) $45°$. (19) $30°$ or $90°$. (20) $45°$.

XXV. (Page 81.)

(1) $\dfrac{\sqrt{3}}{2}$. (2) $-\dfrac{1}{2}$. (3) $\dfrac{1}{\sqrt{2}}$. (4) $-\dfrac{1}{\sqrt{2}}$.

(5) $\dfrac{1}{2}$. (6) $-\dfrac{\sqrt{3}}{2}$. (7) $-\dfrac{1}{\sqrt{2}}$. (8) $-\dfrac{\sqrt{3}}{2}$.

(9) $-\sqrt{3}$. (10) $-\dfrac{2}{\sqrt{3}}$. (11) $\sqrt{2}$. (12) $-\sqrt{3}$.

(13) $\dfrac{1}{2}$. (14) $\dfrac{2}{\sqrt{3}}$. (15) 1. (16) $\dfrac{\sqrt{3}}{2}$.

(17) $\dfrac{1}{\sqrt{2}}$. (18) $\dfrac{\sqrt{3}}{2}$. (19) 0. (20) 1.

(21) -2. (22) $\dfrac{1}{\sqrt{3}}$. (23) 1. (24) $-\dfrac{2}{\sqrt{3}}$.

(25) $\dfrac{\sqrt{3}}{2}$. (26) 1. (27) $-\sqrt{2}$. (28) -1.

(29) 2. (30) $-\dfrac{1}{2}$.

XXVI. (Page 82.)

(1) $n\pi + (-1)^n \cdot \frac{\pi}{2}$. (2) $2n\pi$. (3) $n\pi + (-1)^n \cdot \frac{\pi}{4}$.

(4) $n\pi + \frac{\pi}{3}$. (5) $n\pi + (-1)^n \frac{\pi}{6}$. (6) $n\pi$ or $2n\pi \pm \frac{\pi}{3}$.

(7) $n\pi + (-1)^n \cdot \frac{\pi}{4}$. (8) $2n\pi \pm \frac{\pi}{4}$ or $2n\pi \pm \frac{3\pi}{4}$.

(9) $n\pi + \frac{\pi}{4}$. (10) $2n\pi \pm \frac{\pi}{3}$.

XXVIII. (Page 88.)

(5) $\frac{\sqrt{5} + 4\sqrt{2}}{9}$. (6) $\frac{2\sqrt{7} - 3\sqrt{21}}{20}$.

(7) $\frac{\sqrt{3}-1}{2\sqrt{2}}$. (8) $\frac{\sqrt{3} + \sqrt{899}}{60}$.

XXX. (Page 89.)

(1) 45°. (2) 0°. (3) 105°. (4) 60° or 30° or -30°.
(5) 45°. (6) 60°.

XXXII. (Page 93.)

(1) $2 \cos \frac{1}{2}\left(a + \frac{\pi}{2} - \beta\right) \sin \frac{1}{2}\left(a - \frac{\pi}{2} + \beta\right)$.

(2) $\sqrt{2} \cdot \sin\left(\frac{\pi}{4} + a\right)$.

(3) $2 \sin \frac{\pi}{4} \cdot \cos\left(a - \frac{\pi}{4}\right)$.

(4) $2 \cos \frac{\pi}{4} \sin\left(a - \frac{\pi}{4}\right)$. (5) $2 \sin 20^\circ \cdot \cos 10^\circ$.

(6) $2 \cos 15^\circ \cdot \sin 5^\circ$. (7) $2 \sin \frac{7\pi}{24} \cos \frac{\pi}{24}$.

(8) $2 \cos \frac{19\pi}{60} \cdot \sin \frac{\pi}{60}$.

XXXV. (Page 105.)

2.
(1) $\theta = 45°$ or $-15°$. (2) $\theta = 30°$ or $45°$. (3) $x = 0°$ or $7\frac{1}{2}°$.
(4) $\theta = 15°$ or $30°$. (5) $A = 30°$. (6) $\theta = 0°$ or $7\frac{1}{2}°$.
(7) $\theta = 15°$ or $30°$. (8) $a = 0°, 30°$. (9) $\theta = 18°$ or $234°$.
(10) $a = 0°$ or $15°$ or $60°$. (11) $\theta = \dfrac{\pi}{6}$. (12) $\theta = 0°$ or $30°$.

XXXVI. (Page 106.)

(1) $\frac{1}{4}\sqrt{(10-2\sqrt{5})}$. (2) $\frac{1}{4}(1+\sqrt{5})$. (3) $\frac{1}{4}(1+\sqrt{5})$.

(4) $\frac{1}{4}\sqrt{(10-2\sqrt{5})}$. (5) $\frac{1}{4}\sqrt{(10+2\sqrt{5})}$.

(6) $\dfrac{\sqrt{(10+2\sqrt{5})}}{\sqrt{5}-1}$. (7) 1. (8) 0.

XXXVII. (Page 110.)

1. $\cos\dfrac{A}{2} + \sin\dfrac{A}{2} = +\sqrt{1+\sin A}$;

$\cos\dfrac{A}{2} - \sin\dfrac{A}{2} = +\sqrt{1-\sin A}$.

2. $\cos\dfrac{A}{2} + \sin\dfrac{A}{2} = -\sqrt{1+\sin A}$;

$\cos\dfrac{A}{2} - \sin\dfrac{A}{2} = -\sqrt{1-\sin A}$.

3. $\cos 189° = -\dfrac{1}{4}\left\{\sqrt{5-\sqrt{5}} + \sqrt{3+\sqrt{5}}\right\}$;

$\sin 189° = \dfrac{1}{4}\left\{\sqrt{5-\sqrt{5}} - \sqrt{3+\sqrt{5}}\right\}$.

4. $\dfrac{2-\sqrt{2}}{2\sqrt{3}}$. (5) $-\dfrac{\sqrt{2+\sqrt{2}}}{2}$.

XXXIX. (Page 120.)

(1) $\bar{1}\cdot 2187180$. (2) $\bar{7}\cdot 7074922$. (3) $2\cdot 4036784$.

(4) $4\cdot 740378$. (5) $2\cdot 924059$. (6) $\bar{3}\cdot 724833$.

(7) $\bar{5}\cdot 3790163$. (8) $\overline{40}\cdot 578098$. (9) $\overline{62}\cdot 9905319$.

(10) $\bar{2}\cdot 1241803$. (11) $\bar{3}\cdot 738827$. (12) $\bar{1}\cdot 61514132$.

XL. (Page 123.)

(1) $2\cdot 1072100$; $2\cdot 0969100$; $3\cdot 3979400$.

(2) $1\cdot 6989700$; $\bar{3}\cdot 6989700$; $2\cdot 2922560$.

(3) $\cdot 7781513$; $1\cdot 4313639$; $1\cdot 7323939$; $2\cdot 7604226$.

(4) $1\cdot 7781513$; $\bar{2}\cdot 4771213$; $\cdot 0211893$; $\bar{5}\cdot 6354839$.

(5) $\bar{4}\cdot 8750613$; $1\cdot 4983105$.

(6) $\cdot 3010300$; $\bar{2}\cdot 8061800$; $\cdot 2916000$.

(7) $\cdot 6989700$; $\bar{1}\cdot 0969100$; $3\cdot 3910734$.

(8) $-2, 0, 2 : 1, 0, -1$.

(9) (1) 3. (2) 2.   (10) $x = \dfrac{9}{2}, y = \dfrac{3}{2}$.

(11) (a) $\cdot 3010300$; $1\cdot 3979400$; $1\cdot 9201233$; $\bar{1}\cdot 9979588$.
(b) 103.

(12) (a) $\cdot 6989700$; $\cdot 6020600$; $1\cdot 7118072$; $\bar{1}\cdot 9880618$.
(b) 8.

(13) $3\cdot 8821260$; $1\cdot 4093694$; $\bar{3}\cdot 7455326$.

(14) (1) $x = \dfrac{1}{6}$.   (2) $x = 2$.   (3) $x = \dfrac{\log m}{\log a + \log b}$.

(4) $x = \dfrac{\log c}{m \log a + 2 \log b}$.

(5) $x = \dfrac{4 \log b + \log c}{2 \log c + \log b - 3 \log a}$.

(6) $x = \dfrac{\log c}{\log a + m \log b + 3 \log c}$.

XLI. (Page 127.)

(1) 4·7201799. (2) 2·477736. (3) 1·5054974.
(4) 2·3740165. (5) 1·8293173. (6) $\bar{3}$·8653132.
(7) $\bar{6}$·8190943. (8) 3·5324716. (9) 5·5921478.
(10) ·4119438.

XLII. (Page 129.)

(1) 12954·8. (2) 4624·51. (3) 345·7291.
(4) 393756·9. (5) 3715·9523. (6) ·009646153.
(7) ·00000025725982. (8) 601·9541.
(9) 1090·5286. (10) 262·01818.

XLIII. (Page 132.)

(1) ·6724242. (2) ·9523159. (3) ·8150856.
(4) ·999000. (5) ·6850417. (6) ·7521403.
(7) ·0240028. (8) 1·4225190. (9) ·9230768.
(10) ·8270272.

XLIV. (Page 135.)

(1) 48°. 46′. 34″. (2) 2°. 33′. 45″· (3) 43°. 14′. 8″·18.
(4) 32°. 31′. 13″·5. (5) 24°. 11′. 22″·2. (6) 82°. 22′. 12″·8.
(7) 53°. 7′. 48″·4. (8) 25°. 3′. 27″·2. (9) 73°. 44′. 23″·2.
(10) 77°. 19′. 10″·5.

XLV. (Page 138.)

(1) 9·9163319. (2) 9·6912280. (3) 9·8996023.
(4) 9·9091749. (5) 9·7203429. (6) 8·9610068.
(7) 11·1975684. (8) 9·8027687. (9) 9·9745378.
(10) 8·2814754.

ANSWERS.   217

XLVI. (Page 140.)

(1) $14°.24'.35''$.   (2) $54°.13'.19''$.   (3) $71°.40'.18''$.

(4) $29°.25'.2''$.   (5) $30°.50'.27'''·6$.   (6) $86°.32'.24'''·5$.

(7) $24°.8'.45''$.   (8) $11°.39'.52''$.   (9) $46°.23'.11''$.

(10) $29°.54'.29'''·7$.

XLIX. (Page 157.)

(1) $a=4,\ A=53°.7'.48''·4,\ B=36°.52'.11'''·6$.

(2) $a=8,\ A=28°.4'.20'''·9,\ B=61°.55'.39'''·1$.

(3) $a=20,\ A=43°.36'.10'''·1,\ B=46°.23'.49'''·9$.

(4) $a=24,\ A=73°.44'.23'''·3,\ B=16°.15'.36'''·7$.

(5) $a=56,\ A=59°.29'.23'''·2,\ B=30°.30'.36'''·8$.

(6) $a=12,\ b=5,\ B=22°.37'.11'''·5$.

(7) $a=40,\ b=9,\ B=12°.40'.49''·4$.

(8) $a=48,\ b=55,\ A=41°.6'.43'''·5$.

(9) $a=39,\ b=80,\ A=25°.59'.21''·2$.

(10) $b=9,\ c=41,\ B=12°.40'.49''·4$.

L. (Page 159.)

(1) $b=153,\ A=34°.12'.19''·6,\ B=55°.47'.40'''·4$.

(2) $b=297,\ A=45°.40'.2'''·3,\ B=44°.19'.57'''·7$.

(3) $b=41,\ A=87°.12'.20''·3,\ B=2°.47'.39'''·7$.

(4) $b=527,\ A=32°.31'.13'''·5,\ B=57°.28'.46'''·5$.

(5) $b=141,\ A=82°.41'.44'',\ B=7°.18'.16''$.

(6) $a=748,\ A=75°.23'.18'''·5,\ B=14°.36'.41'''·5$.

ANSWERS.

(7) $a=736$, $A=69^0.38'.56'''\cdot3$, $B=20.21'.3''\cdot7$.

(8) $a=200$, $A=18^0.10'.50''$, $B=71^0.49'.10''$.

(9) $c=565$, $A=29^0.14'.30'''3$, $B=60^0.45'.29'''7$.

(10) $c=565$, $A=44^0.29'.53''$, $B=45^0.30'.7''$.

LI. (Page 161.)

(1) 231·835 feet. (2) 93·97 feet.

(3) 36·6...feet; 70·7...feet; 100 feet. (4) 196 feet nearly.

(5) 460 yds. nearly. (6) $63^0.26'.6''$. (7) 88 yds. nearly.

(8) $33^0.23'.55'''7$. (9) $39^0.5'.47'''9$. (10) 104·93 feet

(11) 45 feet. (12) 150 feet.

LII. (Page 174.)

1. (1) $67^0.22'.48''\cdot5$. (2) $43^0.36'.10'''1$.
   (3) $112^0.37'.11''\cdot5$. (4) $29^0.51'.46''\cdot1$.

2. $A=49^0.7'.10''$, $C=87^0.44'.50''$.

3. $b=79·063$. 4. $b=219·37$.

5. $57^0.14'.21''$ or $122^0.45'.39''$.

6. No, for $B=90^0$. 7. $\cos A = \frac{1}{2}$. 9. $45^0, 60^0, 75^0$.

11. $69^0.10'.10''$ and $46^0.37'.50''$. 12. $55^0.46'.16''$.

13. $A=116^0.33'.54''$, $B=26^0.33'.54''$.

LIII. (Page 176.)

(1) $c=5$, $A=53^0.7'.48'''4$, $B=36^0.52.11''\cdot6$.

(2) $a=48$, $A=41^0.6'.43''\cdot5$, $B=45^0.53'.16'''5$.

ANSWERS.   219

(3) $c=353$, $A=50^0.24'.8''·1$, $B=39^0.35'.51''·9$.

(4) $a=40$, $A=5^0.43'.29''·3$, $B=84^0.16'.30''·7$.

(5) $a=84$, $b=437$, $B=79^0.7'.9''·6$.

(6) $a=460$, $b=429$, $B=43^0.0'.10''·3$.

(7) $a=280$, $b=351$, $A=38^0.34'.48''·3$.

(8) $a=180$, $b=299$, $A=31^0.2'.53''·6$.

(9) $b=231$, $c=569$, $B=23^0.57'.8''$.

(10) $a=480$, $c=481$, $B=3^0.41'.43''$.

LIV.   (Page 177.)

(1) $A=31^0.53'.26''·8$, $B=8^0.10'.16''·4$, $C=139^0.56'.16''·8$.

(2) $A=84^0.32'.50''·5$, $B=25^0.36'.30''·7$, $C=69^0.50'.38''·8$.

(3) $A=76^0.18'.52''$, $B=35^0.18'.0''·9$, $C=68^0.23'7''·1$.

(4) $A=62^0.51'.32''·9$, $B=44^0.29'.53''$, $C=72^0.38'.34''·1$.

(5) $A=150^0.8'.14''$, $B=17^0.3'.41''·5$, $C=12^0.48'.4''·5$.

(6) $a=101$, $c=120$, $B=11^0.25'.16''·3$.

(7) $a=221$, $c=222$, $B=39^0.18'.27''·5$.

(8) $c=78$, $A=136^0.23'.49''·9$, $B=11^0.25'.16''·3$.

(9) $c=408$, $A=77^0.19'.10''·6$, $B=5^0.43'.29''·2$.

(10) $c=120$, $A=110^0.0'.57''·5$, $B=39^0.18'.27''·5$.

(11) $c=102$, $A=79^0.36'.40''$, $B=33^0.23'.54''·6$.

(12) $c=450$, $A=81^0.27'.16''$, $B=10^0.37'.44''$.

(13) $c=312$, $A=33^0.23'.54''·6$, $B=15^0.11'.21''·4$.

(14) $c=326·24$. $A=45^0.46'.26''·5$, $B=29^0.10'.2''·5$.

220 ANSWERS.

(15) $c = 90$, $A = 134°. 45'. 36''·6$, $B = 29°. 51'. 46''·4$.

(16) $B = 67°. 22'. 48''·1$ or $112°. 37'. 11''·9$.

(17) $B = 62°. 51'. 32''·9$ or $117°. 8'. 27''·1$.

(18) $B = 78°. 19'. 24''$ or $101°. 40'. 36''$.

(19) $B = 75°. 18'. 28''·2$ or $104°. 41'. 31''·8$.

(20) $B = 53°. 26'. 0''·6$.

LV. (Page 181.)

(1) 236·602... feet.   (2) 1210 yds. and 1040·5 yds.

(3) 4596 yds. nearly and 4584·48 yds.   (4) 33' nearly.

(5) $\sqrt{3} : 1$.   (6) 107 feet nearly.   (10) $\dfrac{a}{2} \sin \alpha . \sec \beta$.

(13) 4 miles.   (14) $5 (3 - \sqrt{3})$ miles.   (16) $\tan^{-1}\dfrac{4}{3}$.

(20) 51·76 feet.   (21) 10 and 14·14 miles.

(22) $48°. 22'$.   (23) 115·47 yds. and 9·503 yds.

(24) 5·71307 miles.   (25) 15 yds.

(26) 6236·549 ft.; 1095·47 ft.   (27) 85·28 ft. or 28·14 ft.

(28) 108·64 yds. nearly.   (29) 204·2 ft.

(30) $A = 116°. 13'. 20''$, $B = 26°. 20'. 40''$, $c = 4325·26$.

(31) 1 mile and ·923497 mile.   (32) 124·3 feet.

(33) 306·4178 yds.   (34) 34·42284 or 14·524 miles an hour.

(35) 513·7045 yds.   (36) $17°. 47'. 50''$.

(37) 134 yds.   (38) 169·4392 yds.

(39) 76·5455 miles.

LVI. (Page 199.)

1. $30\sqrt{3}$ sq. in.   2. 600 sq ft.   3. $7\frac{1}{2}$ sq. ft.
4. 12 sq. in.   5. 151872.   6. 30600.
7. 12480.   9. 1016·9487.

34. $a = \sqrt{(d_2^2 + d_3^2 + d_2 d_3)}$,
    $b = \sqrt{(d_1^2 + d_3^2 + d_1 d_3)}$,
    $c = \sqrt{(d_1^2 + d_2^2 + d_1 d_2)}$,

    area $= \dfrac{\sqrt{3}}{4}(d_1 d_2 + d_1 d_3 + d_2 d_3)$.

35. $\sqrt{\dfrac{1}{2}\left\{a^2 + c^2 \pm \sqrt{4(a^2 b^2 + a^2 c^2 + b^2 c^2 - b^4) - (a^2 + c^2)^2}\right\}}$.

38. 3992·835 miles.   42. 339·164.

43. $\dfrac{6\pi}{17}, \dfrac{7\pi}{17}, \dfrac{11\pi}{17}, \dfrac{10\pi}{17}$.   47. 2·36 miles.

48. $1°.26'$.   49. 4017·79 miles.   50. 4224 miles.

51. $2°.13'.50''$.   55. $\tan^{-1} ·003$.

APPENDIX.

1. *To find the trigonometrical ratios for an angle of* 18°.

Take the figure and construction used by Eucl. IV. 10 in describing an isosceles triangle having each of the angles at the base double of the third angle.

Hence $\angle BAD = \frac{1}{5}$ of 2 rt. $\angle^s = \frac{1}{5}$ of $180° = 36°$.

Bisect BAD by AE, which will bisect BD at right angles.

Let $AB = m$, $AC = n$, and $\therefore BD = n$.

Then, since rect. $AB, BC = $ sq. on AC,

$$m(m-n) = n^2;$$

$$\therefore m^2 - mn + \frac{n^2}{4} = \frac{5n^2}{4};$$

$$\therefore m = \frac{\sqrt{5}+1}{2} n;$$

$$\therefore \frac{n}{m} = \frac{2}{\sqrt{5}+1}.$$

Now $\sin 18° = \sin BAE = \dfrac{BE}{AB} = \dfrac{\frac{n}{2}}{m} = \dfrac{1}{2} \cdot \dfrac{n}{m}$;

$\therefore \sin 18° = \dfrac{1}{\sqrt{5}+1}$;

$\therefore$ multiplying numerator and denominator by $\sqrt{5}-1$,

$$\sin 18° = \dfrac{\sqrt{5}-1}{4}.$$

So the other ratios may be found.

2. *To explain geometrically why in determining* $\sin \dfrac{A}{2}$ *or* $\cos \dfrac{A}{2}$ *from* $\cos A$, *we get two, but from* $\sin A$ *four different values.*

Let A be an angle whose cosine is known, and describe PAM, the least angle which has the given cosine.

Make $P'AM = PAM$.

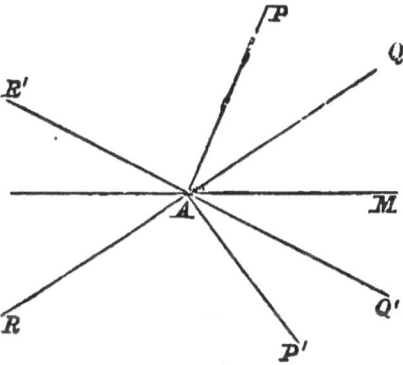

Then A must be an angle whose bounding lines are AM and either AP or AP', that is, it must be either the angle MAP, or the angle MAP', or some angle formed by adding (or taking) a multiple of four right angles to (or from) one of these.

Now bisect MAP, MAP' by AQ, AQ', and produce QA, $Q'A$ to R, R'.

Then $\dfrac{A}{2}$ must have AM and one of the four QA, $R'A$, RA, $Q'A$ for its bounding lines.

Now the ratios of all these angles are of the same magnitude and can only differ in sign, there being a pair of angles which have each ratio + and a pair −.

∴ in determining from the cosine we get *two* values.

Next, let A be an angle whose sine is known, and describe MAP the least angle which has the given sine.

Make MAP' equal to the supplement of MAP.

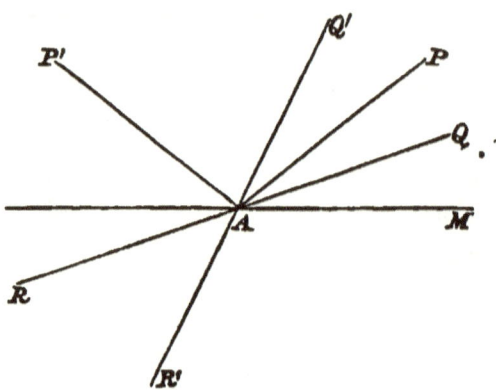

Then A must be either MAP or MAP', or some angle formed by adding (or taking) a multiple of four right angles to (or from) either of these.

Bisect these angles as before.

Then $\dfrac{A}{2}$ must be an angle which has MA and one of the four QA, RA, $Q'A$, $R'A$ for its bounding lines.

Now those which have either QA or RA as one of their boundaries have ratios equal in magnitude but opposite in sign. So also for those having $Q'A$ or $R'A$ as one of their boundaries; but the magnitudes of the ratios of the former sets differ from those of the latter

∴ the ratios of $\dfrac{A}{2}$ may be either of two sets of magnitudes and of either sign and therefore have *four* different values.

www.ingramcontent.com/pod-product-compliance
Lightning Source LLC
Chambersburg PA
CBHW021823230426
43669CB00008B/844